THE ARTS AND SCIENCES OF CRITICISM

The Arts and Sciences
of Criticism

EDITED BY
DAVID FULLER
AND
PATRICIA WAUGH

OXFORD
UNIVERSITY PRESS

809
A 792

OXFORD
UNIVERSITY PRESS

Great Clarendon Street, Oxford OX2 6DP

Oxford University Press is a department of the University of Oxford.
It furthers the University's objective of excellence in research, scholarship,
and education by publishing worldwide in

Oxford New York

Athens Auckland Bangkok Bogotá Buenos Aires Calcutta
Cape Town Chennai Dar es Salaam Delhi Florence Hong Kong Istanbul
Karachi Kuala Lumpur Madrid Melbourne Mexico City Mumbai
Nairobi Paris São Paulo Singapore Taipei Tokyo Toronto Warsaw

and associated companies in Berlin Ibadan

Oxford is a registered trade mark of Oxford University Press
in the UK and certain other countries

Published in the United States
by Oxford University Press Inc., New York

British Library Cataloguing in Publication Data
Data available

Library of Congress Cataloging in Publication Data
Data available

ISBN 0-19-818639-8

1 3 5 7 9 10 8 6 4 2

Typeset in Sabon
by J&L Composition Ltd, Filey, North Yorkshire
Printed in Great Britain
on acid-free paper by
Biddles Ltd, Guildford and King's Lynn

To
WILLIAM AND GEORGE,
MATHEW AND JESSIE

Acknowledgements

WE BOTH wish to acknowledge, at different stages of our work on this book, the tenure of a Durham University Sir Derman Christopherson Foundation Fellowship. We would like to thank the General Lectures Committee of the University of Durham for financing the public lecture series from which this collection of essays began, and the secretary of that committee, Mrs Sylvia Melanby. We are also grateful to the Department of English Studies of the University of Durham, which contributed generously to the financing of the lecture series, and particularly its then chairman Professor J. R. Watson, and its administrative officer Mrs Agnes Delanoy. Although they have not contributed to this collection, lectures were also given in this series by Professors Gillian Beer and Richard Hoggart, to both of whom we are indebted for their stimulating contributions to the project. We are also grateful to our very helpful editors at Oxford University Press, Sophie Goldsworthy and Matthew Hollis, our excellently scrupulous copy-editor Jackie Pritchard, and our desk-editor Janet Moth.

We would also like to thank our departmental secretary Ms Marie Howard and, for various labours of reading and commenting on material, Professor T. W. Craik and Drs Michael Schepers and Derek Todd; and finally our contributors, who were unfailingly helpful and co-operative as we worked on shaping their essays into a unified volume.

The dedication to our children, William and George Fuller and Mathew and Jessie Waugh, is a small acknowledgement of their more diffuse help and support.

D. F.
P. W.

Contents

1

Introduction

DAVID FULLER AND
PATRICIA WAUGH

The underlying purpose of this collection of essays is to reflect, directly and obliquely, on developments in criticism which bear on a debate between different models of knowledge—a science model and its place in the university versus other ways of conceiving knowledge for which the arts have traditionally been seen as vehicles but which the science model makes currently problematic. It has, of course, been open to contributors to challenge this way of conceiving the problem. We invited contributions from outside the literary academy (Doris Lessing, Raymond Tallis, and, in his current work, David Lodge) so that discussion could range beyond points of view directly informed by, but also therefore inevitably caught up in, the institutional construction of the subject on which it was part of our aim to reflect. All of the essays are in some way about what kind of knowledge literature is or claims (implicitly) to be, and how far similar answers to this question predicate comparable conclusions about what criticism should be. Several of the essays are concerned with a specifically aesthetic way of knowing, the value of which lies partly in its very resistance to scientific models of knowledge on the grounds that they are not adequate to the whole of what it is to be human. Literature, on this view, betrays its peculiar contribution to the fully human in so far as it is forced to accommodate itself to such criteria. But the answers about how literature can resist them, and in positive terms what kinds of ways of knowing can best respond to the distinctive nature of aesthetic knowledge, are very varied. Finally, criticism (as David Lodge begins his essay by pointing out) is a sense-making activity which is an inevitable part of all reading. This collection also addresses the issue of how far professional criticism should be a deepened extension of that ordinary reading activity[1]—a discipline, therefore, with a perhaps anomalous status in the academy—or how far professional criticism should be a purely objective and scholarly study, distinctly different not in degree but in kind from non-professional reading, purged of the personal, analogous to other scientific forms of knowledge studied in an academic context.

1. Criticism and the History and Philosophy of Science

The essays in this section represent a varied response to contemporary post-positivist considerations of epistemology and the so-called 'crisis of legitimization' at the centre of postmodernism. They also formulate many of the terms of the questions with which the contributors to the following sections engage. Since the 1960s, critiques of scientific method, counter-cultural opposition to technologization and 'instrumental reason', and developments in science itself have drawn the arts and sciences closer together. Postmodernists speak of the 'aestheticization of science', rhetoricians have pointed out the metaphorical nature of scientific language. In tandem with this recent turn in philosophy of science runs a similar self-reflexive movement in literary criticism: if scientists question correspondence models of knowledge, then it is hardly surprising that literary critics should come to unquiet meditation on the nature of their relations with the work of art. However, analogies between critic and text and scientist and nature, though seductive, are often misleading, since they tend to elide differences between linguistic construction and material being-in-the-world. The essayists represented here all proceed cautious of such dangers. Each discriminates between aesthetic and scientific ways of knowing to explore the limits, advantages, and dangers of mutual borrowings. In different ways each finally affirms the desirability of continuing to recognize the limits of the two demesnes, the separateness as well as the relatedness of the realms of the cognitive

---

[1] Even so impersonal a poet as T. S. Eliot argues that interpretation must incorporate some account of the critic's own feelings ('The Frontiers of Criticism', in *On Poetry and Poets* (London: Faber, 1957), 114). However, contrast the argument of Northrop Frye that criticism 'must be an examination of literature in terms of a conceptual framework derivable from an inductive survey of the literary field' and so can properly be considered a science (*Anatomy of Criticism* (Princeton: Princeton UP, 1957), 7–8).

and the aesthetic. More problematic, and therefore more provocative of dissent, is the question of where this leaves criticism.

Of late this question has provoked dissent not simply among literary critics but also between critics and scientists. The now almost infamous volume of the journal *Social Text* entitled *Science Wars* (ed. Andrew Ross, 1996) provoked impassioned debate on the question of the implications of certain kinds of interdisciplinary transgression across the humanities and the natural sciences. Much of the controversy grew out of an article by the mathematical physicist Alan Sokal later revealed as a hoax by its author and defended as a Swiftian attempt to expose the ideological bias and intellectual pretension of the editors of *Social Text*.[2] This article ostensibly presents an argument demonstrating that the legitimacy of currently fashionable postmodern cultural concepts (indeterminacy, uncertainty, and non-linearity) can be 'proven' by drawing on contemporary mathematical ideas. The New Science, it is claimed, thereby provides an irrefutable challenge to an older empirical scientific tradition and its belief that human beings infer from their immediate sensations the existence of an externally real world which provides some framework for the regularities of our collective human existence. What enrages Sokal about such postmodern arguments is that they are not made in the admittedly fictive spirit of poetry, but in the more narrowly epistemological spirit of (traditional) science, as verifiable truths about the world. What might be a source of fruitful perception if acknowledged as metaphoric becomes the basis for dishonest masquerade. Sokal uses two basic strategies to expose the ill-foundedness of such claims: the leap from scientific axiom to sociological inference without reasoned bridging argument; and the citation of spurious 'scientific' proofs and axioms by literary theorists to ground liberationist claims of a multiculturalist or gender kind. Incredulity towards meta-narratives, it would seem, is still alive and kicking.

The more general aim of Sokal's essay was, on the one hand, to attack the pervasive drift towards epistemological relativism in the human sciences, and, on the other, to resist the recently formulated rainbow coalition of anti-science radicals. Brilliant as it is in itself,

[2] 'Transgressing the Boundaries: Towards a Transformative Hermeneutic of Quantum Gravity', *Social Text*, 14 (Spring/Summer 1996), 217–52; the hoax was revealed in 'A Physicist Experiments with Cultural Studies', *Lingua Franca* (May/June, 1996), 62–4. See also Jean Bricmont and Alan Sokal, *Intellectual Impostures* (London: Profile Books, 1998).

Sokal's parody is ultimately most interesting as a symptom of a number of anxieties and malaises in the contemporary academic world. There have long been anti-science movements contesting issues of science's cultural value—from the Romantic indictment of disenchantment and calculative thinking to the Leavisite questioning of scientific rationalism's capacity to ground any sense of cultural identity. What is disturbing about the current articulation of this tradition is the extension of critique beyond questions of value into the realm of knowledge itself. This has prompted scientists such as Richard Dawkins and Lewis Wolpert to launch counter-offensives against the variety of relativisms which have challenged the orthodox realist or objectivist view of scientific enquiry.[3] Similarly Sokal's ire has been directed, not towards the hermeneutic tradition which has persuasively argued against the kind of scientism which would reduce consciousness and intentionality to mechanical determinism, but rather towards these newly burgeoning cultural relativisms whose common claim is that all knowledge, including science, is culturally situated and its theoretical formulations largely ideologically determined. Sociologists of science interested in the cultural embeddedness of knowledge join forces with those philosophers of science who have sought to demonstrate the ultimate unverifiability, in philosophical terms, of the reality affirmed by scientific claims. Scientific theory, it is argued, may be empirically adequate without necessarily describing the world at all. Scientific discourses use models and metaphors from everyday language which are inevitably already imbued with ideological slants and suggestive connotations. The objectivity of science is thus at best a flattering illusion which convinces us of our human autonomy by affirming our instrumental power over nature. At worst it is an ideological state apparatus whose very rhetoric of truth and understanding preserves our political quietude by conferring on scientists the status of priestly diviners.[4]

What is suggestive for literary criticism in this anti-science movement is the shift from a Romantic tradition, which opposed the

[3] See for example Lewis Wolpert, *The Unnatural Nature of Science* (London: Faber, 1992).

[4] See, for example, Sandra Harding, *The Science Question in Feminism* (Ithaca, NY: Cornell UP, 1986); Andrew Pickering, *Constructing Quarks: A Sociological History of Particle Physics* (Edinburgh: Edinburgh UP, 1984); Steve Woolgar, *Science, the Very Idea* (Chichester: Horwood, and London: Tavistock, 1988); and Barry Barnes and David Edge (eds.), *Science in Context: Readings in the Sociology of Science* (Milton Keynes: Open University Press, 1982).

embodied experience of art to the abstract calculation of science, to a postmodern position where science is itself aestheticized and where both science and art as kinds of knowledge are suborned by an ideological critique which denies the possibility of any genuinely transcendental experience or disinterested epistemological criticism. None of the contributors to this book takes up such a position in its pure form. Rather, pervasive throughout these essays is the influence of a more tempered hermeneutic tradition concerned less with the political or epistemological deconstruction of scientific truth-claims than with the effort to respect scientific models of knowledge whilst disabling their encroachment on or subversion of a humanistic understanding of consciousness. Purpose, belief, aesthetic delight, self-reflexive awareness—none, in this view, can be reduced either to a mechanistic scientific model or to an ideologically determined play of signification.[5]

Patricia Waugh provides a context for debates between rival paradigms of knowledge by re-examining the Snow–Leavis 'two cultures' controversy of the 1960s. She argues that in some form an arts/science clash is an ancient debate about exact and inexact kinds of knowledge which has been reformulated variously in many cultures. The argument is about how far models of exact knowledge and 'research' methods of investigation appropriate for science are properly applicable in the aesthetic realm,[6] and how far we are driven to accommodate aesthetic knowing to scientific models by contemporary institutions of knowledge which are science-dominated. Waugh traces the history of some crucial twentieth-century developments about the nature of scientific knowledge, and shows why these render it no longer satisfactory to see this debate in terms of a simple arts/sciences split. She also, however, argues against the claims about radical uncertainty and complete relativism which some contemporary literary-critical movements hold to be consequences for criticism of modern views about the supposedly theory-dependent nature of

[5] Cf. Charles Taylor, *Philosophy and the Human Sciences: Philosophical Papers*, 2 vols. (Cambridge: Cambridge UP, 1985); and Anthony O'Hear, *Beyond Evolution: Human Nature and the Limits of Evolutionary Explanation* (Oxford: Oxford UP, 1997).

[6] The inappropriateness of the term 'research' to advanced study in the arts is discussed from a humanist viewpoint by F. R. Leavis, 'Research in English', in *The Critical Moment: Essays on the Nature of Literature* (London: Faber, 1964); and by George Steiner, *Real Presences: Is There Anything in What We Say?* (London: Faber, 1989), esp. 34–7. The issue is taken up, from a different point of view, in the essay by Timothy Clark below.

scientific 'fact'. Finally she shows, in a reading of *To the Lighthouse*, how Virginia Woolf, both overtly and in the very texture of her novel, reflected the interests of contemporary science in order to challenge habits of perception, though these interests, hazily reconstructed, are now often read as confirming the easy relativism that Woolf actually sought to oppose. Waugh argues that partial readings of Woolf exclusively in relation to contemporary preoccupations (formerly Woolf as subjective impressionist, currently Woolf as feminist social critic) index a more general critical failure—the failure to attempt that paradoxically disinterested engagement which reflects the unique nature of aesthetic knowledge. Art can, she argues—and this is a repeated theme of the collection—both embody and, in a situated way, reflect on experience: engagement pre-empts desiccated pedantry; disinterestedness releases from solipsistic self-reflection. Together they enable a properly relished aesthetic pleasure to challenge dead habits of perception and moribund systems of value.

Like Patricia Waugh, whose essay defends the aesthetic against the intrusions of scientific epistemologies, David Cooper maintains their polarity but concentrates on the clarification of the proper sphere of scientific knowledge in the context of the contemporary (post-Snow/Leavis) two cultures debate. In *A Defence of Poetry* Shelley declared of poetry that it 'comprehends all science' and is 'that to which all science must be referred'.[7] Although Cooper does not allude to this claim, his essay is a defence of scientific knowledge against the more extravagant and confused legacies of Shelley's perspective on the relations between the arts and sciences. He draws on (strong) pragmatist arguments in philosophy of science to refute postmodern relativists and contructivists of the so-called 'strong sociology of knowledge school'. For Cooper a rigorous pragmatism will serve as a valid response both to traditional (Humean) scepticism and to the postmodern drift towards the aestheticization of science and the declared bankruptcy of epistemology. Indeed, the tone of his essay hints amazement that such defence should be required, that so many intellectuals have fallen victim to the seductive rhetoric of the postmodern: like the Emperor's New Clothes, it produces an astigmatism which misperceives gaudy rhetorical draperies as substantial evidence. One tacit premiss of Cooper's argument is that, simply

---

[7] *A Defence of Poetry*, in *Shelley's Poetry and Prose*, ed. Donald H. Reiman and Sharon B. Powers (New York: W. W. Norton, 1977), 503.

because we cannot know everything, we should not assume, either that we cannot know at all, or that there is nothing to know: we should not conflate epistemology and ontology. Although science can never 'know' the whole world (to this extent the postmodern critique of the hubris of grand narrativizing is justifiable), science can know some of it. Science is often accurate, its predictions often do correspond with events in the world, they often do tell us about the world which exists outside of science's own models and metaphors.

Like Waugh, Cooper notes the softening of the two cultures debate since the 1960s, and that one negative consequence of this has been the attempt to assimilate science to literary criticism by extending the deconstructionist version of the relation of the critic to art by analogy to the relation of the scientist to nature. If we accept that criticism must always construct its object of knowledge (so this argument runs) we should also recognize that 'nature' is whatever is constructed as such by the scientific community of the day. Cooper dismantles such arguments by dwelling on the central trope of modern epistemology, the metaphor of the mirror. This metaphor provided the focal point for Richard Rorty's seminal critique of objectivity in both its realist and idealist modes in what would become a bible of postmodernism, *Philosophy and the Mirror of Nature* (1980). Rorty claimed that it was time to renounce for ever the outworn image of mind as a glassy essence, either passively reflecting the external world (the old view in its Lockean or empiricist form), or refracting it through the distortions of its own lenses (mind after Kant). Once we give up such hankering for truth as correspondence we may get on with the business of cultural conversation and the proper social construction of knowledge. Cooper's essay seeks to defend science against the Rortian turn whilst acknowledging the cogency of sceptical critiques of Snow's complacent positivism. That science draws on metaphor to offer an account of its procedures does not mean that science has the same ontological status as art. Cooper builds his case against the aestheticization of knowledge in effect by drawing out the implications of the confrontation between Karl Popper and Thomas Kuhn. Popper's idea of the role of conjecture in science accepts that there is an imaginative or aesthetic dimension in the discovery of scientific laws, but, in line with his concept of falsifiability, he insists that what establishes an argument as 'scientific' is its availability for refutation. For Kuhn, conversely, there can be no final court of appeal because it is impossible to step outside of a theoretical paradigm in order to provide the conditions for independent testing.[8]

Debates about the role of the imagination or the 'aesthetic' element in science reach back to Francis Bacon's assertion that truly scientific endeavour should seek for disconfirmation of initial hypotheses—that science, like art, should rouse us from our habitual and prejudiced ways of seeing. Cooper suggests, however, that in the postmodern turn in science aesthetic criteria such as elegance or coherence have displaced entirely the desirability of refutation, or even the common-sense recognition that, whatever the truth-status of scientific theories, on a pragmatic level science has been hugely successful in giving us knowledge of our world. Science works. Even if we are no longer prepared to accept its grander and more heroic narratives, and may well deplore the consequences of their misapplication to history, we should recognize the sheer hard work involved in the scientific effort to establish the difference between truth and fiction. We should acknowledge the existence of different ways of knowing, even the desirability, in some senses, of the existence of the 'two cultures'.

Raymond Tallis comments on the debate from the distinctive perspective of an 'outsider' (his own self-designation). He speaks as a medical practitioner, a scientist intent on testing the pronounce-ments of contemporary literary theorists against the rigorous empir-ical codes of modern medical research. Like David Cooper, he defends scientific practice, but he goes further than Cooper in his prescriptive recommendations for the reform of degenerate tendencies which threaten the health of contemporary literary studies. Tallis assumes as axiomatic the centrality of empirical testing to the advance of knowledge, and argues that the extension of this particular kind of rigour to literary criticism might curb a theoretically induced and hubristic critical preference for apocalyptic and globally resonant but often slenderly evidenced pronouncements—not simply about literary texts, but about the entire nature of Western culture, art, and know-ledge. For Tallis, the very defence of 'intuitive' or 'tacit' knowing at the heart of literary culture is largely responsible for the current methodological chaos of the discipline: a tradition of accepting evi-dence-poor assertion has facilitated the postmodern predilection for

---

[8] See Karl Popper, *Conjectures and Refutations: The Growth of Scientific Know-ledge* (London: Routledge & Kegan Paul, 1963); Thomas S. Kuhn, *The Structure of Scientific Revolutions* (1962; 2nd edn. Chicago: Chicago UP, 1970).

evidence-free generalization on the grand scale. Without a clear framework of truth and value (his argument runs) English has become a moral and epistemological heart of darkness, a methodological vacuum of subjectivism and nihilism increasingly colonized by purveyors of spurious metaphysical games.

In many ways Tallis's essay occupies a direct line of descent from C. P. Snow's Rede lecture of 1959, though the focus of his critique is the post-structuralist intellectuals of the ultra-sceptical Left (Barthes, Lacan, Derrida) rather than the modernists of the culturally pessimistic right (Pound, Lawrence, Wyndham Lewis). For both Tallis and Snow, however, literary intellectuals are all too ready to promulgate a sense of the inevitability of cultural degeneration and decline, whereas scientific communities are associated with the positive forces of collaborative effort and ameliorative practice. Such arguments have always raised intellectual hackles (in the case of Snow and Tallis intentionally so), but they also challenge literary intellectuals to formulate more precisely their own kinds of defence. Tallis's position is not, however, identical with that of Snow, for Tallis's intention is not to denigrate literary culture *per se*, but to curb its hubris, to warn critics off territory not rightfully part of their appropriate demesne. In *Newton's Sleep* (1995) Tallis staunchly defended the distinctive contribution to cultural well-being of imaginative artists, arguing that literature provides a unique kind of experience in its capacity to combine simultaneously a full sense of living presence with a meditative reflection which neither compromises nor reduces this particular sense of 'being there'. Moreover, Tallis sees the humanities as carrying the important cultural burden of exploring and debating questions of human value, purpose, and meaning.[9] He laments, therefore, that the present generation seems so bent on its own self-annihilation, on destruction rather than conservation and building up, and suggests that theorists undergo the curative intervention of science by taking lessons in precise empirical method.

Implicitly then, Tallis's essay constitutes an attack on the abuse of science in literary theory, on the dangerous pseudo-scientific practices of charismatic theorists such as Lacan, who spin their magical and irrefutable (because untestable) diagnoses of cultural morbidity with insouciant disregard both for the particularities of individual works

[9] Compare the arguments of the biologist Peter Medawar, *The Limits of Science* (Oxford: Oxford UP, 1985).

in so far as they resist the ideological schemes such theorists wish to impose on them, and for the unique and complex values of different phases of the broader literary culture. Tallis's Zolaesque 'j'accuse' lays at their feet the blame for much currently voguish relativism and nihilism. Of course it is not difficult to predict the kinds of counter-argument which are likely to be invoked against Tallis's accusation: that literary criticism is inevitably indeterminate, given that language constitutes both the medium and the object of its analysis; that no amount of scholarly evidence in literary studies (however necessary as the foundation for judgement) could, in itself, constitute an interpretation of the value or significance of a work of art; that even under the aegis of the regulatory ideal of a 'view from nowhere' the subjective elements, which in scientific practice constitute confirmatory bias, in literary criticism can never be ruled out; moreover, given that the possible determinants of meaning are quite properly various, it would in any case be inappropriate to aim for their eradication. Nevertheless, Tallis's provocative essay raises many important questions about the kinds of knowledge appropriate to science, cultural history, and literary criticism. One measure of their problematic nature is perhaps the extent to which Tallis's own argument is sometimes forced to proceed (as he acknowledges) using the rhetorical manœuvres which he deplores in his opponents: hyperbole, *reductio ad absurdum*, selective quotation, and some measure of generalization from a small number of examples. If literary critics need the methods of science (this seems to suggest), then sometimes science needs the methods of literary criticism—especially when it seeks polemical defence and legitimization. Implicitly as well as explicitly the two cultures debate is here alive and flourishing.

Jacques Berthoud concentrates on one aspect of Tallis's critique, attacking as logically incoherent Lacan's attempt to present psychoanalysis in the guise of a 'conjectural science' which proclaims the death of the individual subject—an extirpation comparable to the post-structuralist attempt, which soon followed, to destabilize and disintegrate meanings by extinguishing the author. Lacan argues that the individual is a set of mutations continuously in process: subjective consciousness—the humanist illusion of a stable core to the ego—is an effect of language. The system of language creates the world, within and without. Mind and world are not, as for Kant, correspondently structured. Understanding is not even, as for Nietzsche, the necessary projection of mental fictions on to a chaos of sensation.

Lacan severs all connections. Jacques Berthoud attempts to steer a path between this radical, and on his view unscientific, claim, and the common sense but naive view of language as simply reflecting the world. By so doing, he seeks to maintain the idea of the individual as an active agent partly creating meaning, not a passive automaton 'spoken' by the language system.

While for Lacan the subject arises entirely out of the impersonal signifying network, Berthoud counters with a subject able in some measure to process it. But language can only construct the world, Berthoud argues, in so far as it is tied to the world. A system of unfixed terms, so-called sliding signifiers such as Lacan developed from Lévi-Strauss—each adjusted only in relation to other elements of the language, not in relation to reference or use—cannot create the reality it purports to name. Berthoud develops Peirce's distinction between natural and coded signs along lines suggested by Vincent Descombes to distinguish signs which represent concepts from those which make a statement. Lacan's error is to move unconsciously between these two, that is to slither from Saussurian *langue* (the system of language itself) to *parole* (individual usage), a distortion of Saussure designed to do away with the (in a degree) autonomous humanist subject, the individual—of whom the poet is the primary example—whose inventive struggles intentionally disrupt the cliché-imprinting power of system, and, in so doing, force new perceptions. Berthoud's critique is echoed in Paul Fry's account of de Man in Part II. As Fry there argues, such anti-intentionalist polemics do not destroy all notion of intention: they simply transfer intention from individual utterance to the system of language itself. By maintaining Saussure's distinction between *langue* and *parole*, Berthoud argues, a proper recognition of human agency can be preserved. Any speech act exists with a speaker and a hearer, in a world.

2. Criticism and the Aesthetic

While the essays in Part I are largely concerned with the discrimination of different ways of knowing and with criticism as a particular kind of knowledge, those in Part II are more concerned with experience, and particularly with the problem of how to communicate the unique experience involved in the encounter with works of art. Significantly, almost all are by writers who are literary practitioners (as novelists or poets) or artistic performers as well as critics. Each is concerned with the experience of inhabiting the work as it comes into being either on the page or in the world. If criticism is born out of a dialectical relation between the impulse toward objectivity and a recognition of subjective engagement, the essays in this part recommend proceeding from situatedness toward transcendence.

Michael O'Neill takes up from Patricia Waugh the issue of the nature of aesthetic knowledge, and develops in his own way Harold Bloom's recent re-emphasis of the aesthetic: literature is not to be mistaken for philosophy or politics carried on by other means. But O'Neill opposes Bloom's post-Freudian pessimism that all poems are born out of an Oedipal struggle which makes them misreadings of other poems. Poetry is a valid way of knowing, about poetry as about the world, and a peculiarly valuable one because the usual prose of critical analysis misses, and may even inhibit, a fully adequate response. Accepting that intuition is the product of a partly intellectual process of cultivation, O'Neill's argument implies—like the essays of Paul Fry and David Fuller—that we must recognize limits to what can be fully intellectualized in the understanding of art. The implication, all but inherent in the critical act's claim to reveal what was previously hidden, that criticism is a superior form of knowledge, is here inverted. Critical prose offers a form of knowledge which is easier to grasp but more partial. In criticism as elsewhere, the medium is (at least in part) the message: rarely is critical prose adequate to express the complex emotional and intellectual experiences evoked by the imaginative and implicatory nature of its poetic subject. Criticism is accordingly an art, and one in which understanding cannot be separated from the creative use of language by which it is conveyed. The critic's language, in prose as in poetry, should not only (or even necessarily) analyse: it should register the critic's whole intellectual-emotional response. Accordingly O'Neill confronts the problem of criticism's claim to objectivity, especially in so far as this relates to the way language is used: the attempt at a scientific mode is inimical to the adequate practice of what is necessarily an art, because criticism relates in part to matters of feeling, whether the poet's or the critic's. With worthwhile criticism it is finally a question of 'the quality | of the affection— | . . . that has carved the trace in the mind' (O'Neill quotes Pound adapting Guido Cavalcanti). The medium of criticism, be it poetry or prose, must be adequate to express that. If (as Wallace Stevens claims) it is in the nature of poetry that it 'must resist the intelligence almost successfully', or if (as T. S. Eliot has it) the meaning of a poem is the piece of meat with which the burglar distracts the guard-dog,[10] then critics should be less confident that analytical prose, the tool of a would-be objective rationalism, is a wholly competent medium for their art. As Friedrich Schlegel puts it—more unequivocally than O'Neill, who, though himself a poet, extrapolates from his poem-critiques in prose, and admits a number of prose writers to his critical pantheon—'Poesie kann nur durch Poesie kritisiert werden.'[11]

As a novelist and one of the first critics to introduce structuralism to the world of English letters, David Lodge is uniquely placed to consider literary criticism both as an art and a science. Although Lodge was one of the first apologists for distinctively modern forms of literary theory he also subsequently expressed disquiet at the extent to which theory has become a New Scholasticism, remote from the public world and enmeshed in arcane linguistic edifices of its own construction. Indeed, as comic novelist, Lodge has derived much imaginative capital from this situation, depicting the modern world of university letters as an Academy of Lagado, its professors strenuously trying to build houses from the roof downwards, its junior researchers bent on the reconversion into food of human waste. In this essay, however, Lodge approaches the situation with even-handed clarity: he surveys the apparently entropic scene of proliferating critical discourses and attempts to reimpose order by drawing up a map of the various relations which have existed between criticism and creative writing. Lodge sees no point in restoring order through authoritarian suppression or cowardly retreat: in the spirit of his *Working with Structuralism* he takes up his theodolite and sets about a practical survey. Literary criticism, he argues, can be regarded as complementary to the text or as in opposition to it, as an artistic practice in its own right or as a part of the creative process. Lodge explores these claims without arriving at a hierarchy of judgement. Though one senses preferences when he speaks *in propria persona* as

---

[10] Wallace Stevens, *Opus Posthumus: Poems, Plays, Prose*, ed. Samuel French Morse (New York: Alfred Knopf, 1957), 171; T. S. Eliot, *The Use of Poetry and the Use of Criticism: Studies in the Relation of Criticism to Poetry in England* (London: Faber, 1933), 151.
[11] 'Poetry can only be criticized by means of poetry': *Kritische Fragmente, Charakteristiken und Kritiken I*, ed. Hans Eichner (Zurich: Thomas-Verlag, 1967), 164.

a creative writer, evidently he believes that there are good and bad practitioners of every mode.

In complementary mode criticism functions as handmaiden to the work, usually claiming to offer on the one hand scholarly contextualization, on the other explication or close reading. Lodge regards these modes as complementary because both offer a mantle of protection for the work—guaranteeing its authenticity, justifying its complexity, preserving it for posterity. For this reason perhaps these were the critical practices which founded the institution of university letters. As early as the 1950s Randall Jarrell was proclaiming his time 'The Age of Criticism'—somewhat derogatorily, and with an apprehension of worse to come. Lodge looks back from 'The Age of Theory' with evident affection and nostalgia for this time of innocence.[12] He explores the assumptions of critics from the 1920s and 1930s onwards who were among the earliest and greatest practitioners of the complementary mode. However, what he discovers in their writing is a contradictory logic which, even without institutional pressures, would almost of itself generate a countermovement, his category of 'opposition'. In attempting to respect the literary work as an object in its own right, complementary critics (Eliot, Empson, the New Critics) discovered instead that, as a structure of values, the text seemed always to resist 'objectivity', seemed always (in part at least) to be constructed by the choice of critical frame or vocabulary. The more the critic strove for certain knowledge of the literary artefact the more he or she would arrive at uncertainty even about its ontological status and about what criticism can know. This is the period when so many critics sought to define or fix the quality of 'literariness': as 'wit', 'paradox', 'irony', or 'defamiliarization'. This is also the period when the pressures of positivistic science began to be felt insistently within the burgeoning discipline of academic criticism, and when the first tensions emerge about the function of criticism and the special nature of the literary 'object'.

Lodge's second category, criticism as opposition or 'mastery', is a development of this. Here criticism moves on to the offensive, equipping itself with arms borrowed from the sciences and the full regalia of professional skills (methodologies, theories, and excavatory sys-

---

[12] Cf. Frank Kermode, for whom the question 'what is to become of literary criticism?' is 'really a question of how it can survive in a time when its most influential exponents are doing their best to abolish it' ('Theory and Truth', *London Review of Books* (21 Nov. 1991), 9–10).

tems) which have provided the familiar vocabularies of knowledge in
the modern university. At this stage of the analysis Lodge feels the
need for the protection of his creative writer's status, the need
(faintly) to protest and to remind such critics that, as they blanket
over the text with increasingly elaborate camouflage, they may inadvertently starve it of oxygen. The writer feels dispossessed, powerless
in the face of such technological onslaught to protect the fragile
object which now lies buried beneath this most recent of Platonic
censors. Moreover it is not just academics who are on the offensive.
Lodge points to a similar impulse at work in the wider culture of
letters—in literary journalism and in the adjudication of literary
prizes. As he has written elsewhere, one of the consequences of the
academic flight into theory and away from close engagement with
contemporary creative writing has been an abandonment of analysis
and evaluation of literary works to the more predatory, sensation-
and reputation-seeking world of the mass media.[13]

As theory loosens the boundaries between language and metalanguage, literature and criticism, and as mastery takes on a fanatical
edge, critics begin to view their own activity as a form of creative
writing. Criticism, it is now claimed, is not ontologically distinct
from literature. Opposition becomes substitution. A parallel may
be drawn here with changes happening generally in universities
from the mid-1970s. Modern academic literary study began in the
age of positivism with an increasingly professional assertion of the
objectivity of criticism,[14] its status as quasi-scientific in an institution
where only the hard sciences were accorded the status of certain
knowledge. In the formalist-structuralist years of the late 1960s
and early 1970s criticism as 'science' could be opposed to literature
as 'art', though critiques of method were even then, and even in the
hard sciences, loosening assumptions about objectivity. As structuralism released its many versions of textuality, distinctions between
truth and rhetoric were subverted and criticism aspired to be more
radically improvisational, to create hypothetical worlds of its own
rather than compliantly service a stable aesthetic demesne which was
itself the creation of a stable canon of 'creative' writers.

However, as criticism asserted autonomous creative powers

[13] 'The Novelist Today: Still at the Crossroads', in Malcolm Bradbury and Judy
Cooke (eds.), *New Writing* (London: Minerva/The British Council, 1992), 203–15.
[14] See, for example, John Crowe Ransom's 'Criticism Inc.', in *The World's Body*
(London: Charles Scribner's Sons, 1938), 327–50.

creative writers increasingly included overt critical self-reflexivity in their own writing (the age of metafiction, surfiction, self-conscious poetry). Instead of regarding this as a negative condition of identity-crisis and territorial skirmishing between criticism and art, one might put a more positive gloss on it by attending to Lodge's account of his fourth category, criticism as part of creation. In considering criticism as an activity always involved in any creative process Lodge brings his essay explicitly round to the two cultures debate and to recent scientific work on human consciousness. In the philosopher Daniel Dennett's work mind is a hyper-evolved but still algorithmically functioning computer which works by almost instantaneously shuffling through and discarding multiple possibilities for the solution of each problem it encounters. Consciousness works like a writer—correcting, deleting, and substituting, so that the creative process can be seen as the outcome in part of a sophisticated but nevertheless mechanical procedure. In this model, the mechanical and the inventive are fundamentally related, the critical and the creative become necessary aspects of each other: on this view mind is situated across a network of interfaces occupied by both the arts and the sciences. If consciousness, unlike God, is finally open to explanation, then any progress in our knowledge of it must depend on the capacity of scientists and artists to talk to one another. Lodge's essay ends, therefore, optimistic about the potential future of relations between the arts and the sciences.

Even more evidently than David Lodge, Doris Lessing is a voice from outside the academy. Her very manner exhibits no desire to feel at home in an institutional context the scientific paradigms of which can undermine the central concern of her essay: personal authenticity of literary experience. Lessing argues that the change in mode of the critical stance from intuitive to conscious knowledge, while it may involve a gain in coherence, can also entail a loss of vitality. Her starting point, autobiographical writing, illustrates the relativity of interpretation to point of view: what is true of how we interpret and reinterpret our own histories, as a present self looks back from a different viewpoint, is also true of how different readers read other people's fictions. Critical thinking, therefore, moves between a Scylla and Charybdis: on the one hand making a work real by adapting it too much towards one's own experience, using reading merely to elaborate and confirm one's own ideological conceptions; on the other attempting an objectivity which cuts one's reading off from any reality, actual or imaginative. Doris Lessing avoids the term subjective, perhaps only because of the confusions to which it can give rise—from 'true to my personal experience, but perhaps true only for me'; through the grand claims (of Romanticism) that individual experience is at bottom representatively human, or (of certain religions) that it is finally identifiable with the Divine Ground; to the anti-humanist objection that, there being no such thing as an individual, the illusion experienced as subjectivity is made up of forces (social, linguistic) expressing themselves equally in all other illusory subjects. Lessing instead invokes Goethe to propose what she calls 'passive' reading—reading which uses one's own experience with an openness to the individual and historical otherness of the work. This is reading that Edward Said has recently characterized as that of the true amateur,[15] the reader actuated by a love of literature, who recognizes that in the 'human sciences' (so-called) truths are as often lost as found, and that part of the struggle of criticism must be to know, really, in a way true to one's own experience, what has been known by others, lost and found and lost again and again. Such criticism is likely to be anarchically eclectic, antithetical to notions of special expertise and professionalized method, and availing itself as occasion demands of literary, intellectual, and social history, knowledge of a writer's whole *œuvre* and biography, an intuition arrived at by wide reading and the effort to understand many different kinds of work, and the critic's own experience of life—a criticism casting around, experimenting, and (like Doris Lessing's own) idiosyncratic. Only this kind of reading is that true imaginative extension which enables one to recognize that people in different individual or historical situations experience what it is to be human differently—the liberal point of reading.

Paul H. Fry's essay is a meditation on the debate about intentionality provoked by E. D. Hirsch's *Validity in Interpretation* (1967). Hirsch defended the concept of authorial meaning both against the more provisional claims of critical significance and the various modernist and New Critical theses of impersonality. The debate which followed focused on the circularities of Hirsch's arguments, on the fact that, in trying to establish meaning as authorial intention, the critic is driven into the explication of proliferating contexts which

---

[15] 'Amateurs and Professionals', in *Representations of the Intellectual: The 1993 Reith Lectures* (London: Vintage, 1994), 49–62.

finally cannot be separated from those Hirsch assumed to constitute significance. The preposition 'beneath' of Fry's title is a clue to his own intentions. His thesis is that, although the post-structuralist and political criticism which dominates the contemporary scene involves an even more radical anti-intentionalism in its assaults on the concept of authorial intention, in fact this criticism cannot function without a determining concept of intention. It has simply disguised this dependency by projecting intentionality onto various apparently impersonal realms of being: for example, on to cultural or social speech-communities, or on to quasi-transcendental orders such as the Saussurian notion of *langue*. In emphasizing the belief that art exists 'beneath' interpretation (implying ground) Fry seeks to articulate an idea of the literary work as constituting a created order from which intentionality (even as *primum mobile*) has withdrawn. Literature has no meaning, since meaning cannot exist without intention. Literature may be understood as generative of interpretation (which is contingent upon it), but does not require it. Occupying its own necessary realm, literature provides a unique kind of experience which has nothing to do with (and does not require an account of) who or what intended it to mean.

Fry's essay is, therefore, informed by a similar performative paradox to Michael O'Neill's: he sets out to communicate an account of aesthetic experience which suggests that literature is finally incommunicable except in its own terms. Whereas O'Neill's answer is that, in the end, only a poet can be a fully adequate critic of poetry, Fry dwells, often in ironic and wittily self-subverting fashion, on buried assumptions about the relations between language and intention which inform contemporary criticism. For Fry the disjunction between literary and ordinary uses of language is ontological and apparently absolute: the literary work, he suggests, does not seek to communicate, but provides us with a unique, if momentary, 'ostensive' experience, an experience of plenitude, of inhabiting not a mimetic reflection of the world but a continuation of it. The contemporary critical emphasis on the materiality of the linguistic sign might appear to facilitate such an understanding in that it seems to posit the autonomy of linguistic orders. However, it is Fry's view that a persistent if generally unacknowledged belief that language was invented for communication has obscured the ontological experience of art and guaranteed an insistent assumption that criticism must always offer an interpretation, an account of the meaning of this act of communication which is the work. Fry's revaluation of experience over meaning situates his ideas in a tradition of aesthetics which has two divergent emphases: on the one hand, the Paterian emphasis on sensation, more recently articulated in Susan Sontag's 'Against Interpretation',[16] and, on the other, the more mystical, Heideggerian belief in the capacity of the literary work to offer the experience of plenitude. It is this latter view (which appears modified in poets such as Charles Olson and critics such as Owen Barfield) which is closest to Fry's.

In Fry's view, contemporary criticism has fallen into a pathological condition of interpretation-compulsion and is in danger of never recovering sufficiently to remember that art is this unique kind of experience. He dates the onset of the symptoms of the latest variety of this disease from the publication of Jacques Derrida's thoroughgoing antifoundationalist statement 'Structure, Sign and Play in the Discourse of the Human Sciences' (1966).[17] Derrida's essay so unsettled the relation between intention and meaning that Fry sees the subsequent history of criticism as a desperate attempt to rehabilitate intention (and therefore meaning), its almost imperceptible transference from an ostensibly discredited concept of authorship to various supposedly impersonal sources. Interpretation-compulsion flourishes in this new environment, because, though the desire for meaning rages unabated (if subterraneously), the sources of intention are now much more resistant to final determination. Interpretation-compulsion thus becomes an addiction which feeds off itself, onanistically seeking, in the disease it has become, its impossible cure. Fry sees emerging from this febrile response to the new indeterminacy a gradual bifurcation of criticism into two schools which now dominate the critical scene. On the one hand is an earnestly politicized and culturally situated school of 'relevance' whose linguistic assumptions Fry traces to the arguments put forward by Steven Knapp and Walter Benn Michaels in 'Against Theory' (1982); and on the other a school of hedonism and significatory promiscuity whose assumptions about language are referred to Paul de Man's 'The Resistance to Theory' (1982).

Fry sees these two essays as the landmark critical productions of

[16] 'Against Interpretation' and Other Essays (New York: Farrar, Straus & Giroux, 1966).
[17] In Richard Macksey and Eugenio Donato (eds.), The Languages of Criticism and the Sciences of Man: The Structuralist Controversy (Baltimore: Johns Hopkins UP, 1970).

the 1980s and the determining force behind critical developments in the 1990s. Nevertheless, he finds Knapp and Michaels guilty of the pervasive and mistaken assumption that all language exists to communicate. In their case the mistake flourishes because of their over-reliance on ideas about language derived from the 'speech-act' theory which developed from the philosophical writings of J. L. Austin and John Searle. Because Knapp and Michaels understand literary works as special kinds of 'speech acts' they assume that there is an intention behind their meaning; further, that this cannot be separated from their meaning and can only be accounted for by elaborating the specific contexts which ultimately determine the act of speaking. For Fry this is a transference of intentionality—from individual author to speech-community—which legitimizes criticism exclusively as the investigation of ideological determinations (or, in its most degenerate form, as upholder of ideological purity or political correctness). In Fry's view, however, language does not always constitute a speech act and is not always primarily communication: literary language he defines as a performance which exceeds determination by context and is always in excess of intention.[18] For Fry literary language does not offer an account of the world: it is an experience in excess of the world, an opening out into a realm of its own which is yet an extension of the world. All too often, however, and in consequence of our pursuit of what we take to be the meaning, we miss the experience.

Fry is also anxious to dissociate his defence of aesthetic presence from de Manian deconstruction. De Man's anti-intentionalism constitutes an austere, ironic, and even tragically aware critique of what he regards as the impossible yearning for linguistic and metaphysical presence. Conversely, Fry's notion of 'ostension' carries the belief that literature offers a unique experience of presence—so long as we open ourselves to the right kind of appreciation. In Fry's view post-structuralist accounts of literary language err in that the interpretative drive, and thus the search for intentionality, is once again furtively at work in them even as they appear to be (as Derrida expresses it) 'under erasure'. Here intention is transferred to the system of language itself: language is conceived simultaneously

---

[18] A similar argument was actually implied in Austin's original account of illocutionary acts: Austin half-acknowledges that contexts are potentially endless and therefore never definitive, and that our evident pleasure in language may be attributable to its inexplicable condition of extra-referential excess (*How to Do Things with Words* (Oxford: Oxford UP, 1962), *passim*).

both as an impersonal order, or *langue*, and a kind of protean virtual reality, daemonic, and yet personalized by a vital unpredictability, the actuating principle of which is the impulse to outwit any attempt to pin it down or fence it in.

Fry's opposition to both the relevance and the freeplay schools of criticism may be prompted by his sense of their shared agonistic relation to the literary work itself: both constitute varieties of a hermeneutics of suspicion. In their desire to be more clever than the text itself both schools fail to appreciate that criticism could be other than this. Regarded in this light Fry's essay recalls us to that humility in relation to the work of art which is a precondition for the experience of wonder which art can induce, the sense of being transported to another realm which is both beyond and yet an expansion of everyday experience. Fry is certainly not the first critic to suggest how literature might give back the world by taking us out of it, but he is perhaps the first to reiterate this ancient view of art in opposition to the contemporary anti-humanist schools of criticism.

By way of introduction to his theme of 'Poetry, Music, and the Sacred' David Fuller begins with a commentary on Les Murray's 'Poetry and Religion'. The poem contains what might be interpreted as a warning to contemporary methodologically minded critics to keep off. A poem, Murray tells us, embodies 'a law against its own closure': poetry will always exceed interpretation. So begins Fuller's meditation on a dominant theme of this group of essays: how to reconcile the often contradictory demands of art as experience and criticism as knowledge. Fuller argues that in the modern academy too much emphasis has been placed on knowledge of art at the expense of the experience of it, and, like Michael O'Neill, he sees one remedy for this imbalance in looking to art itself to suggest modes of critical practice. Unlike O'Neill, however, whose exploration is of the (poet) author as critic, Fuller considers readerly modes of engagement with literary works, drawing on analogies with musical performance to investigate ways in which the critical act might arise directly out of immersion in the work of art.

Fuller is not looking entirely to banish criticism. He is simply mindful of the need, within the constraints of the modern academy, to reinstate the participatory knowledge of the Homeric rhapsode as a counterweight to the currently imperialist overextensions of the Socratic. It might be argued that in its original form Platonic dialectic served to confirm the wonder and mystery of the Good, but once its rational-sceptic instruments are deployed to undermine all wonder then an abyss of endless self-reflexivity and nihilism beckons. Without the possibility of belief in an ideal Form of Justice Socrates' interrogation of the pragmatist arguments of Thrasymachus and Glaucon may be construed as no more than an elevated semantic quibble.[19] Similarly, without the possibility of belief in art as a form of the sacred, as an experience of pure essence, critical interpretation becomes an endless and tenebrous stream of voids chasing each other: 'Mirror on mirror mirrored is all the show.'[20] Like Fry, Fuller is concerned therefore to defend the concept of presence and to talk about ways in which a plenitudinous experience of art might be communicated through a critical practice. His concern is with the sense of how our spiritual awareness might be remythologized by the imaginative experience of art—an achievement possible only through complete participation as a foundational aspect of the full critical process. As T. S. Eliot puts it: 'you don't really criticize any author to whom you have never surrendered yourself.'[21] In Fuller's account such acts of surrender require perpetual refreshment and renewal.

More than Fry, however, Fuller does concede that there is a place for the Socratic spirit in critical practice: where Fry's 'ostensive' moment takes us wholly into a distinct ontological realm (and thus has affinities with the Kantian aesthetic as well as the Homeric rhapsode), Fuller's account of aesthetic participation grounds the experience of the sacred in earthly encounters with the material body of the work. Socrates complained that the rhapsodic relation to art entirely precluded critical judgement: *mimesis* is a term used not only to designate art as reflection but also art as an illusion so absolute as to obviate the possibility of critical, and thence ethical, thinking. The recitation of words so deeply committed to memory that you become the poem while the poem lasts seemed to Plato prohibitive of the structures of arrest which he associated with the critical spirit. This required a capacity for abstract disengagement which might relate the concrete particularity of the temporal moment—the singular just act for example—to a spatially conceived or distilled concept of pure justice to be apprehended through the

[19] *The Republic*, bks. 1 and 2.
[20] Yeats, 'The Statues', in *Collected Poems* (London: Macmillan, 1950), 375.
[21] Letter to Stephen Spender, quoted in Spender's 'Remembering Eliot', in Allen Tate (ed.), *T. S. Eliot: The Man and his Work* (London: Chatto & Windus, 1967), 38–64 (p. 55).

exercise of rational intelligibility. However, Fuller offers an account of aesthetic participation which allows for the exercise of self-conscious critical awareness paradoxically through that very unselfconscious immersion in the work of art which for Plato was absolutely at odds with this. Performance, in its use of memory and voice, serves as the hinge which opens doors onto both realms.

Fuller negotiates this move through the construction of a second analogy: having approached poetry through its relation to the sacred he then situates it in relation to the experience of musical performance. Fuller's essay is itself fugue-like: the themes of music, poetry, and the sacred are expanded and developed in a constellatory network. The essay begins with a personal account of his dissatisfaction at trying to reconcile that sense of beauty encountered in the experience of art with the formal requirements of the study of an academic discipline. In this essay, however, he synthesizes out of the ingredients of that dissatisfaction the model for a critical practice which might satisfy an aesthetic desire frustrated by too early or too exclusive a demand for detached reflection. In an analogy between the performance of music and of poetry Fuller finds the means of reconciling the demand that criticism should constitute self-conscious knowledge with the imperative that art should constitute an unselfconscious and rhapsodic experience of aesthetic intoxication. To play a musical instrument successfully the performer must inhabit a work with an immersed and self-renunciatory concentration. But also required is a kind of living memory which enables every detail to be held always in a knowing and creatively shaped relation with the whole. Fuller reformulates a McLuhanite cliché: that the thought is in the medium, the medium is the thought. This insight is close to O'Neill's sense that only a poem can know a poem, but Fuller is interested in how performance may know a poem too. Reading aloud, he argues, offers the experience of immersing oneself in the creation of another mind combined with a form of critical reflection as one explores ways of realizing the artefact through the resources of the living voice.

3. Criticism and the Ethical

The essays in Parts I and II—largely concerned with the relations between criticism as knowledge and art as experience—orient themselves toward what Kant called the faculties of the cognitive and the aesthetic. Those in Part III foreground what is a more peripheral concern in the earlier essays: the relations between each of these and the third Kantian category of knowledge, the ethical. Criticism here is seen to function as a force against misappropriation: by drawing attention to the imaginative nature of the work of art it guards against art's speculative projection onto history. Irresponsible aesthetic myth-making confuses the Kantian realms and produces dangerous political ideologies. Criticism is Janus-faced: it has responsibilities to the work and to the world. It does not take place in a vacuum, and must therefore articulate and defend its practices as part of an idea of the community it serves.

Seán Burke reverses the judgement of Plato. Plato's Socrates constructed his argument for banishing the poets in relation to his society's misunderstanding of poetry as a vehicle of ethical and even practical knowledge. Poetry must be aware of its own fictiveness, or criticism should function adequately to remind us of this. It is not then (as the *Republic* argues) the poets who are dangerous: it is those philosophers—such as Plato himself—who seek to present dialectic as a form of knowledge not requiring the interpretative supervision of a critical tradition but as analogous to the theorems of mathematics—truths which, being wholly impersonal, are not open to the interpretative abuse of philosophy, for example when it is misunderstood as directly translatable into social practice.[22] Works of philosophy, like works of art, ethically require a concept of authorship. Despite his claims for the scientific status of dialectic, Plato implicitly acknowledges this in instituting the academy as guardian of authorial legacy against the word's promiscuous dissemination. Though the Kantian categories of the cognitive, the ethical, and the aesthetic cannot (as Kant supposed they should) be kept wholly separate, they must not be confounded.

That the prophetic philosopher—Hegel, or Marx—would not accept this separation is certain. Whether the prophetic artist—Blake, Whitman, Lawrence—would accept it may be doubtful. Though a simple pill and cherry theory is clearly never adequate—fiction is not ideas, whether moral or practical, made palatable—still, for a philosophical novelist such as Sartre the pill and the cherry

---

[22] Cf. Jean-François Lyotard's argument that totalitarian and fascist politics project onto the social level aesthetic or intellectual myths of wholeness: *The Postmodern Condition: A Report on Knowledge*, trans. Geoff Bennington and Brian Masumi (Manchester: Manchester UP, 1985), appendix.

account for a great deal. *Les Chemins de la liberté* makes available the ideas of *L'Être et le néant* to a readership that will not read pure philosophy. The novelist of ideas is an extreme case, but not *sui generis*. When Milton described poetry as potentially 'doctrinal and exemplary to a nation'[23] he may not have meant that the reader could learn from *Paradise Lost* how to prune a garden, but neither was he taking the aestheticist positions of Oscar Wilde or Wallace Stevens. The poem is aesthetic-ethical: the reader is to experience how a paradise within is destroyed and can be built. The moralist novelists from Fielding to Tolstoy expected their readers to learn—to love or to feel the failings of characters who exemplify modes of sensibility and behaviour which are to be embraced or to be repudiated. There are real grounds for Plato's doubt. He was not simply too literalistic about the nature of fiction, or only responding to its peculiar status in his own society: he was recognizing a problem which, Burke argues, is equally, and perhaps more insidiously, applicable to philosophy itself. Criticism, on this view, must therefore be ultimately—even for the most convinced aesthete—an ethical activity. It is a form of dialogue with the work the function of which is to ruffle, to regulate, to unmask with its scepticisms the truth-claims of all forms of knowledge which are not purely cognitive. Seen in this light, criticism is not a parasitic, second-order activity: it is a vital complement to dangers inherent in the imagination's characteristically more immersed and unselfconscious way of knowing.

Timothy Clark presents the problems of English as a discipline in relation both to cultural shifts outside the universities and to the wider problems of the universities themselves over the last twenty years. He accepts in part an Arnoldian or Leavisite view about the way English is implicated in a whole cultural situation, but Clark partially reverses this view's usual terms. English as a discipline is not only a potential arbiter of cultural values: shifting cultural values are themselves arbiters of what should take place in English studies. In this account English is scarcely a discipline at all. This is its problem, because the ideology of professionalism prompts attempts to establish for English untenable disciplinary boundaries which would cut it off from those broad intellectual and cultural issues for which it is a focus. But that literary studies is hardly a discipline is also its great

---

[23] *The Reason of Church Government*, book ii, *The Works of John Milton*, 18 vols. (New York: Columbia UP, 1931–8), iii, pt. 1, p. 237.

strength: literary studies is, on this view, a peculiarly vital point of intersection for cultural critiques, and its inherent instability as a discipline raises valuable questions about the institution's usual intellectual compartmentalizations.

Clark also argues, however, that these powerful potentials of the subject are currently threatened, even neutralized, by bureaucratization. He offers a critique of this drift by attempting to reassess, in relation to contemporary cultural circumstances, the Romantic and idealist programmes of the late eighteenth- and early nineteenth-century founders of the German university system, who presented the university as a place of disinterested research and cultural legislation structured on an assumption of the unity of all knowledge.[24] Clark sees literary studies as having been constructed by a concatenation of conformist pressures the aim of which has been to place it within institutional paradigms of knowledge which are faint and distorted echoes of these large-minded programmes. He focuses on discipline boundaries. Many other such pressures can be suggested: the desire, even within a narrowly conceived discipline, to specialize yet further so as wholly to master some small area, making one's knowledge complete and invulnerably 'scientific'; the assumption that knowledge in the arts is, like knowledge in the sciences, progressive, which is used to validate the constant production of new interpretations prompted not by disinterested scholarly discovery, genuine originality of individual vision, or real shifts in cultural circumstance, but by the dynamics of publishing (which requires, as much as any commercial enterprise, changes of fashion), and the demands of individual and institutional prestige.

When English was first established as a university subject the supposed need for a recognizable cognitive core was filled by Philology (the implied analogy was with the study of classical languages). For the New Critics the cognitive core was the study of texts considered in isolation from those contextual elements that might seem to annex English to some other discipline—to History, or to Philosophy. While some contributors to this collection see the current fashion for literary theory as the new Philology, symptomatic of mistaken forms of professionalizing, Clark argues that (on the con-

---

[24] The development of the British university system is discussed, with greater stress on its intellectual foundations within Britain (in the writings of Coleridge, Carlyle, Arnold, and Mill), by Ben Knights, *The Idea of the Clerisy in the Nineteenth Century* (Cambridge: Cambridge UP, 1978).

trary) the dominance of theory is a response to over-professionalization: it is an attempt to reposition literary studies in a wider cultural
forum.

Clark argues in dialogue with commentators who regard the
bureaucratization he identifies as presenting an opportunity—a
chance to break down the departmental boundaries which he and
they agree in seeing as arbitrary institutionalisms with at best a
limited intellectual validity. Clark is himself doubtful about the
claimed opportunities. Nevertheless, he ends by sketching a programme for university education, based on his view of English as
inherently interdisciplinary, in which all the arts and sciences are
drawn into closer relationship.

The arts and sciences debate emerges throughout this volume as a
particular configuration of the broader relationship between knowledge and experience. Most contributors accept that gain in one direction may entail loss in the other, though the overwhelming consensus
advocates a return to meditation on the particularity of the experience
of art, and on the kind of knowledge that is made available through
it. Michael Bell's essay suggests that it may be possible to reconcile
these apparently conflicting demands. The art historian Adrian
Stokes described the tension involved in such an ideal response:

Our relationship to all objects seems to me to be describable in terms of two
extreme forms, the one a very strong identification with the object, whether
projective or introjective, whereby a barrier between self and not-self is
undone, the other a commerce with a self-sufficient and independent object
at arm's length. In all times except the earliest weeks of life, both of these
relationships, in vastly different amalgams, are in play together, as is shown
not only by psychoanalysis but by art, since the work of art is, *par excellence*,
a self-sufficient object as well as a configuration that we absorb or to which
we lend ourselves as manipulators.[25]

Michael Bell's consideration of the relations between literature,
criticism, and myth bears upon this observation. Stokes's account
of the earliest weeks of life offers a model of the experience of a world
in which distinctions between self and other, subject and object, have
yet to make their appearance. The infancy of the human race has
often been described in similar terms by those seeking to explain the
configuration of knowledge and experience which constitutes the
mythic consciousness. Myth is usually regarded as a pre-conceptual

[25] *Three Essays on the Painting of our Time* (London: Tavistock, 1961), 10–11.

awareness in which knowledge and experience exist as aspects of each other and there is no distinction between the experiencing subject and the experienced world. The advent of modernity, it has been assumed, entails a fall into consciousness in which this awareness has been largely sacrificed to the theoretical and self-conscious knowledge associated with the sciences. Sociologists such as Anthony Giddens have described modernity as a condition of disembeddedness in which self-reflexive knowing must be at the expense of unselfconscious being. Many of the essays in this volume argue that in our ideal relation to art we momentarily recover this mythic consciousness, yet in the detachment and objectivity of our critical modes it slips away and eludes us. Bell's defence of modernist myth, however, is built upon the radical claim that, in this particular mythic mode, criticism is part of the participatory experience, that the logical contradiction of being self-conscious and unselfconscious at the same moment is thereby undone or transvalued. To appreciate modernism in this way may provide us with an alternative model of critical practice, one in which the aesthetic, cognitive, and ethical remain separate but are not estranged from each other.

Central to Bell's argument is a reassessment of the Nietzschean legacy which involved repudiating the aestheticist version current in most postmodern criticism and instead offering us a Nietzsche whose thought is closer to such post-Kantians as Hans Vaihinger. In *The Philosophy of As If*[26] Vaihinger argued for the cultivation of a component of critical self-consciousness in the construction of fictions, a self-reflexive awareness of their provisional and heuristic nature which constitutes an ethical contract ensuring protection against a dangerous degeneration into unselfconscious myth. Bell introduces a significant modification: in his version of modernist myth, in art at least we can have it both ways. Bell sees the modernist literary work as uniquely able to express the vital habitation of a world whilst simultaneously conveying awareness of living in a particular world-view. The condition is represented conceptually in Heidegger's 'The Age of the World Picture'.[27] What is there described discursively as a speculative vision is actually embodied in the modernist literary work: being and knowing are reconciled.

[26] *The Philosophy of As If: A System of the Theoretical, Practical and Religious Fictions of Mankind*, trans. C. K. Ogden (London: Routledge & Kegan Paul, 1924).
[27] *'The Question Concerning Technology' and Other Essays*, trans. William Lovitt (New York: Harper & Row, 1977), 115–55.

For Bell this is the condition expressed in Nietzsche's mature writing on the aesthetic. In this body of work the aesthetic is never an autonomous realm separate from life and in opposition to it, but is always in an aspectival relationship with actual existence. A life lived under the sign of the aesthetic would be an ethical life, lived for its own sake and valued accordingly. The aesthetic is a mode of experience which is always accompanied by a judgement on that experience. Bell concludes his essay by calling for a criticism which can respond to and learn from this double consciousness. Instead of reducing art to ideology criticism must recognize that, in the realm of the aesthetic, knowledge and experience can coexist—as they must in any mature critical practice.

Part I

Criticism and the History and
Philosophy of Science

2

Revising the Two Cultures Debate
Science, Literature, and Value

PATRICIA WAUGH

On 7 May 1959, C. P. Snow delivered the annual Rede lecture in
Cambridge entitled 'The Two Cultures and the Scientific Revolution'.
Snow's argument was that although the scientific revolution had
opened up new and exciting possibilities for the social and technological transformation of post-war Britain, the nation continued to
stagnate under the rule of a backward-looking and blinkered cultural
élite, trained in the exegesis of classical and modern literature, paralysed by a cultural pessimism which refused to acknowledge the
scientific concept of progress. Snow clearly saw his historical intervention as updating T. H. Huxley's 'Science and Culture' which had
been delivered as a response to Matthew Arnold's own 1882 Rede
lecture, 'Literature and Science'. When Leavis offered his own out-
raged, if Arnoldian, response to Snow in the Richmond lecture of
1962, the replaying of the original controversy seemed complete.[1]
   The two cultures controversy, however, goes back much further
than the end of the nineteenth century. It is arguable that no culture
has been without its version of the debate: every culture has witnessed
struggles for dominance between rival paradigms of knowledge which
have also been struggles to establish a structure of values which might
determine the educational curriculum. In antiquity, an emergent
rationalism vies with a literary culture concerned with the training
of the orator-lawyer; in the Renaissance, an emergent humanism with
an entrenched Scholasticism which is the basis of a theological
training; and since the nineteenth century aesthetic and humanistic

---

[1] See C. P. Snow, *The Two Cultures*, introd. S. Collini (Cambridge: Cambridge UP,
1993); and F. R. Leavis, 'Two Cultures? The Significance of Lord Snow', in *Nor Shall
my Sword: Discourses on Pluralism, Compassion and Social Hope* (London: Chatto &
Windus, 1972).

cultures have found themselves in opposition with the empiricist and rationalist foundations of the 'research' model of scientific training. The conflicts have been most intense when one form of knowledge lays claim to the exclusive title to all knowledge: Leavis's moral version of aestheticism is a response to what he regarded as the scientism of Snow's 'technologico-Benthamism' and Snow set his forward-looking and democratic positivist science against what he perceived to be a regressive and élitist culture of letters.

The Snow–Leavis controversy was essentially a debate about kinds of knowledge and the value of different kinds of knowledge and continued to play with a distinction between exact and inexact ways of knowing which is almost as old as Western culture itself. Aristotle's *Nicomachean Ethics*, for example, opens with the argument that although 'exactness' is the aim of science, it would be inappropriate to look for more exactness than the matter is capable of, and exactness is not appropriate for non-scientific disciplines. In the *Phaedrus* too, Socrates says there is a form of discourse appropriate to science and another which produces variant readings. There is only a minimal sense of individual intention in Plato, but thereafter one can see the gradual emergence of a recognition that whereas science involves the 'objective' study of natural objects in the world, the object of literary study is the intentional activity of other minds. The problem for literary *criticism*, in particular, emerges as the question of how far it is appropriate to subject the intentional activity of consciousness to the procedures of 'objective' research. Its first systematic interrogation was in Kant's *Critique of Aesthetic Judgement*, which attempted to formulate the precise nature of aesthetic knowledge in relation to the claims of a specifically modern form of science. Kant argued that the animating principle of literary works is that they 'occasion much thought, without however any definite thought, ie. any *concept*, being capable of being adequate to it'.[2] Literary knowledge exists as a bodying forth irreducible to conceptual truth, a creation of shared value (the beautiful), and an intuition of worlds beyond the actual (the sublime). Leavis would refer to this sphere of knowledge as the 'third realm', a realm beyond both the abstract cognitive certainties of science and the personal realm of private feeling: 'the collaboratively created human world, the

---

[2] *Critique of Aesthetic Judgement*, trans. J. H. Bernard (New York: Hafner, 1908), 157.

realm of what is neither public in the sense of belonging to science (it can't be weighed or tripped over or brought into the laboratory or pointed to) nor merely private and personal (consider the nature of language, of the language we can't do without—and literature is a manifestation of language).'[3]

Snow and Leavis represent a tail-end of the peculiarly modern version of an ancient debate about the value of different kinds of knowledge. A glance back at those first eighteenth-century documents (Baumgarten's aesthetics, Rousseau's discourse on the arts and sciences, Kant's three critiques), however, reveals the extent to which modern aesthetics emerged in a culture where science had already laid claim to certain (and therefore superior) knowledge. From the eighteenth century onward the two cultures debate has tended to proceed with a culture of letters defending the value of a conceptually indefinable form of knowledge: the idea of the aesthetic as a kind of shared symbolic knowledge created through and sustaining of culture, offering a joyful release from the scientific picture of nature which Schiller painted as a 'monotonous round of ends'.

Against the already established scientific vision of a universe of physical determinism, laws of causality, and blind mechanical motion, to be charted and measured through a strict inductive method and hypothetico-deductive rational analysis, Schiller opposes an aesthetic realm of play, symbolic transcendence, reconciliation, and participatory knowledge: in other words the aesthetic becomes the optimally expressive (and moral) realm of value, freedom, intentionality, and purpose, for: 'though it may be his needs which drive man into society, and reason which implants within him the principles of social behaviour, beauty alone can confer upon him a social character.'[4] Indeed, in this very division is built a myth of the origins of modernity which Leavis will inherit with his idea of a seventeenth-century dissociation of sensibility. The birth of modern science, in the first moments of Cartesian doubt and with the foundational enumerations of Newton's *Principia Mathematica*, delivers into history a twin: a redemptive aesthetic which would compensate for science's disenchantment of the world and its projection of human consciousness into the alienated and mechanistic Laplacean blankness of

---

[3] *Nor Shall my Sword*, 98.
[4] *On the Aesthetic Education of Man, in a Series of Letters*, ed. and trans. Elizabeth M. Wilkinson and L. A. Willoughby (Oxford: Clarendon Press, 1967), 215.

interstellar cold. In this universe, as William Empson has put it, 'one was only a pile of billiard balls, jerking about according to mathematical rules: scientific determinism spelled horror and despair'.[5] More amusingly, it gave James Joyce his jocoserious definition of Cartesian and Newtonian man as a 'conscious rational reagent between a micro and a macrocosm ineluctably constructed upon the incertitude of the void'.[6] Newtonian science had provided a world-picture governed by the certainty of mechanical law, but which seemed to offer no obvious place within its materialist parameters for human consciousness, purpose, intentionality, or meaning. The incertitude of the void is the abyss which opens between the Cartesian subject and the Newtonian universe, and the specifically modern aesthetic is formulated as a heroic struggle toward the plenitudinous form of a concrete universal where, somehow, the wound of self-consciousness might be healed, where embodied experience might be reunited with the reflective idea of itself, mind with body, and consciousness with cosmos. Literature exists in this heroic vision to give presence to what is made unavailable by science; it is the attempt, in the words of the French New Novelist Alain Robbe-Grillet, to 'sublimate a disparity'.[7]

However, the Snow–Leavis debate stands on a threshold of which it is either unaware or to which it is intentionally blind: their controversy represents the last moments of a 200-year-old version of the ancient debate about exact and inexact kinds of knowledge which was about to be radically challenged by new developments in both cultures. Neither Snow nor Leavis adds anything substantially new to the debate they inherit. Snow simply assumes the epistemological security of positivistic science and, in the tradition of what Leavis refers to as 'crass Wellsianism', is eager to promote its absolute centrality to the technologically transformed society of the future. Leavis's outrage is not so much about science, as about Snow's complacent scientism: his assumption that empirical science is co-extensive with knowledge *per se* and therefore adequate for knowledge of everything; the assumption that empirical knowledge is also sufficient for its own explanation and has no need for justification or

---

[5] *Argufying: Essays in Literature and Culture*, ed. John Haffenden (London: Chatto & Windus, 1987), 528.

[6] *Ulysses*, ed. Hans Walter Gabler with Wolfhard Steppe and Claus Melchior (Harmondsworth: Penguin, 1986), 572.

[7] *'Snapshots' and 'Towards a New Novel'*, trans. Barbara Wright (London: Calder & Boyars, 1965), 83.

interpretation; and, of the two cultures, as Snow said in a later commentary, that 'one is cumulative, incorporative, collective, consensual, so designed that it must progress through time' whilst the other remains 'non-cumulative, non-incorporative, unable to abandon its past but unable to embody it . . . to be represented through negatives', and essentially lacking 'the diachronic progress which is science's greatest gift to the mind of man'.[8]

Leavis's largely *ad hominem* critique of Snow's lecture, however, actually left intact the epistemological grounds of his version of scientific knowledge and simply attacked its overextension and failure to provide a vocabulary or experience of cultural value. Yet, buried in his assault are the presuppositions of Leavis's own valuation of knowledge. Snow's greatest crime is his insensitivity to language, his technocrat's lumpen prose. For as far as Leavis consciously articulates his own defence of literary culture it is in the now familiar terms of the 'value' of a kind of knowledge which is strictly indefinable, which cannot adequately be discussed because it only exists as a practice. This is the 'tacit' understanding which shapes a culture: a knowledge to be experienced in the intricate tissue of the highest uses of language, a knowledge valuable precisely because it is beyond objective criteria of verifiability, beyond theoretical or conceptual articulation.

1. The Contemporary Two Cultures: Shifts in Scientific Culture

Even in 1959, however, Snow's conception of science was limited and outdated and Leavis's vision of a consensual or common literary culture would soon disappear with an explosion in the 1960s of new political voices, the youth, jazz, pop, and mass-media subcultures, alternative cultures which seemed to distribute the values of the aesthetic beyond the boundaries of a high culture of letters or the demesne of academic literary criticism. Fortified by the countercultural critique of technology as the strong arm of capitalism, the aesthetic stood poised for expansion both into the realms of popular culture and those of science. In Snow's classic model of empirical science, the external world may be accurately and exhaustively

---

[8] 'The Case of Leavis', *TLS* 3,567 (9 July 1970), 739–40.

described, its facts captured in the transparent propositions which are the truths of its discoveries. Facts exist in the world independent of intentionality and are recoverable through an 'objective' process of controlled experiment involving the theory-free testing of hypotheses through neutral observation reported in value-free language. Complacently secure in the 'exactness' of his professed discipline, and writing under the penumbra of the rekindled light of Ayer's positivism, Snow is thus able to launch his attack on the narcissistic, 'feline and oblique' culture of modern letters.

However, this model of science had been under intellectual stress since the late nineteenth century, challenged by the burgeoning discipline of philosophy of science and by discoveries in the physical sciences in the 1920s and 1930s. Developments in both had already eroded the distinction between 'exact' and 'inexact' forms of knowledge and, in the period immediately after Snow's lecture, philosophers such as Paul Feyerabend would declare that there is no distinction between the knowledge available to science and that of literary culture. Richard Rorty would argue that the future of philosophy is as an adjunct of literary criticism rather than of science.[9] The two cultures divide seemed to be loosening with the blurring of distinctions between 'natural' and 'intentional' objects and 'exact' and 'inexact' method. By the 1980s, and across a range of intellectual disciplines, a pervasive scientism begins to be displaced by a no-longer defensive aestheticism. Not surprisingly, the fallout from these critiques of science was enthusiastically taken up by contemporary literary critics (in numerous versions of so-called 'postmodernism'), newly on the offensive, eager to confer on their own practices the authority of a scientific knowledge which now seemed indistinguishable from traditional constructions of the aesthetic.

Philosophical and sociological 'science studies' began to develop as cognate disciplines in the 1960s on the heels of the Snow–Leavis controversy and in the context of the vigorous counter-cultural assaults on the instrumental nature of technology. At the same time, the Heideggerian critique of the scientific 'research' model of knowledge was rejuvenated and made available for literary critical assimilation in Hans Georg Gadamer's critique of objectivity in *Truth and Method* (1960). If all knowledge arises from fundamentally

---

[9] Paul Feyerabend, *Against Method* (London: Verso, 1978); Richard Rorty, *Philosophy and the Mirror of Nature* (Oxford: Blackwell, 1980).

'tacit' structures of cultural belief, though conceptual definition is possible, it always arrives too late: the moment we formulate a conceptual definition and, Orpheus-like, turn to grasp our object, it has been expanded in the process of phenomenological encounter and has already moved on. From the substantial ground of cultural tradition we reach out for the Eurydice of exact knowledge: in attempting to grasp her we are left merely with the spectral shapes of our own desire. Thomas Kuhn's *The Structure of Scientific Revolutions* (1962) would also assert the cultural situatedness of all knowledge, though, unlike Gadamer, his analysis of scientific communities would focus on ruptures in rather than the continuity of knowledge. Kuhn introduced the idea of the 'paradigm', whose literary counterpart would be developed later in Stanley Fish's institutional notion of the 'interpretive community'. Here again we have the idea that scientific ideas exist relative to particular frameworks of knowledge or paradigms which constitute the boundaries of the scientific community. Facts exist within models agreed by the community and change occurs when the pressure from anomalies in observation and theorizing becomes so insistent that eventually it forces a revolutionary shift in the overall paradigm: Kuhn's axiomatic example is the shift from Newtonian to post-Einsteinian physics. In Kuhn's view, therefore, science moves not cumulatively, as in Snow's account, but in discontinuous leaps. He introduces the concept of incommensurability as an account of the way in which, as an entire world-view is shifted, scientific vocabularies regarded as exact and universal, terms such as 'mass', for example, come to carry radically different, indeed incommensurable, meanings within different paradigms. In effect, scientific paradigms constitute irreconcilable 'language games' and non-reconcilable world-views. We can see how these critiques of science might be regarded as bringing scientific knowledge closer to the kinds of models of 'inexact' knowledge associated with the disciplines of the humanities. There can be no theory-free observation, for there are always underlying and ultimately inarticulable belief systems and presuppositions which determine the interpretation of what is considered to be data. So the context of discovery and the question of intentionality become relevant issues for science too. Similarly, the suggestion that there can be no correspondent or neutral language of science opens up scientific language to rhetorical analysis. If no theory can be tested against theory-independent facts, it would seem to be impossible to offer final proof that theoretical constructions are actually in contact with what they set out to explain. Fictionality moves across from the demesne of literature to that of science. If logic cannot proceed from the empirical data to the postulates of the deductively formulated theory, but vice versa, then the same data can be used to support competing theories: we cannot necessarily say that one theory is more 'true' than another. An abstract model is projected onto the world and not surprisingly the world appears to confirm the model: not because the underlying structure of nature consists of regular and abstract laws, but because the mind discovers in nature what it has put there. In a radical extension of Kantianism, it may then be argued that scientists simply impose models on the world rather than discover them in the world.

This assault on the certainty of scientific knowledge has led to current constructivist claims that objectivity and rationality are culturally produced systems, that science cannot arrive at knowledge of a mind-independent natural reality, that its methods are always relative to shifting and heterogeneous theoretical frameworks, and that the 'objects' of scientific knowledge are therefore as 'intentional' as those of a literary text. The classic scientific distinction between contexts of emergence (beliefs, values, cultural ideas) and those of justification (that the proof of a scientific fact has nothing to do with the context of its discovery) disappears. In other words, scientific knowledge and language are no more exact than aesthetic knowledge and language. Well, philosophers make such claims, but scientists, of course, do not necessarily accept them. However, changes in physics itself, often regarded as the 'aristoscience' because of the exact nature of its knowledge, have provided even more persuasive grist for the mill of 'framework relativism'. Despite the fact that he was trained in Rutherford's laboratory, Snow's positivist and technology-oriented account of the 'revolution in science' ignored almost entirely *the* revolutionary period of twentieth-century science, between 1900 and 1930 (the period he focuses on for his attack on the culture of letters). Moreover, he ignored altogether its enormous influence on subsequent theories of knowledge and, in particular, on the perceived relations between scientific 'exactness' and non-scientific 'inexactness'.

I will begin by picking out the discoveries most relevant for the present discussion, and then attempt to assess the impact of these critiques of knowledge on the contemporary study of literature. In 1900, Max Planck observed that electromagnetic radiation is emitted in discrete packets or quanta and that this seemed to introduce the notions of discontinuity, randomness, and acausality into the fundamental structure and activity of matter. Werner Heisenberg's Uncertainty Principle suggested that all physical qualities that can be observed are subject to unpredictable fluctuations, again suggesting that there is an ineradicable indeterminism in the behaviours of the fundamental particles such that at the quantum level no definite predictions can be made about the behaviour of any system. He went on to question the traditional scientific separation of subject and object by suggesting that the interaction between observer and observed 'causes large changes in the systems being observed'.[10] Neils Bohr's Principle of Complementarity (actually directly appropriated by the literary critics I. A. Richards and William Empson in their discussions of irony, ambiguity, and paradox) developed the argument that there is an ineradicable ambiguity in all quantum systems. Though an electron could be a wave or a particle, it could not be both at the same time, and its realized form would depend on the condition of observation (literary theorists may recognize the similarity between this view of the universe and the concurrently developing field of phenomenological aesthetics with its idea of the reading process as a play of intentionalities which produces a concretization of the virtual structure of the literary text). There is no way to observe or measure a system without also changing the system in some way. Incompatible conceptualizations can both represent 'truth'.

Bohr's interpretation was that this discovery necessitated 'the final renunciation of the classical ideal and a radical revision of our attitude towards the problem of physical reality': it promised the end of Cartesian dualism, of materialist science and the treadmill of Newtonian determinism.[11] Heady possibilities of interpretation were seized upon: particularly the idea that consciousness might be reconciled with matter not simply in the organicism of the work of art, but in the scientific understanding of the cosmos. Again we see that the natural object/intentional object distinction seems to break down at this fundamental level of matter. If consciousness and matter arise out of the same fundamental particles, mutually partake of the same condition of virtuality, then the universe would seem to be

---

[10] Heisenberg, quoted in Karl Popper, *Quantum Theory and the Schism in Physics*, ed. W. W. Bartley (London: Hutchinson, 1982), 41.   [11] Bohr, quoted *ibid.*, 40.

42   PATRICIA WAUGH

snatched back from Newton and returned to Heraclitus. If the quantum world is fundamentally indeterminate then what was previously regarded as the intentional and free space of the aesthetic would now seem to be integral to what had been thought of as the mechanical and causally determined world of physical science. Moreover, if this quantum world seems to be at odds with the laws of Newtonian mechanics then it might be claimed that classical science is not universally 'true', but that its 'facts' are simply intelligible with reference to its theoretical frame: what is 'true' in one world is not necessarily 'true' in the other. Again, as in the formalist understanding of the literary text, internal coherence rather than exact external correspondence might be our only form of certainty. As Heisenberg put it: 'The concepts may. . . be sharply defined with regard to their connections . . . which can be expressed by a mathematical scheme . . . But the limits of their applicability will in general not be known.'[12] The quantum seemed to present an epistemological limit: a certainty of Uncertainty, the realization there can be no single model of explanation. Undoubtedly, commonsense perception is unable to account for activity at this level, although consciousness seemed more fundamentally implicated in it than classic realist science could ever have dreamed of. Indeed, Heisenberg claimed there is no picture of nature which is not a picture of our relation to nature (an idea which would become fundamental to the thought of Martin Heidegger). Like aesthetic knowing, Uncertainty transforms science too into participant knowing. If we cannot step outside of our systems of measurement, then, as the astronomer Arthur Eddington would observe in 1928: 'the world of physics is a world contemplated from within, surveyed by appliances which are part of it and subject to its laws.'[13] Should we regard the universe as ontologically commensurate with a work of art? Does the New Science suggest the collapse of distinctions between aesthetic and scientific knowing? Can science explain consciousness? Is consciousness in the world and, if so, how can we conceive of the world with our consciousness in it? I will come back to these problems in my final defence of a uniquely aesthetic way of knowing.

My own defence of aesthetic knowledge will involve a critique of

---

[12] *Physics and Philosophy* (1959; Harmondsworth: Penguin, 1990), 80.
[13] *The Nature of the Physical World* (Gifford Lectures, 1927; Cambridge: Cambridge UP, 1930), 225.

many of the claims that science has been 'aestheticized' and will argue
for the need to continue some form of the Kantian separation of the
categories of knowledge. First, though, we should turn to consider
some of the consequences for literary criticism in this 'postmodern
turn' in the problem of knowledge. Radical Uncertainty would
become central to 'the postmodern condition', especially as presented
in Jean-François Lyotard's influential 'Report on Knowledge', the
subtitle to his book of that name, published in 1979. Lyotard's
book has a crucial, though generally unacknowledged, place in the
two cultures debate in that it took Kuhn's critique of scientific knowledge overtly in the direction of Wittgenstein's concept of language
games and towards a fully fledged aestheticism. Lyotard argued that
the models of scientific certainty underpinning the progressivist
beliefs of Enlightenment had collapsed undermining the entire
Enlightenment belief in the possibility of human emancipation
through the application of a universal rationality to culture and
society (precisely Snow's belief in the nature and cultural value of
science and technology). Lyotard insisted that the pre-emptive doubt
of classic realist epistemologies—that knowledge could lead outside
of itself to discover truth in the world—should be renounced entirely
for a radical postmodern Uncertainty whose central claim was that
we cannot, indeed, step outside of our systems of measurement. But
the very examples used to proclaim the exhausted legitimacy of
scientific method are simultaneously adduced as key factors in the
scientific legitimization of Lyotard's own version of indeterminacy.
Like many literary theorists after, Lyotard aestheticizes science and
then uses the fact that it is still, after all, science, to offer a new
legitimization of the aesthetic, to give it the borrowed authority of
science, on the grounds that aesthetic knowing was always the kind of
knowing that is the only knowledge available. (Science has now,
somewhat belatedly, arrived at such recognition.) He achieves this
flattering (for literary criticism) reversal by first substituting for the
supposedly discredited epistemologies of classic realist science a
model of knowledge derived from the radical reading of the New
Physics: uncertainty is not a consequence of the limits of our perception, as Einstein, for example, saw it, but a fundamental condition of
being. However, Lyotard has carefully tailored his scientific examples
to suit his argument and highlights only those aspects of the New
Physics which most favour the strong Uncertainty thesis: that there is
no fundamental distinction between natural and intentional objects,

that the natural is as much a construct as the intentional object which is a work of art. How does he achieve this sleight of hand?

New Science, Lyotard explains, is concerned with 'undecidables, the limits of precise control, conflicts characterised by incomplete information, fracta, catastrophes, and pragmatic paradoxes' and provides the outline of a world which, in its very essence, is radically uncertain, 'discontinuous, catastrophic, non-rectifiable and paradoxical'.[14] In fact, by reading modern science wholly in terms of the strong interpretation of indeterminacy, Lyotard is still working with a correspondence model of truth even as he denies its very possibility. He still longs to find a language authorized by its mirroring of the external reality we call 'nature', but now nature itself exists in a condition of radical indeterminacy. Effectively then, Lyotard continues a tradition of commentary beginning at the time of the Copernican Revolution (that the New Philosophy calls all in doubt), of trying to read human purposes into the scientific picture of nature. Bertrand Russell, Ernst Cassirer, Karl Popper, Erwin Schrödinger, and other philosopher-scientists had warned against this kind of interpretation of the New Physics as early as the 1930s, pointing out its openess to false analogization. Of indeterminacy, Russell said it is simply a principle of measurement and has absolutely nothing to do with freedom or reconciliation: we cannot derive from it a new ethics of free will or chance and randomness, and in any case what kind of ethical responsibility could be involved in a world which was entirely random and indeterminate?[15]

But this is entirely what is implied in Lyotard's embrace of Uncertainty, in the idea that matter and consciousness are inseparable, for example, and that chaos, catastrophe, and complexity seem to offer some kind of picture of a vestigial, if limited, possibility of freedom when opposed to the deterministic and causally absolute picture of Newtonian science. Mysticists, popular New Agers, postmodernists, and even serious scientists have all climbed onto this contemporary bandwagon. For its vision is seductive: the realm of intentional knowledge, consciousness, and the realm of causality and physical matter, are reimagined as no longer closed to each other. The universe itself is indeterminate and this is meant to imply, somehow, that the

---

[14] *The Postmodern Condition: A Report on Knowledge*, trans. Geoff Bennington and Brian Masumi (Manchester: Manchester UP, 1985), 60.
[15] *Religion and Science* (1935; Oxford: Oxford UP, 1961).

potential for liberation associated by a Romantic-aestheticist tradition with the autonomous space of artistic creativity is now to be
relocated within the space of the scientific understanding of the
structure of nature. Lyotard, a disaffected Marxist, seems almost to
be trying to reground a liberatory principle plucked from Hegel's
dialectic of history and regrafted onto the very form of the cosmos
itself. This new revolutionary potential seems no longer to require
what is normally regarded as an agent: that is to say, the intentional
consciousness of a discrete historical being. But if we look at the
more modest interpretation of the Uncertainty Principle and the
Principle of Complementarity, the effect of the observer on the
observed is actually simply the effect of an instrument of measurement. Presumably then, if consciousness is reduced simply to this
kind of structural function, it is hardly surprising that the kind of
agency and intentionality associated with a humanist understanding
of consciousness disappears into the impersonal web of 'language
games', the idea that has propelled so many of the latest fashionable
ideas in literary criticism (including the death of the author, linguistic
determinism, radical alterity, to name but a few). The attractions of
this premature act of reconciliation, however, are self-evident: if
Newtonian science seemed to alienate consciousness from a deterministic physical universe, Lyotard's version of postmodern science
suggests it was only one kind of language game, the working out of
an enclosed logic which is inapplicable in the universe of the Newest
Sciences. Universal rationality was a prison from which we are now
liberated, and in the new model of an Uncertain universe, indeterminacy is not simply the limits of our knowledge but an inherent
condition of nature. Whereas the classic modern 'incertitude of the
void' called forth a painful but doggedly pre-emptive doubt, postmodern Uncertainty is a paradoxically comfortable and reassuring
condition. We simply give up worrying, for nature itself is radically
uncertain and our best response is to be pragmatic and decide which
version of it is most useful for our immediate purposes.

2. *Literary Criticism and 'Postmodern' Science*

Like science, literary culture too has shifted in significant ways since
the Snow–Leavis debate. For Snow, 'literary culture' meant a culture
of letters. But this culture had actually already begun to divide

internally at the end of the nineteenth century, most obviously with the split between the radically individualist (and anti-academic) Paterian aesthetic of sensational contemplation, and the new, rigorous and methodologized, scholarly study of letters within the universities. By the 1960s, however, the culture of literature had become almost entirely situated within the university, chained to a knowledge institution whose paradigm of understanding had become even more emphatically that of 'research'. If we think about the traditional model of scientific research training, though, we can see how many of its features seem the antithesis of the kind of model of 'inexact' knowledge central, as we have seen, to the tradition of modern aesthetics. For this is a kind of knowledge based on objective and publicly available evidence; requiring training in appropriate methods of retrieval and marshalling of data; concerned with predictable and repeatable patterns of events rather than unique or singular experiences or objects; involving precise reasoning from data to laws or from hypothesis to controlled experiment and avoiding arguments from authority; all to be written up with a precise and unambiguous terminology, a style, established with Boyle's Royal Society papers in the seventeenth century, which requires the negation of authorship through a radical impersonalization of discourse.

Throughout the twentieth century, the pressure of this research model has produced controversies and insecurities about the appropriate 'method' for literary criticism as a discipline, just as the fragmentation of cultural consensus about the canon has thrown up anxieties about what is to be regarded as its object of study. Until the current shift toward deconstruction, postmodernism, and New Historicism (which take their cue variously from the formulations of indeterminacy), in every critical movement, through formalism, New Criticism, structuralism, and Marxism, there has been conflict about how to reconcile the need for 'exact' definitions of method and object of study with the 'inexact' model of literary knowledge and value formulated in the (moral) aestheticist traditions through Kant, Schiller, Arnold, Pater, and Leavis (and not forgetting Dr Johnson who famously said that mathematics is central to some things, but morality to all). Not surprisingly then, literary critics have welcomed the shift towards 'inexactness' in science and have appropriated contemporary arguments and concepts as a way of reconciling their own institutional tensions about the nature of literary critical practice. However, there were bound to be problems because, as I have argued, the specifically scientific concept of 'indeterminacy' does not allow for the kinds of understanding of intentional consciousness, of unique experience, of feeling, of cultural embodiment and value which have traditionally been the demesne of literary culture. Whatever kind of a 'science' literary criticism aspires to be, it cannot engage at all with literary texts if this intentional dimension is ignored or dealt with merely as a 'principle of measurement', whether this is the play of the signifier, ideology, or any other impersonal vehicle. In a liberal democratic culture increasingly dominated by models of measurement and quantifiable knowledge yet equally by demands for ever more effective forms of communication, it seems more important than ever to resist the easy seductions of the new scientized aesthetic and to return to the issue of the value of the non-quantifiable kind of knowledge embodied in literary texts and the question of how we might talk about it as literary critics. Aesthetic indeterminacy is created in the play of intentionality which is the distinctive feature of all art; aesthetic knowledge, and presumably, therefore, literary critical practice, must arise out of the unique nature of this mode of indeterminacy and requires understanding within its own terms.

The impact of postmodern relativism seems, however, to have produced a generally pragmatist orientation in literary criticism, one which has all too often abandoned questions about the specific nature of literary knowledge or of anything resembling Hirsch's understanding of 'validity in interpretation'. Science too, of course, increasingly frames its defence in pragmatic rather than epistemological terms. So if, for example, philosophers raise sceptical questions about the theoretical explanation of why water boils at a certain temperature, they cannot dispute the fact that it does so boil: science does accurately predict physical occurrences at this level; it works and can be used. Literary critics cannot predict the effects of literary texts in this way, but, as they give up on worrying about the kind of knowledge available in literature or the possibility of validity in interpretation, many orient themselves to some version of pragmatism: if we cannot say that one interpretation is 'more true' than another, we can say that the text is more useful for one set of purposes than for another; that it 'works' on this pragmatic level. Literary texts can be put to various uses: moral, political, sociological (or even those of career advancement). But the problem with this kind of argument is that it licenses us to judge the text entirely in terms of how well it performs the job we ask of it and to abandon all consideration of whether this is, in the first place, an appropriate job to demand. According to Stanley Fish, for example, we should stop worrying about 'truth' or 'knowledge' and accept that we must simply learn to be good professionals and to read texts as well as we can within the rules and conventions of the institution *as it exists in our moment of belonging*: 'Interpretation is not the art of construing but the art of constructing. Interpreters do not decode poems; they make them.'[16] One problem with this argument is that, on such a definition, 'good' may mean nothing more than 'conformist'. Of course, another use sustaining this orientation toward relativism may be that it appeals to the contemporary desire of literary critics to read texts politically, to give literature and their own practices the same kind of political function in their world that it had, say, for Sir Philip Sidney in his. And though relativism and politicization would seem to be naturally opposed (given that even if it undermines the normative definition of truth, a marginal position cannot claim any greater truth-status for itself), the assumption now seems to be that relativism at least evens up the contest: in serving to expose the traditional claim to knowledge as ideological, the marginalized position is put on a par with the established one. Is the pursuit of 'disinterested' knowing or experience for its own sake equivalent to political apathy or withdrawal into an ivory tower? May not the pursuit of any kind of knowledge or experience at least initially for its own sake actually enhance our existence as political beings in the full meaning of that word? I will come back to this issue and attempt to defend the value of disinterestedness in the last section of this essay. First, though, what are the consequences for literary criticism of abandoning all impulse towards such an ideal or condition of knowledge or experience?

First the somewhat overworked notion of incommensurability. For literary criticism, specifically, it means that even when we think we are making generally applicable observations, we are only ever talking about intelligibility or value within the rules or terms of a given language game. How pointless therefore (so the argument runs) to compare readings of texts from within different interpretative models. Why waste breath trying to say that one is better or more true than another when we can acknowledge from the start that we simply

[16] *Is There a Text in this Class?* (Cambridge: Cambridge UP, 1980), 327.

prefer this reading because it suits our own tastes or immediate pragmatic purposes better than that one? Better get rid of the word 'true' altogether: after all, we know at heart that it simply reflects our own desire or the value of the group with which we identify. Given the remaining choice between emotivism or pragmatic institutionalism, better to go for the latter or we may be tainted with the brush of 'individualism' (now unavoidably and inextricably contaminated with capitalism). 'True' is relative to the system and cannot be definitively separated from belief: to be authentic therefore we should quite self-consciously 'privilege' the reading that suits our purposes and admit the indistinguishable fictionality of all interpretative models. Only imperialists believe in truth.

As with 'truth', so with 'value'. If we cannot recognize the meanings (or even the existence) of other language games (texts, cultures, periods) from within our own, then we cannot arrive at evaluation. The 'Other' thus becomes a sacred but empty category—a relation of difference with no positive terms—as inaccessible to reasonable understanding as to careful observation or even old-fashioned human sympathy (this is the worst kind of solipsism, for we are simply constructing the 'other' through the projection of our own desire).[17] Various anti-humanist irrationalisms have been proposed as the way out of this world of cultural solipsism, and the 'sublime', in particular, has been rejuvenated within postmodernist discourse (to be glimpsed, but not to be represented). But without reasonable criteria for evaluation, are we not inevitably pitched toward the abyss of nihilism?

Enter thirdly, and consequently, the appeal of the 'pseudo-scientific'. Karl Popper developed his notion of falsifiability (that a theory is only scientific if it is open to refutation, or is 'falsifiable') in response to Humean scepticism about verification, but also specifically in reaction against psychoanalysis (and later, Marxism) as discourses which claim the authority of science but whose terms are so ill-defined or extendable they are simply not open to any kind of refutation. 'What is the point', he said, 'of criticising a theory rationally if we know from the start that it is neither refutable by pure reason, nor testable by experiment', or, one might add, even by human experience.[18] In pseudo-scientific practice, Doubt, the difficult business of trying to know as an open-ended struggle, actively seeking

[17] See Christopher Norris, *Truth and the Ethics of Criticism* (Manchester: Manchester UP, 1994).   [18] *Quantum Theory and the Schism in Physics*, 200.

disconfirmation of premises and hypotheses against the test of experience (or the text), is given up and the model simply confirmed every time it is applied. One is spared the patience of continual rereading as a means to challenge prejudice. But if the truth of an observation is only ever relative to the theory through which it is constructed, then we must accept, in any case, that all theories give us more knowledge of themselves than of the world or text to which they are applied. So theory as substantive dogma or pseudo-science may as well become what it is: an end in itself. How convenient that such perfectly self-contained systems are so amenable to the pedagogic demands of mass higher education whilst seeming to satisfy also its criteria for serious 'research'. Who would not find it easier to learn the abstract concepts of Freudian psychoanalysis than to fathom the poetry of even a single undistinguished human consciousness? Who, indeed, would not find it easier to explain the concept of the 'Oedipus complex' than fathom Freud's own profound and human engagement with the tragic emotions of Sophocles' ancient drama? The dangers of pseudo-scientific misapplication are that whilst appearing to open up the world they often serve only to close the world down, to make it safe by reintroducing as 'method' that habit whose veil literature is traditionally supposed to lift from our eyes. They may actually blind us to what Samuel Beckett in a brilliant essay on Proust (1931) saw as the nature of art: to present 'the object . . . perceived as particular and unique and not merely the member of a family . . . [D]etached from the sanity of a cause, isolated and inexplicable in the light of ignorance, then and only then might it be a source of enchantment.'[19]

3. Reading Woolf: The Dialectic of Consciousness and the View from Nowhere

In this final section I will attempt to defend the existence and value of a specifically aesthetic kind of knowing through a reading of Virginia Woolf's *To the Lighthouse*. I have chosen Woolf's novel as a text which self-consciously explores the problem of knowledge in the terms of the modern two cultures debate and, in so doing, engages with many of the same scientific ideas examined earlier in their

---

[19] *'Proust' and 'Three Dialogues with Georges Duthuit'* (London: John Calder, 1965), 22–3.

postmodern interpretation by Lyotard. In Woolf's novel, however, those same ideas are harnessed not to a pervasive notion of Uncertainty but to a rigorously dialectical exploration of modern Doubt as the disinterested impulse to know, and taking specific forms in science and art. Indeed, I will argue that what emerges is a much more persuasive defence of a disinterested but specifically aesthetic kind of knowledge than in the notions of indeterminacy borrowed from modern science to underpin Lyotard's postmodern concept of Uncertainty. Woolf's novel was published in 1927: the year when the philosophical impact of quantum theory was given its first elaborate popular expression by the astronomer Arthur Eddington in the Gifford lectures which were later published as *The Nature of the Physical World*; the year when Heisenberg's Uncertainty Principle first attracted controversial interpretation, and when Woolf's meditations on the philosophical discussion evenings with Bloomsbury's Cambridge realists and aesthetes begin to indicate her awareness not only of contemporary scientific ideas, but also of the contours of Bertrand Russell's theories of knowledge and of G. E. Moore's work on ethics. What was produced in each of these engagements with the problem of knowledge was a sense of the profound strangeness of the world we so often unthinkingly inhabit, and of the need to suspend our habitual modes of perception in order to try to understand what Russell referred to as the 'gulf between the world of physics and the world of sense': a gulf over which he later declared his entire work to be an attempt to build a bridge.[20] It will be my argument that Woolf saw art in a similar light and believed that the literary work was uniquely able to hold in balance a scientific 'view from nowhere' as the impulse to break out of habitual seeing, and an anchoring of this impersonal view in personal or subjective consciousness: that it could embody (a crucial word) a uniquely detached view of the world which not only includes human consciousness, but also includes our possession of that conception as part of what enables us to understand. The contemporary American philosopher Thomas Nagel in his own defence of the value of 'disinterested' knowing has put into conceptual terms what I take to be the aesthetically embodied quest of Woolf's novel: how might one, he asks, 'combine the perspective of a particular person inside the world with an objective view of that same world, the

---

[20] Bertrand Russell, *My Philosophical Development* (London: Allen & Unwin, 1959), 151.

person and the view included? It is a problem that faces every creature with the impulse and the capacity to transcend its particular point of view and to conceive of the world as a whole.'[21] We might tentatively respond that neither in science, nor even in philosophy, could this task be accomplished. Only in art do we have this kind of experience, and that is the unique knowledge which it has to offer. It is also why there seems to be an 'aesthetic' component in most creative and, indeed, ethical activity. I will try to show what I mean by 'aesthetic knowledge' by looking more closely at Woolf's work.

Repeatedly in her non-fictional and fictional prose, Woolf asks these kinds of questions. In A Room of one's Own (1928), she famously urged the woman writer in the twentieth century to 'see human beings not always in their relations to each other but in relation to reality . . . for no human being should shut out the view'.[22] Elsewhere in this text, she talks of this problem as the difficulty of seeing the spot at the back of one's head, and in her diary she mused on a 'consciousness of what I call "reality": a thing I see before me: something abstract; but residing in the downs or sky; besides which nothing matters'.[23] Yet this aspect of Woolf's work tends to be overlooked; she tends to be read as a novelist of flux, of subjective impressionism. Woolf has been the key modern writer for contemporary feminist criticism and it is Woolf as purveyor of the fluid 'feminine' sentence, or as the social critic of Victorian mores, or of relational form, the Paterian or Bergsonian Woolf reappropriated from an earlier symbolist reading, who is the most familiar figure in current critical discussions. Her interest in science or the problem of knowledge sometimes receives comment, but usually in order to confirm this kind of interpretation: the concentration tends to be on the imagery of flux and waves, of random atoms and uncertainty, for this seems to connect with the kinds of conceptualizations of indeterminacy which I discussed earlier, and to provide a kind of cosmic base for her vision of intersubjective relationship. But Woolf is neither a refashioner of Bergsonian élan vital for écriture feminine, nor is she a forerunner of the Lyotardian postmodern. Shifts in our own cultural preoccupations have wakened us to Woolf the feminist, but if this awakening produces a narrowly pragmatic approach to her

[21] The View from Nowhere (Oxford: Oxford UP, 1986), 3.
[22] A Room of one's Own (London: Hogarth Press, 1928), 118.
[23] The Diary of Virginia Woolf, iii, 1925–1930, ed. A. O. Bell and Andrew McNeillie (London: Hogarth Press, 1980), 196.

as a writer, then we will simply close down other ways of seeing which anchor her feminism in specific intellectual and aesthetic concerns remote from our own but which may actually expand our own if we can grasp them as intentional contexts. What seems perpetually to fascinate Woolf is the confrontation of what she repeatedly refers to as the 'ordinary mind' of everyday waking consciousness ('examine . . . an ordinary mind on an ordinary day', she tells us in a famous essay on modern fiction),[24] with the immense strangeness of a universe which seemed increasingly to be beyond the grasp of commonsense experience or perception. (It is no surprise therefore that she has Mr Ramsay chuckling at the thought of David Hume, the empiricist, grown fat and stuck in a bog.) All around, the intellectual currents which pressed on her emphasized this need to respect strangeness, to attempt to break out of habitual ways of seeing. Of philosophy, Russell wrote in his popular 'shilling shocker' *The Problems of Philosophy* that it 'keeps alive our sense of wonder by showing familiar things in an unfamiliar aspect', or as Eddington would assert in 1927: 'if we are to discern controlling laws of nature not dictated by the mind it would seem necessary to escape as far as possible from the cut-and-dried framework into which the mind is so ready to force everything that it experiences.'[25]

Writing on the problems of biography even, she reiterates in a graphic image this sense of the immense difficulty of bringing together the impressionistic and 'ordinary' sensory world and the strange and remote world of scientific knowledge: 'if we think of truth as something of granite-like solidity and of personality as something of rainbow-like intelligibility', then, she adds, the challenge is how to 'weld these into a seamless whole . . . the problem is a stiff one'.[26] The problem of knowledge as the issue of whether it is all flowing or whether it resolves itself into 'angular essences' is the quest of getting to the lighthouse on its 'stark bare rock', its ground of granite, from which its 'misty eye', its rainbow illumination of the world, stares out into the darkness of the surrounding sea.[27] But this

[24] 'Modern Fiction', in *Collected Essays*, vol. ii (London: Hogarth Press, 1966), 106.
[25] Bertrand Russell, *The Problems of Philosophy* (1912; Oxford: Oxford UP, 1967), 91; Eddington, *The Nature of the Physical World*, 209.
[26] Virginia Woolf, *Roger Fry: A Biography* (London: Hogarth Press, 1940), 149.
[27] *To the Lighthouse* (London: Hogarth Press, 1927), 286. All other quotations from the novel are taken from this edition; page references are given in parentheses in the text.

problem of knowledge not only informs the overall quest shape of the novel, but provides also the aesthetic logic for its three-part structure. The 'perspectivism' of Woolf's writing, the continuous experiment with point of view, is often noted as the hallmark of her style, but if we think of this formal device within the terms of the problem of knowledge, then it can be seen as the first step toward a 'view from nowhere': it is an analogue for minds of the centreless conception of space for physical objects. Within the scope of the novel form, however, these 'perspectives' can then be explored from within as situated consciousnesses in the world. A similar effect is created through her sophisticated and subtle use of free indirect discourse with its sometimes complicit, sometimes ironic blending of an authorial voice from nowhere with the situated voice of a particular character. The continuous sense of shifting between impersonal and personal viewpoints in her novels is echoed in their imagery of fading, distance, and threshold, and in their concern with permanence and transience (that a stone, as Mr Ramsay observes, worrying about his own authorial legacy as a philosopher, will outlast Shakespeare) (p. 59). Even the structural relations between characters may be understood in this light: the artists with their impulse toward identification—Lily the painter, Mrs Ramsay, artistic arranger of dinner parties and human destinies, Augustus Carmichael, the symbolist poet; and the scientists with their concern for detachment—Mr Banks the biologist, Mr Ramsay, the logical atomist-style philosopher, and his pupil Charles Tansley.

The Woolfian universe then is one where private consciousnesses, like locked rooms, but with small illuminated windows, look out on vast wastes of space: matches illuminating the dark, 'the two senses of that vastness and this tininess' (p. 119), to use Woolf's own phrase. This is a world of ever-shifting perspective, full of vanishing points, of images and moments of fading, of brilliant thresholds plunging into darkness, of momentary completion dissolving into time, of memories slipping in and out of consciousness. Repeatedly characters stand on the edge of darkness, 'in the failing light they all looked sharp-edged and ethereal and divided by great distances' (p. 115); or, in the midst of the ordinary, a game of tennis, for example, 'when solidity suddenly vanished, and such vast spaces lay between them' (p. 152); or Mrs Ramsay looking back from the doorway into the triumphal room in which she has made of the moment of her dinner party something permanent, and seeing it decompose and fade before her eyes into the mysterious flow of time (p. 178).

The problem of knowledge is explicitly referred to as Lily ponders Mr Ramsay's description of his work as thinking 'of a kitchen table when you're not there' (p. 40). Lily's mind wonders over the table as process and flickering impression: its texture of silvery bark, the fish-shaped leaves, over lovely evenings with flamingo-like clouds, and she has to make a strenuous effort to imagine Mr Ramsay's austere formal table on which she confers the value of 'muscular integrity' (p. 41). Lily's is the meandering of ordinary consciousness; it is what anchors us in the world of response, feeling, and sensation. But, we are told that Mr Ramsay, who looks for a table which cannot be seen, 'could not be judged like an ordinary person' (p. 41), indeed has been 'born blind, deaf and dumb to the ordinary things' (p. 111), and, for him, it is minds which 'tamper with the facts', which refuse the ethical and imaginative challenge of the 'view from nowhere', of the thought-experiment of self-negation, which are extraordinary: the 'extraordinary folly of women's minds' (p. 53), he thinks, as Mrs Ramsay insists on judging from within the world of human feeling and sensory perception. Here we have the problem of knowledge precisely as articulated in Eddington, Russell, Schrödinger, and other philosopher-scientists of the day: how to reconcile the formal and logical account of reality available in the bleached-out structures of mathematical science (the world of the extraordinary) with the world of ordinary sense-perception, of colour, taste, and sensation? Through the form of the aesthetic Woolf recreates the problem as one about the value of different ways of knowing. Tables, of course, have for long served as exempla in philosophical discussions of knowledge and truth, and indeed Eddington's first Gifford lecture would begin with a long meditation on the problem: imagine two tables, he told his audience, the commonplace table, a thing which occupies space, and the scientist's table, 'mostly emptiness' and 'sparsely scattered in that emptiness are numerous electric charges pushing about with great speed'.[28] Woolf's question is: how can this shadowdance of atoms represent the 'granite' of absolute knowledge, the solid 'view from nowhere'; how can the thing of substance be a product of the 'rainbow' of impressions, the shifting perspective of numerous onlookers?

Woolf is not a scientist, but she constructs an aesthetic from a scientific problem and then offers the resulting work of art as a kind

[28] *The Nature of the Physical World*, p. xvii.

of enacted and embodied answer to the problem. This is achieved through her use of the resources of the aesthetic as a structure and texture woven of language, of image, symbol, juxtaposition, irony, character, narrative voice: the problem receives its answer as the work of art. Just as the question of the table functions at the level of explicit metacommentary, to guide our understanding of the epistemological issue as we read, so too she provides a metacommentary on her own aesthetic answer in the representation of Lily Briscoe's quest to complete her painting: 'Beautiful and bright it should be on the surface', thinks Lily, 'feathery and evanescent, one colour melting into another like the colours on a butterfly's wing; but beneath the fabric must be clamped together with bolts of iron. It was to be a thing you could ruffle with your breath; and a thing you could not dislodge with a team of horses' (p. 264): rainbow and granite, impression and structure, the world seen through consciousness and the world viewed from nowhere. In order to paint, Lily must 'subdue all her impulses as a woman to something much more general' (p. 86), driven as she is to discover 'the thing that matters; to detach it; to separate it off; clean it of all the emotions and odds and ends of things' (p. 174), to 'find the thing itself before it has been made anything' (p. 297). In order to complete the painting, she discovers that she must 'lose sense of personality, consciousness . . . name' (p. 246). But the operation involves 'a razor edge of balance' (p. 296): for what is presented here as an aesthetic problem is epistemological, existential, and ethical too. The problem of knowledge is how to connect the impersonal view from nowhere, the world of science, with the world of sense, of cultural embodiment, of human consciousness and value.

Abandonment or exclusion of either perspective is represented as incompleteness in each of these spheres: yet how can they be connected? As Russell said, the 'the world of physics is, *prima facie*, so different from the world of perception that it is difficult to see how one can even afford evidence for the other', but as the physicist Erwin Schrödinger wrote of the scientific attitude, 'it gives a lot of factual information, puts all our experience in a magnificently consistent order, but it is ghastly silent about all and sundry that is really near to our heart'.[29] To go too far toward the view from nowhere

[29] Bertrand Russell, *Mysticism and Logic* (London: Longmans, 1918), 53; Erwin Schrödinger, *Nature and the Greeks* (1954) and *Science and Humanism* (1951; Cambridge: Cambridge UP, combined Canto edn., 1996), 95.

is to lose touch with the human world altogether, to enter a different kind of prison, to lose all sense of ego to the point of experiencing meaninglessness, nihilism, the sense that there is no place for one's own or another's subjectivity: Mr Ramsay standing on the edge of the spit and thinking how 'we know nothing and the sea eats away the ground we stand on' (p. 72), so he must retreat from the impulse and return to be taken back 'within the circle of life' of his family; or Mrs Ramsay, losing all fret, all stir, all personality, reduced to a 'wedge shaped core of darkness' (p. 99) suspended between negative capability and self-annihilation. To go far out but with an inability to leave behind the framework of immediate or subjective preoccupations is to experience the absurdity of one's own petty egotism: it is Charles Tansley with his insecurities and ambitions and his lurking knowledge that his anxiousness to impress and to receive academic recognition is unworthy, experienced by others as the 'ugly talk' which Mrs Ramsay cannot bear of academic ambition, of 'fellow-ships, readerships and lectureships' (p. 24); or Augustus Carmichael writing his lyric poetry of symbolic transcendence, egotistically unaware of the comic disjunction between his bodily grossness and his artistic pretension as he greedily helps himself to more soup, and basks, indifferent to the world of suffering around him, 'like a creature gorged with existence' (p. 274). Yet not to move toward the view at all, to shut out the real, in Woolf's phrase, is to enter into that prison, the closed and shuttered room of private consciousness, the narcissism that overwhelms us when we are unable to connect with anything outside of ourselves. But the complex texture of her prose presents each of these relations in unstable and ambiguous aspect: heroic, absurd, noble, or egotistic. What do we make of Mrs Ramsay carefully helping Mr Banks to a 'specially tender piece' and thinking that it partook of eternity (p. 163): is the collocation of eternity and meat heroic vision or absurd narcissism? Woolf's skilful blending of authorial and individual voice in the intricate modulations of her use of free indirect discourse entices the reader to attempt a judgement: but does she imply sympathy, or simply irony about human pretension, or both? For each of these examples represents a human attempt and failure to connect the world of science with that of sense. Maybe reconciliation or even contact is impossible, but as Lily says of staying with the Ramsays, so it is with the reading of Woolf's novel: 'to be made to feel violently two opposite things at the same time' (p. 159); to experience for ourselves the problem of knowledge.

What is offered in the literary text is the simultaneous apprehension of experience and of the idea of it, participation with detachment: the perspective of 'a particular person in the world with an object view of that same world, the person and the view included'.

Interestingly, of course, Roger Fry, who was trained in science and in art, had articulated this view of the aesthetic of post-impressionism in his *Vision and Design* (written for the second post-impressionist exhibition of 1920). Fry's 'vision' is analogous to Woolf's 'rainbow', his 'design', her 'granite', and for him the aim of contemporary post-impressionist painting is their reconciliation: 'these artists do not seek to give what can, after all, be but a pale reflex of actual appearance, but to arouse the conviction of a new and definite reality . . . they wish to make images which by the clearness of their logical structure, and by their closely-knit texture, shall appeal to our disinterested and contemplative imagination . . . they aim not at illusion but at reality.'[30] But for Woolf, there was also an ethical imperative because the attempt to find in the aesthetic a means of holding 'vision' and 'design', of the scientific 'view from nowhere' with the situatedness of consciousness in the world, is also the problem of how we situate ourselves between what might become, in one direction, nihilistic detachment or, in the other, solipsistic or narcissistic self-importance. Woolf writes repeatedly of the menace of the 'dark bar' of the 'I' which threatens ever to cast its shadow across the writer's page and of how it might be dispelled by a more cosmic perspective which offers release from egotism without capitulation to or sense of absorption in an indifferent nature.[31] The capacity of the aesthetic in its ability to offer us experience and the idea of it is, as Kant said, the poet's venture 'to realise to sense, rational ideas of invisible beings . . . he tries, by means of imagination . . . to go beyond the limits of experience and to present [ideas] to sense with a completeness with which there is no example in nature'.[32] Literature makes experience strange in this completion by lifting it out of itself, but if we insist on accepting relativism as the justification for reading according to a preformulated or narrowly pragmatist account of knowledge as use or desire we can only see from the place where we began.

[30] Roger Fry, *Vision and Design* (1920), ed. J. B. Bullen (Oxford: Oxford UP, 1981), 167.
[31] This theme runs through *A Room of one's Own*. See also her essay 'Street Haunting', in *The Death of the Moth and Other Essays* (London: Hogarth Press, 1942), 23–4 and 27–9.   [32] *Critique of Aesthetic Judgement*, 157–8.

To return then to the two cultures debate: literary critics have learned from classic science the value of Doubt as pre-emptively driven to overcome its own epistemological limits. Lily completes her painting once she learns respect for Mr Ramsay and recognizes that 'he must have had his doubts about that table . . . whether the table was a real table; whether it was worth the time he gave to it; whether he was after all able to find it' (p. 241). We can see doubt, the struggle to know, as keeping us alive as the impulse to resolve it; the Uncertainty of relativist postmodernism as a kind of comfortable acquiescence, an assumption of reconciliation which reduces the strangeness of natural and aesthetic worlds to our familiar models and simply dissolves the problem of consciousness and intentionality by writing it out of consideration. The problem for literary criticism, as for literature itself, is how to bring that scientific impulse back from nowhere and into a relation with our human situation, to the kind of in-dwelling of embodied consciousness, where we begin from, as individuals and inhabitants of a culture. Aesthetic knowledge is unique because of its capacity to make these connections in the way it does: literature has its own kind of indeterminacy and literary criticism does not need to authorize what it does by appeal to the scientific forms of this idea. What might be more valuable than the appeal to New Science is a reminder of the regulative ideal of the 'view from nowhere' as the broad imperative of all science and an important impulse in literature too. Perhaps as literary critics we should try to respect both this impulse and the recognition of our inevitably situated condition of seeing, accept the need therefore for Leavis's participatory 'experience' *and* the kind of 'scientific' impersonalism elaborated here as the view from nowhere. Perhaps we need to explore the ways in which criticism speaks its own forms of free indirect discourse. Neither the monologue of an imperialistic postmodern aestheticism nor that of an aggressive positivistic scientism can substitute for the requirement of genuine dialogue and recognition of sameness and difference across the two cultures divide. Genuine mediation is hard. As Harold Bloom has written: 'The only humane virtue we can hope to teach through a more advanced study of literature than we have now is the social virtue of detachment from one's own imagination, recognising always that such detachment made absolute destroys any individual imagination.'[33]

[33] *The Anxiety of Influence: A Theory of Poetry* (London: Oxford UP, 1973), 86.

3

Science, Interpretation, and Criticism

DAVID E. COOPER

I

Reflecting on the 'two cultures' debate of the 1960s Patricia Waugh notes that C. P. Snow's image of science was, even then, a fading one. Nor, she observes, was this seized upon by Snow's arch-critic F. R. Leavis who, indeed, subscribed to the same image of science, taking issue only over the relevance of science, so pictured, to the 'judgements about life' which define a civilized culture and which, in his view, are the domain, principally, of literary criticism.

While it is not without some diehard defenders today, and while it might continue to shape the 'man in the street's' picture of scientific enquiry, the kind of view assumed by Snow has, in the intervening years, become increasingly incredible to many of those who reflect on the nature of science. In this essay I want to look at some considerations which have contributed to the incredibility of this view of science—considerations which at the very least soften the old 'two cultures' contrast between scientific and literary understanding, and which, in their more dramatic renderings, serve to assimilate science to literary criticism—indeed to render the former a branch of the latter. As an example of these claims at the more dramatic end of the spectrum, consider those of the postmodernist Jean Baudrillard. According to him, all 'referentials' have been 'liquidated': that is, we have renounced the very idea that words and theories can refer to anything 'real'. Revelling in the 'hyperreal', we now see all human constructions—including scientific theory—as mere 'simulacra', no more capable of truth and objectivity than literary fantasies or

Disney cartoons.[1] Scientific study of the world, therefore, is no different in status from exploring the world of a novel or the world of Donald Duck.

My essay has the form of a crescendo, though the reader may think it closes with a disappointingly muted coda. I shall start with some more modest considerations that soften any sharp contrast between scientific and literary understanding, building up to those which, on the Baudrillard view, might serve to elide the one into the other.

But, before that, two preliminaries—the first by way of a historical observation. That there are now voices speaking of science as a branch of literary criticism should come as no surprise to people familiar with the usual fate of attempts to divide knowledge into different kinds—into, say, a priori versus empirical knowledge, or factual versus evaluative knowledge, or (the case which concerns us) scientific versus humane understanding. For the tendency is for the one kind of knowledge to drive out the other: for people to insist, say, that there is only a priori knowledge, so-called empirical knowledge being mere uncertain opinion; or that science alone is the repository of knowledge, the so-called understanding of humanists being a matter merely of subjective response or emotional expression. Sooner or later, this aggression gets avenged: so that one then hears, for example, that there is only empirical knowledge, the so-called a priori truths of mathematics and logic being mere conventions people happen to have agreed upon.

As a second preliminary, we need to have before us that picture of science to which C. P. Snow subscribed: a picture found increasingly incredible, and one whose dismantling will serve at least to soften the contrast between scientific and humane enquiry, and hence between two cultures of enquiry and understanding. I shall call it the 'mirroring picture' of science. The metaphor of the mirror suggests two main components. The first is that scientific theories are, or strive to be, accurate mirrors of—representations of—how things are. Reality is determinate: there is a way things are, and in principle nothing prevents us from coming to know what this is. A true science is one that mirrors, corresponds to, this reality. In practice, we may not be too confident how much of science is true in this sense—but the explanation for this is provided by a second component. Our theories will not mirror the way things are unless we and our

---

[1] *Selected Writings* (Cambridge: Polity, 1988), 166 ff.

investigations and experiments are free from defects, distortions, prejudices, and follies. Now it may be that we shall never be able to hold up to nature a perfectly clean and polished mirror, but given the success of scientific method over the last few centuries—its record of conquest over obstacles to objective enquiry—the perfect mirror remains an intelligible and sensible ideal.

II

It is with considerations germane to the assimilation of scientific to literary understanding that I begin, considerations concerning the role of metaphors and ideal models in the sciences. Nobody would deny that these are often of great importance in the development of theories in various sciences: for example, the metaphor of light as waves in optics, of deep and surface syntactic structure in linguistics, of the model of perfect competition in economics. The traditional view has been, however, that metaphors and models, however heuristically valuable, are nevertheless dispensable with in principle. Like diagrams and the coloured balls chemists use to represent molecules, metaphors and models are among the props of science, but not of its essence.

This traditional wisdom has been challenged in recent years. It has been argued, notably by Mary Hesse,[2] that metaphor is essential to scientific enquiry, that there could be no understanding of phenomena except in the light of imaginative ways of seeing-as, of novel and at the time figurative redescriptions of phenomena. What were once metaphorical references, like those of Newton to 'force' and 'mass', may eventually pass into the established, 'literal' lexicon of science: but this must not delude us into ignoring the indispensable role played by the metaphors in nurturing and subsequently guiding the relevant area of scientific enquiry. Shelley may have exaggerated in speaking of metaphors as 'creating anew the universe', but maybe it is only through metaphors that we can create and renew our descriptions of the universe.

Again, it has been argued, this time by Nancy Cartwright, that ideal models belong to the very fabric of science: for it is only to ideal models that the laws of physics strictly apply. If these laws govern

---

[2] *Revolutions and Reconstructions in the Philosophy of Science* (Brighton: Harvester, 1980).

anything in the real world, this will be the behaviour of things in the controlled, quarantined conditions of the laboratory, where to a degree 'real life mimics explanatory models'. Generally, what these laws 'govern has only the appearance of reality and the appearance [the ideal model] is far tidier and more readily regimented than reality itself'.[3] In fact, models as untidy and unregimented as reality itself would be useless, for purposes of prediction, say.

What impact do these considerations have upon the mirroring picture of science, and how do they serve to soften the contrast between scientific and humane enquiry? Insistence on the essential role of metaphor spoils the image of reality imprinting itself on the mind of the impartial scientist-observer. If Hesse is right, it is only when the mirror has, so to speak, been doctored so as to receive data through the filter which a metaphor provides that anything will show up on the mirror at all. Unless we first see the data as—or by analogy with—this or that, we shall never see them at all. The effect of treating the laws of physics as idealizations is to deny that science is or could be a strictly accurate representation of reality. An accurate mirror of reality would be as fuzzy and untidy as it is—and hence useless. The mirror science holds up to reality, if it is to be any use to us, must, as Nietzsche long ago observed, simplify and so distort reality: it is tidier, more regimented than the real thing.

If science explores the implications of guiding metaphors and reflects on idealized models abstracted from the *tohu-bohu* of nature in the raw, then it is surely not without its affinities to the labours of the literary critic. It is hardly controversial to reaffirm the point, made familiar to us by Shelley and others, that a central aspect of the critical task is reception of and reflection on the metaphors and other 'figurative curtains' which, for Shelley, distinguish poetic works. And the idea that a literary work—a tragedy, say—is an idealized model of human beings, their passions and motives, goes back to Aristotle's *Poetics*. Indeed the point that science is useful precisely because it idealizes and abstracts echoes Aristotle's view that tragedy is more valuable than mere history: for history—a messy unstructured record of accidentally related events—does not enable us to discern universal truths about the human condition in the manner of the well-wrought tragedy, whose very artificiality equips it to render salient the essential aspects of that condition.

---

[3] *How the Laws of Physics Lie* (Oxford: Clarendon Press, 1983), 162.

III

I turn to another consideration, one with perhaps more radical implications for the mirroring picture of science and science's proximity to literary criticism. Some years ago I was bearded by a member of a fundamentalist Christian sect who asked me if I accepted every word of the Old Testament. No, I replied: after all there are inconsistencies; for example, Noah's ark would have to be many times larger than it is described as being in order to accommodate two of every animal species. Quick as a flash, the fundamentalist retorted that there was no inconsistency here: what happened was, you see, that as the animals trooped into the ark, they all shrank to a fraction of their usual sizes. The story is humorous—but the point illustrated is a serious one: that any theory can be held onto, in the teeth of whatever evidence, provided something else is given up (such as the belief that creatures do not suddenly shrink). Philosophers of science speak, in this connection, of the 'underdetermination of theory': take any theory which is compatible with 'the facts', the data—you can then construct any number of other theories, incompatible with the first, but equally compatible with 'the facts'. For example, a Creationist worth his salt will have little trouble accommodating—'explaining away'—the data cited by the Evolutionist.

This does not mean that Creationism is as plausible as Evolutionism—nor, more generally, that any two theories consistent with the data are equally viable. What it does mean is that the mirroring picture of scientific knowledge is deficient: what it ignores is that different mirrors held up in front of the same scene—the same data—may register it very differently. The scene itself—the facts themselves—can never decide in favour of one representation, one theory, rather than another which is equally consistent with the facts. And this means, in turn, that if we are to prefer one theory over another—as of course we do and must—we need to employ criteria over and above adequacy to the evidence.

There may be many such criteria, but two seem especially central—simplicity and coherence. Given two theories equally consistent with the observed data, we will go for the one which is simpler, more elegant, and coheres better with what we already think we know than the other. (These two criteria may conflict, and then the sparks fly. They did around 1600, when the Copernican system gave a simpler explanation of our observations of the planets than the Ptolemaic, but cohered much worse with what people thought they already knew—especially about God and his plan. And the sparks can still fly today, in medicine say: Yin and Yang cosmology offers a simple and elegant explanation of certain medical phenomena—but no one has any idea how to fit it into orthodox medical science.)

How does all this bear on the relation of science to literary criticism? Attempts are sometimes made to formalize notions like simplicity and coherence: to treat the coherence of beliefs with one another, for example, as a matter simply of logical consistency. But such attempts are surely misconceived: the coherence we seek among our beliefs is more amorphous than, less specifiable than, logical consistency. In aiming at coherence, says Hilary Putnam, 'we aim at a *Weltanschauung*',[4] an overall picture that satisfies us, and into which some beliefs fit far less well than others, even if they are not strictly inconsistent with it. If this is so—if the coherence so central to theory choice in the sciences is something informal, something one 'has a nose for', a matter of fit and harmony—then the role of coherence in science does not sound so very different from its role in literary criticism. David Hume, in his marvellous essay *Of the Standard of Taste*, included among the qualities of the true critic that practical, uncodifiable good sense which equips the critic to tell whether a literary work 'hangs together'—whether, say, a certain chapter or scene chimes with the overall tone of the work.

What I am saying here about coherence can be generalized. Putnam writes that 'the "real world" depends on upon our values':[5] even to have a notion of the real world we must deploy criteria of rational acceptability which discriminate between better and worse accounts of the world. And Putnam's point is that these criteria—coherence, simplicity, elegance, relevance, and so on—reflect our sense of what is valuable, what is virtuous, in cognitive activity. But then is it not these same criteria which also reflect our sense of what is aesthetically virtuous and which, traditionally at least, critics have employed in their appraisals of literary works? (I am aware that in some critical circles today it is incoherence, aporia, and self-subversion which are regarded as the marks of literary depth and merit: but then, in those circles, science too is exhorted to eschew coherence and consensus

[4] *Pragmatism: An Open Question* (Oxford: Blackwell, 1995), 15.
[5] *Reason, Truth and History* (Cambridge: Cambridge UP, 1981), 135.

and seek dissonance and subversion instead. So, however backhand-
edly and aberrantly, the affinity between criteria of appraisal in art
and science is retained.)

IV

The mirroring picture of science, then, had two components: a view
of reality as having a determinate nature there to be captured by
science, and a view of how science must proceed for the mirror truly
to capture nature. The objections so far adumbrated have focused on
this second component: the idea that we can arrive at a true depiction
of the world by holding up a clean mirror to it overlooks the muteness
of the world—the failure of the data it affords us to motivate acceptance of one theory rather than another; a failure, a muteness, that
must be compensated for by the active construction of metaphors and
models, and by the deployment of criteria, like coherence, which
receive no mention in the mirroring picture. What has not yet been
challenged is the first component: the idea of a determinate world
there to be got right, of a determinate nature there for science to
correspond to. It is to the challenge to this idea, and its implications
for science's affinities to literary criticism, that I finally turn.

There are in fact many ways to challenge it. One goes in two stages.
The thought at the first stage goes back to Kant: it is that there is no
way we can, as it were, get out of our own skins in order to check the
correspondence between our image of the world and the world itself.
The world that we experience is one always already shaped by our
concepts and classifications of things: and there can be no primordial
encounter with nature in the raw which would enable us to assess the
fit between the world, on the one hand, and those concepts and
classifications on the other. As Richard Rorty puts it, 'we cannot
find a skyhook which lifts us' above our beliefs so as to assess their
'correspondence with reality as it is in itself'.[6] The scientific image of
the world is no better off here than the pre-scientific, everyday one:
for the former necessarily builds upon the latter.

This Kantian view, however, remains, as it stands, compatible with
the idea of a determinate reality: for it might be argued—and in effect
was argued by Kant himself—that while our refined, scientific con-

---

[6] *Objectivity, Relativism and Truth* (Cambridge: Cambridge UP, 1991), 38.

ception of reality cannot be checked against reality, it is the only one that rational beings like ourselves could entertain. In broad outline, that is, the concepts and classifications we apply to the world, suitably honed by science, are the only ones available. What reality 'in itself' might be like, God only knows (indeed, he may be what it is): but the reality which matters to us—empirical reality as we encounter and experience it—can only be the way enlightened rational beings do encounter it.

So a second stage is needed in the demolition of the mirroring picture. The *coup de grâce* is administered by the pragmatists' recognition of 'the interdependence of concepts and interests'. The reason why the world cannot, as one philosopher puts it, announce 'I am like this', rather than that—why there cannot be 'the correct reading' of the world—is because the concepts in terms of which we experience the world reflect our interests in it, interests which we can at least imagine might have been very different.[7]

If there is no sense to comparing a view of the world with the way the world independently is, and if there can be different views of it which reflect different constellations of concepts and interests, the mirroring picture must be finally abandoned. And there is no doubt that it is this line of thought which conspires towards the more radical assimilations of science to literature: towards, for example, Rorty's pronouncement that chemistry and literary criticism are 'equal comrades . . . distinguished only by [their] interests, not by cognitive status',[8] and towards those ultra-radical pronouncements which in effect equate science with literary criticism.[9]

How does this happen? How does a critique of the mirroring picture of science lead to the reduction of science to something else? We can see how by reflecting on the fate of an infamous remark of Jacques Derrida—'il n'y a pas de hors-texte'. This is often translated as 'There is nothing outside/beyond the text', but this is to give it a twist which Derrida probably did not intend. What he intended, I think, was that there is nothing 'untexted', and this was his rather dramatic, Gallic way of expressing the broadly Kantian idea I articulated earlier: namely, that we never encounter the world in the raw,

[7] Jane Heal, *Fact and Meaning: Quine and Wittgenstein on Philosophy of Language* (Oxford: Blackwell, 1989), 148.   [8] *Objectivity, Relativism and Truth*, 83.
[9] See for example the arguments of the school of the so-called 'strong sociology of knowledge': David Bloor, *Knowledge and Social Imagery* (London: Routledge & Kegan Paul, 1976).

but always as already conceptualized and interpreted. In that sense, the world is analogous to a text which, by definition, is something which has to be interpreted.

But Derrida's remark has been given a twist that turns it into an ultra-radical slogan. Rendered as 'There is nothing outside/beyond the text', it is construed as saying that all texts—those of science and history as much as novels and poems—are fictions. A work of fiction is one that is not about reality: its words do not refer to, and are neither true nor false of, real things. In that case, however, the reasoning goes, a work of history or of chemistry is also a work of fiction: for have we not acknowledged that the world is a text—not something we encounter as it is, for there is no way that it is except as a 'construct' of our language, of the concepts and classifications encoded in that language? There is nothing, therefore, for the texts of history or science to be about—except themselves. As one literary critic puts it, since 'what language refers to—any language—is . . . textualized', it is never about the things of 'actuality', but only about 'history texts, newspaper accounts, letters . . . and legend'.[10] Or, as Baudrillard had it, all extra-textual 'referentials' having been 'liquidated', we can only experience and talk about 'simulacra'. 'Truth, reference and object[ivity] have ceased to exist.' The scientist or the historian may believe he is investigating the real natural or human world: but in effect he is only exploring other texts—the writings, views, and conceptual edifices of his predecessors and colleagues. And that, of course, is the profession of literary criticism. Science, history, every form of enquiry have become branches of literary criticism.

V

What has gone wrong? Unless we subscribe to Bertrand Russell's flippant dictum that it is the very point of philosophy to take us from sensible premisses to conclusions so paradoxical that no one can believe them, we shall want to challenge a train of thought that has led us from the serious Kantian-cum-pragmatist criticism of the

---

[10] Linda Hutcheon, *A Poetics of Postmodernism: History, Theory, Fiction* (New York: Routledge, 1988), 144; quoted in Joseph Margolis, *Interpretation Radical But Not Unruly* (Berkeley and Los Angeles: University of California Press, 1995), 161. I am indebted to Margolis's book for my remarks in Section V.

mirroring picture to a nihilistic denial of distinctions between fact and fiction, truth and legend, world and text, scientific enquiry and literary appreciation. I suspect that all sorts of things have gone wrong on the journey—not least, a casual playing about with ambiguous terms like 'fiction' (something can be a fiction in the sense of being, in some sense, a human product, without thereby being a fiction in the sense of something disjointed from actuality). But it is with just one aspect of the ultra-radical, nihilistic position that I shall, in conclusion, concern myself.

There is irony in the objection I want to raise, for it is to the effect that, in an important sense, the ultra-radicals have not been radical enough: they have not, that is, really managed to break with—to uproot themselves from—the very notions of truth, reference, fact, objectivity, and the like which they purport to be discarding or 'liquidating'. Recall, first, that terms like 'truth', 'fact', and even 'objectivity' are familiar ones, belonging to the vernacular, and not technical, professional terms. There have of course been professional, philosophical theories about the meanings of these terms, including the theories associated with the mirroring picture—truth as correspondence, objectivity as a matter of presuppositionless enquiry into a mind-independent reality, and so on. And let us grant, in the light of our Kantian-cum-pragmatist objections to the mirroring picture, that these are bad theories of truth, objectivity, and so forth.

Does it follow that we should discard these terms and deny that science or history can be true, objective, factual, referential? That would only follow if one could see no alternative way of understanding the terms to those offered by the bad, rejected theories. The ultra-radicals, the nihilists, fail to explore alternative ways, are so hooked on the traditional, mirroring theory of truth and objectivity that, in rejecting this theory, they are compelled to reject the terms themselves.

The authentically radical position, by contrast, is not to discard the terms—not to proclaim, say, that facts are really fictions, or that we never really refer to anything—but patiently to articulate accounts of truth, fact, reference, and so on which are not in hock to bad theory: a frankly pragmatist account of truth, perhaps, or an account of objectivity in terms of ideal consensus. Unfortunately, this is hard, painstaking work. And of course, it is much easier to announce the death of truth, the liquidation of reference, the end of objectivity, the 'priority of fiction over reality' (de Man). It is also absurd to do this, and it is to do something almost obscenely devoid of a modicum of humility. For it is in effect to rubbish the ordinary and very ancient thinking of the human race—a race that has got along well enough by thinking with the help of notions like truth and reference. Some philosophers exhibit an unfortunate tendency to misconstrue those notions. But to reject that ancient thinking along with those misconstructions really would be to sacrifice what is enduring and valuable for what is fashionable and meretricious.

4

Evidence-Based and Evidence-Free Generalizations

A Tale of Two Cultures

RAYMOND TALLIS

1. *Introduction*

To an outsider, it seems that, since the study of literature was first established as an academic discipline, there has been almost continuous disagreement over the best or most appropriate approach to criticism. Recently, the very legitimacy of appreciation, evaluation, and interpretation of individual works and individual authors has been questioned. Dissent within literary studies has acquired a bitter edge and there are deep divisions amongst academic critics.

The major catalyst has been the emergence of a family of approaches to literature arising out of post-Saussurian schools of thought: structuralist and post-structuralist literary criticism and theory; and the various brands of criticism that have been directly or indirectly inspired by them. The striking feature of these new schools is a shift from the endeavour to understand individual works of literature on what is perceived to be their own terms towards an aspiration to an 'overstanding' of literature as a whole. Literary criticism and traditional scholarship have been displaced by literary theory which has in turn given place to something called 'Theory'.

The emergence of Theory was announced by Richard Rorty over twenty years ago in a widely cited article. Theory, according to Rorty, is a general method of approaching texts or discourses, 'a kind of writing . . . which is neither the evaluation of the relative merits of intellectual productions, nor intellectual history, nor moral philosophy, nor social prophecy, but all of these mingled together in a new genre'.[1] The ascent of Theory has been reflected in an increasing tendency to look *through* individual works of literature to the structures of the system(s) of discourse which are said to underlie them, or *past* them to the wider cultural—intellectual, social, political—formations which they are thought involuntarily to mirror or express.

This shift was decisively signalled a couple of decades ago by Barthes's enormously influential *S/Z*,[2] which atomized a novella by Balzac, breaking up the text into lexias or 'units of reading' and allocating those lexias to five classes—the semes, and the hermeneutic, the proairetic, the symbolic, and the cultural codes. Barthes's approach was implicitly and explicitly an expression of his belief that the significance of an individual work of art is best sought through seeing it as part of a larger discursive formation or social text rather than as a stand-alone artefact produced by an individual consciousness. 'The author' is merely a site where boluses of the collective consciousness, packets of the nth hand—shot through with various kinds of unconsciousness—are sequestrated, brand-marked, and emitted. A poem or novel is but a faint precipitate out of the supersaturated solution of the already-written, the already-read. In the absence of an individual author intending, making, shaping the work, there is only the operation of impersonal systems acting through the work. The work, consciousness, the self, the reader, are structured by language, or, more generally, by the sign systems of the collective consciousness and unconsciousness.

Barthes's methods and their underlying rationale, once revolutionary, are now the almost universal convention. The massive and overwhelming influence of Lacan and Derrida and their innumerable epigones has made the emphasis in literary studies on various forms of collective unconscious—linguistic, psychoanalytical, historical, and so on—the norm. The post-structuralist challenge to the distinction between structure and content, and even between the signifier and the signified, has prompted critic to parrot critic in asserting that literary art is about signifiers without signifieds and has little or nothing to do with any reality outside of the text, except in so far as reality is more text. Because, moreover, the conditions that have

---

[1] 'Professionalised Philosophy and Transcendental Culture', *Georgia Review*, 30 (1976), 757–69 (pp. 763–4); repr. in R. Rorty, *Consequences of Pragmatism (Essays, 1972–80)* (Brighton: Harvester, 1982).
[2] *S/Z: An Essay*, trans. Richard Miller (New York: Hill & Wang, 1974).

given rise to the systems that underlie literary texts are self-contra-dictory—for a variety of Marxist, Freudian, and other reasons—texts are doomed to be at odds with themselves (unless they are written by practitioners of Theory). A crucial function of the critic is therefore 'deconstruction': this is (to use Barbara Johnson's neat encapsula-tion) to 'tease out the warring forces of signification within the text'. The critic will use deconstruction and other techniques to read the work 'against the grain', so as to challenge the already-written, the already-read. This is a good—'radical', 'subversive', 'revolution-ary'—thing to do because the already-written and the already-read incorporate the 'taken for granted' and the taken for granted is bad since, in an unjust world, taking things for granted, like confusing history and nature, is to collude with injustice.

The result of much of this work has been predictably dull: *S/Z* is more like *S/ZZZZZ* . . . But the idea of unpacking from within the text the (textual) world around it and the conventions that structure it has remained attractive to advanced critics, as has the related assumption that works of literature are, above all, texts, and their interpretation should be guided by the fact that texts do not refer to an outside world, except inasmuch as the latter is composed of more text, and that any and every text is to be understood in relation to the systems of signification that regulate discursive practice.

Not everyone, however, is happy with this approach to literature and a few critics have been brave enough to express their unhappiness robustly in print. They feel that Theory is, above all, mechanistic and reductionist—which is hardly surprising since every text is approached with the aim of drawing the same preformed conclusions. And although 'overstanding' now has numerous brands—feminist, post-colonial, Lacanian, Marxist, New Historicist, etc.—this modest variety has done little to alleviate the monotony. Under the homo-genizing gaze of the overstanding critic, the differences between Jane Austen and Wilbur Smith, or between Henry James, Barbara Cartland, and the Venerable Bede, are less important than their deep similarities: all five failed to challenge the colonial enterprise; none of them understood the first thing about the Oedipalized negotiation of the transition from the mirror to the symbolic stages, though their work shows they were up to their eyes in its consequences—to the point of believing the fictitious self to be real; all five were blissfully innocent of the ways in which their texts undid themselves; none of them challenged the confusion between nature and culture that enabled the historically derived to be passed off as the eternally true; and they all took for granted the taken for granted, thereby colluding with those power/knowledge structures that keep the oppressed in their state of oppression.

Approaching works of literature with preconceived ideas, and preventing the interpreted works from speaking for themselves, not only guaranteed a monotonous similarity of interpretation; it also encouraged the imposition of interpretations on the basis of very scanty independent evidence. Critics who are not progressive enough to reject close and careful readings of individual texts have bitterly resented the anti-scholarly habit of using tendentious readings of classic or canonical works to support vast presuppositions about the nature of society, the relationship between language and the world, the origin of the self, the interaction between knowledge and power, and so forth. Advanced critics have in their turn accused traditional scholars of timidity and of a failure to recognize the implicit theory within their own practice and to reflect upon it.

My own position is highly sympathetic to the concerns of traditional scholars, a position that has firmed up since I have observed how Theory has managed to survive, indeed to flourish, even when many of its fundamental assumptions have been examined and shown to be groundless and/or self-contradictory;[3] how its practitioners have carried on regardless,[4] with the flow of publications undiminished; and how, to an outside eye, professional advancement seems to be assisted rather than hindered by commitment to criticism that works within, rather than contests, the assumptions of Theory.

This remarkable indifference to counter-argument may in part be because, as I have argued elsewhere, Theory is consonant with wider trends within the humanities: the pathologization of culture and the marginalization of the role of the conscious agent in all activities, including such distinctively and seemingly highly conscious ones as

[3] See, for example: Brian Vickers, *Appropriating Shakespeare: Contemporary Critical Quarrels* (New Haven: Yale UP, 1993); J. G. Merquior, *From Prague to Paris: A Critique of Structuralist and Post-structuralist Thought* (London: Verso, 1986); Raymond Tallis, *Not Saussure: A Critique of Post-Saussurean Literary Theory* (London: Macmillan, 1988; 2nd edn. 1995); Raymond Tallis, *In Defence of Realism* (London: Edward Arnold, 1988; 2nd edn. Lincoln: University of Nebraska Press, 1998); John Ellis, *Against Deconstruction* (Princeton: Princeton UP, 1989).
[4] See Raymond Tallis, 'The Survival of Theory', in *Theorrhoea and After* (London: Macmillan, 1998).

writing literature.[5] There are, however, other possible explanations, and, in the present chapter, I shall advance a less ambitious 'internalist' thesis: that Theory, far from being an aberration from, is a culmination of certain tendencies that have always been present within literary and cultural studies. In particular, I shall suggest that the widespread and uncritical acceptance of the evidence-free assertions of the founders of Theory is an extension of a much longer tradition of accepting evidence-poor assertions; that, because of their methodological weakness, literary studies have always been at risk of being expropriated by fashions led by charismatics and charlatans. More specifically, I shall argue that the discrepancy between the scope of the general statements made within literary and cultural studies and the minute size of the database upon which such statements are founded is not new. What is novel about Theory is only that its 'truths' are of a wider, indeed, global scope: that it looks beyond literature and, on the basis of few or no facts, makes assertions about, for example, the nature of discourse, or of the metaphysical mind set of Western Culture. That, in other words, the difference between Theory and what preceded it is in many cases only a matter of degree rather than of kind.

My general point will be that it has always been possible 'to get away with murder' in a discipline that has no tradition of adequately testing general statements. I shall conclude that one of the most pressing projects within the humanities as a whole (for the problem, of course, extends far beyond literary studies) in the wake of Theory, is, perhaps, to learn how to determine the legitimate scope of general statements—which are often implicitly causal and quantitative— when there is rarely access to adequate empirical evidence.

2. Evidence-Based Medicine

As medicines become more powerful, the opportunities for doing good with the right treatment and doing harm with the wrong one increase and the burden of responsibility carried by clinicians grows proportionately. The rise of consumerism, in which patients are in more equal partnership with their doctors, means that the latter are

---

[5] *Enemies of Hope: A Critique of Contemporary Pessimism* (London: Macmillan, 1997).

more explicitly accountable to patients for the decisions they make. For these and many other reasons, doctors have become more concerned about the quality of the evidence upon which therapeutic choices are made.

The only truly robust method for obtaining good evidence is the double-blind randomized controlled trial which entered clinical science in the 1940s. Prior to being made widely available, new drugs, for example, are required to be evaluated by assigning carefully matched patients randomly either to the drug under study, or to a placebo, or to the best existing treatment. During the period of the trial, neither the patient nor the assessing doctor knows which treatment the patient is receiving. This 'double-blind' arrangement is essential to ensure that enthusiasm for the new treatment does not bias the observers: it embodies the medical profession's own suspicion of itself and its awareness of the potential of both patient and doctor for self-deception and for consciously and unconsciously shaping observations to conform with their wishes. The double-blind arrangement, in short, reflects an acute awareness of the occupational hazard of all empirical enquiry, that of confirmatory bias. In the last few decades, the design of such trials has become considerably more sophisticated, with a better understanding of the ways in which to balance treatment and placebo groups to eliminate bias; with more precise power calculations to determine the numbers of patients that need to be studied to avoid false negatives or false positives; with the use of quality of life and other qualitative outcome measures to complement the more traditional quantitative parameters; and so on. The culmination of this trend has been a series of 'mega-trials' involving tens of thousands of patients in many different centres and often in many different countries.

Mega-trials were pioneered in Italy and they have dramatically influenced our management of common and life-threatening conditions such as heart attacks. One such mega-trial was the International Stroke Trial (IST). For some time, doctors had wondered whether it might be useful to give aspirin acutely in patients with strokes due to clots in the cerebral arteries. There were good reasons for thinking that this might be a desirable thing to do: aspirin has anti-clotting properties, and animal experiments had shown that early restoration of blood flow may prevent or reverse some of the damage caused by stroke. There were, however, anxieties about the potential of aspirin for causing cerebral haemorrhage even in patients with thrombotic strokes. Similar arguments related to the anti-coagulant heparin. In order to determine the appropriateness of using either aspirin or heparin or both in acute stroke, Charles Warlow and colleagues in Edinburgh established a trial which included 467 centres in 36 countries. Patients were randomized to receive aspirin or no aspirin plus or minus heparin. A prior power calculation indicated that roughly 20,000 patients would be needed and these were recruited over several years. Nearly a decade after the trial was first proposed, the results from IST were reported in *Lancet* in 1997.[6] They were clear-cut: heparin was not beneficial and was possibly dangerous, and aspirin produced a small but clear-cut benefit and should be used in acute stroke. The following week the Chinese Acute Stroke Study (CAST), designed on very similar lines, likewise involving about 20,000 patients, was published.[7] It, too, showed the benefit of aspirin, thus confirming the robustness of both trials and also how international good science is.

Of course not all good trials have to be so large. Where much greater benefits are expected in individual patients, or more complex outcome measures, employing interval rather than categorical scales, are used, smaller numbers may suffice to produce robust results which avoid both false positives and false negatives. It all depends what the power calculation, and the prior hypothesis, require. Sometimes the results of several small trials may be pooled to generate a 'virtual trial' of sufficient power. This approach, however, has potential pitfalls, particularly if the individual trials use different criteria for patient selection or different outcome measures. The science of so-called meta-analysis is therefore now very sophisticated. One of its most important contributions has been to correct the bias that comes from favouring the publication of positive results over negative ones, thereby giving a drug or some other therapy a better press than it may deserve.[8] In meta-analysis, the search for unpublished studies and for raw data from published trials is highly systematic, involving not only

[6] International Stroke Trial Collaborative group, 'The International Stroke Trial (IST): A Randomised Trial of Aspirin, Subcutaneous Heparin, Both, or Neither among 19,435 Patients with Acute Ischaemic Stroke', *Lancet* (1997), 349: 1569–1581.
[7] CAST (Chinese Acute Stroke Trial), 'CAST: Randomised, Placebo-Controlled Trial of Early Aspirin Use in 20,000 Patients with Acute Ischaemic Stroke', *Lancet* (1997), 349: 1641–9.
[8] Trisha Greenhalgh, 'How to Read a Paper: Papers that Summarise Other Papers (Systematic Reviews and Meta-analyses)', *British Medical Journal* (1997), 315: 672–4.

massive electronic medical databases, registers of clinical trials, 'grey literature' (theses, non-peer reviewed journals), and literature in all languages but also unpublished sources known to experts in the field whose knowledge is tapped as systematically as possible. Once all the data have been gathered, pooled, and analysed, it is possible to indicate whether or not the treatment has a beneficial effect to a measured degree of certainty ('confidence intervals') and the scale of the average benefit patients might expect.

This is scrupulous scholarship of the highest order, and so it should be: patients' lives and happiness are at stake. Even so, doctors are conscious that the evidence from clinical trials is still imperfect, and there has been much criticism, not only of the inadequacies of techniques such as meta-analysis,[9] but also of the wider assumption that all decisions made with individual patients can be entirely based on evidence from clinical trials. No amount of general evidence can predetermine the outcome of the discussion between patient and doctor or take into account all of the factors that are relevant for an individual person.[10] This is, of course, true, but the aim of evidence-based medicine must be to narrow the meshes within which decisions are made rather than to reduce clinical decision-making to the enactment of an algorithm. A doctor who is any good should be able to work within a framework of probability rather than apodeictic certainty.

3. Evidence-Free Theory: Two Case Reports

The contrast, when one moves from clinical science to Theory, is such that it is difficult to believe the two pursuits belong to the same stage of evolution of the human species. I do not for a moment wish to suggest that the evidence-free theories of post-Saussurian thought—parroted by generations of teachers to generations of students—are typical of literary scholarship. What they illustrate is the vulnerability of the humanities to colonization by charlatans and how far charlatans can travel unchallenged—because of the lack of a tradition within the literary studies of requiring evidence proportionate to the scale and scope of assertions. Ironically, the demand for evidence

[9] Editorial, 'Meta-analysis under Scrutiny', *Lancet* (1997), 350: 675.
[10] J. A. Knotterus and G. J. Dinant, 'Medicine Based Evidence: A Prerequisite for Evidence Based Medicine', *British Medical Journal* (1997), 315: 1109–10.

seems to fall off as the scope of assertions expands. Rigorous scholars may argue forcefully over the interpretation of a particular word in *Hamlet*, while statements with a global reference will be allowed to pass on the nod—perhaps because the demand for evidence seems almost comical—at any rate misplaced.

Let me illustrate the contrast between Theory and the kind of rigorous scholarship that is regarded as industry standard in the comparatively soft science of clinical medicine with two case reports on well-known practitioners.

Prelude: The Omniscient Roland Barthes

Barthes was one of the major figures in literary studies over the last forty years. These are some of the assertions he made publicly and yet escaped mockery:

1. About all language: 'But language—the performance of a language system—is neither reactionary nor progressive; it is quite simply fascist; for fascism does not prevent speech, it compels speech.'[11]
2. Of all signs since medieval times: 'Replacing the feudal index, the bourgeois sign is a metonymic confusion' (*S/Z*, 40).
3. Of all writing: 'Writing is in no way an instrument for communication.'[12]
4. Of all art in the West: 'In the West at least, there is no art that does not point to its own mask' (*Writing Degree Zero*, 41).
5. Of all writers after 1850: '[After the 1850s] the writer falls a prey to ambiguity, since his consciousness no longer accounts for the whole of his condition' (ibid. 66).
6. Of the relationship between all writing and all power: 'Power, or the shadow cast by power, always ends in creating an axiological writing, in which the distance that usually separates fact from value disappears within the very space of the word' (ibid. 26).

Barthes is not alone in his claims to omniscience. Derrida and Lacan are, if anything, more sweeping in their pronouncements. They have

---

[11] Inaugural Lecture, Collège de France, in *Barthes: Selected Writings,* ed. and introd. Susan Sontag (Oxford: Fontana, 1983), 461.
[12] *Writing Degree Zero*, trans. Annette Lavers and Colin Smith (London: Jonathan Cape, 1967), 25.

taken care, however, to avoid the lucidity that makes Barthes perhaps an easier target, and for this reason have become more potent role models, more widely imitated, and are worthy of more detailed study.

Case 1: Lacan and the Insufficiency of Facts[13]

Lacan's presence in literary studies is particularly instructive. He wins the prize for obscurity, and the few conclusions that seem half-way comprehensible are glades of seeming lucidity in a thicket of argument composed of allusions and enthymemes—a prose style that was described by a disciple as follows:

> A complete account of the characteristic features, syntactic and other, of Lacan's style would include: the ambiguous *que*, disturbances of conventional word order, literal and metaphorical senses interwoven, periphrasis, ellipsis, leading notions alluded to rather than declared, abstractions personified, persons becoming abstractions, synonyms being given widely different meanings . . . All this keeps the signified as a palely fluttering presence behind the rampaging signifier.[14]

In such circumstances, the illusion of meaning created by a bald assertion, however daft, must be gratefully received. What is interesting about Lacan is that his assertions seem unchallengeable because they are apparently rooted in science. Lacanian critics, who are humanist scholars, take them as read; they do not, perhaps, feel qualified to challenge the white-coated boffin. Supporting evidence is never sought. Which is as well—as there is no such evidence.

Consider the claims—central to Lacanian literary criticism—that the self is a signifier without a signified, that it is a fiction, that its unconscious is structured like a language, that the world of words creates the world of things. So far as these widely quoted and much-invoked positions have any evidential base, it should be available in Lacan's *Écrits*.

Lacan claimed to base his beliefs mainly in his theories of child development in which he brought together structuralist linguistics

---

[13] For a detailed critique of Lacan's Mirror Phase see Tallis, *Not Saussure*, ch. 5, 'The Mirror Stage: A Critical Reflection'. See also the damaging evidence for Lacan's fraudulent approach to 'science' in Elizabeth Roudinesco's *Jacques Lacan*, trans. Barbara Bray (London: Polity, 1997), reviewed by Raymond Tallis, *Times Higher Education Supplement*, 31 Oct. 1997.

[14] Malcom Bowie, in John Sturrock (ed. and introd.), *Structuralism and Since: From Lévi-Strauss to Derrida* (Oxford: Oxford UP, 1979), 145.

and Freudian psychoanalysis. He argued that there were two crucial stages in child development: the Mirror Phase, when the child first acquired the notion of a unified self; and the Symbolic Phase when that self was preserved, in the teeth of its ontological groundlessness, by being inscribed in language and was consequently rewarded by receiving a name and a place in the family, and by an entry ticket into society and culture. The Mirror Phase is supposed to begin at about six months and end at eighteen months. The child, seeing itself in a mirror, identifies with the image and internalizes an image of wholeness that is in advance of its undeveloped physical self, its unmediated sense of being a helpless mess. It embraces this image with jubilation and identifies (or misidentifies) with it. The wholeness of the specular image, Lacan says, is the first version of the fiction of the ego, of the unified or coherent self. In fact, Lacan says, contrary to what the mirror tells the child, we are not whole, we are profoundly split; worse, this thing that is split is not something positive—it is a negative, a lack. We are a nothing cut into many pieces; so our lives, which presuppose enduring identities, are founded upon lies which are compounded when we move from the Mirror to the Symbolic phase: then we are best understood as signifiers without signifieds.

The evidence that Lacan gives for this theory is shaky to say the least. He contrasts the behaviour of infants with that of other animals and claims that there is a distinctive jubilation exhibited by human infants faced with their own mirror image. Actually, there are no data to support this claim: a child looking at itself in the mirror is very easily distracted to more interesting things, for example, a passing cat or a rustling sweet paper or (according to the classic experiments of Lewis et al.[15]) the reflection of a toy in the mirror. Moreover, Lacan himself notes the specific delight—the 'Aha erlebnis'—experienced by chimpanzees in this situation, although he claims that the chimp does not pursue this any further, unlike the human baby. This, again, is at odds with experimental observations by Gallup et al.[16]

Lacanians, faced with the threat of empirical refutation, argue that

[15] The experiments are summarized in M. Lewis and J. Brookes, 'Self-Knowledge and Emotional Development', in M. Lewis and L. A. Rosenblum (eds.), *The Development of Affect* (New York: Plenum, 1978), 205–26. (Mirror recognition and self-naming in fact develop at almost the same time, which hardly supports Lacan's notion of a sequence in which a mirror stage is followed by a symbolic stage.)
[16] Gordon G. Gallup, 'Self-Recognition in Primates: A Comparative Approach to the Bidirectional Properties of Consciousness', *American Psychologist*, 32 (1977), 329–38.

the theory is not an empirical theory at all but a metaphor or even 'a diachronic fable of a synchronic functioning' (see *Not Saussure*, 146). One wonders then why specific empirical claims, including assertions about the duration of the mirror and other phases, are made and why 'facts' are invoked to support it.

If Lacan's hypothesis were genuinely scientific—as opposed merely to clothing itself in the rhetoric of science—one would have expected a vast number of observations to support the pivotal assertion that the child has a special relationship to its mirror image. These would have to be obtained in such a way as to ensure that confirmatory bias was guarded against, and the findings would have to be subjected to statistical analysis to be sure that any association between the encounter with the mirror and certain patterns of behaviour was more than might be noted by chance. None of this is offered by Lacan. Nor have Lacanians even attempted to obtained such data in the sixty years or so since Lacan first put forward his theory.

Arguments about the factual basis for the Mirror Phase would be of greater moment if the theory itself were not fatally flawed by explanatory inadequacy. What Lacan does not explain is how the infant connects all the different images of itself—corresponding to the various occasions of its being exposed to reflecting surfaces—with the same self if there is no real basis for that self. Such images will take many different forms depending upon the position in which the child is held up, the background lighting, and the nature of the reflecting surface: a mirror, a teapot, a puddle, etc. Without the prior and persisting intuition of a self, to which all the different images refer, the child could not derive a sense of wholeness from a series of quite different images of parts of its own body. Where, if the self is a fiction—dreamed up by a nothing that only imagines it is a some-thing—does the very idea of identity come from? Why am I on the lookout for candidate entities to identify (or misidentify) with? What is it that is doing the identifying, or misidentifying? Nor does Lacan explain how or why the child connects that image with other con-current experiences—that of its full stomach, its sore bottom, its wriggling legs. Nor—and most damningly—does he account for the connectivity over time, the link between the successive moments of its being. In other words, the specular explanation of the so-called fiction of the self requires the prior existence of precisely that which it has to explain—the synchronic and diachronic unity of appercep-tion, of consciousness, that is an unassailable fact, not a fiction, of our ordinary life in which we take responsibility for our actions. (Lacanians are, of course, entirely insincere in pretending to hold that the self is a fragmented nothing that has no unity: they still believe that there is a difference between their ordinary selves and those of sufferers from end-stage dementia; like the rest of us, they claim ownership for their actions, their works, and their possessions; and they have a sense of rights that would not be coherent if there were no continuous self to assert entitlement. Some of them even have a sense of responsibility that, likewise, presupposes the notion of a real self extended over time.)

As if the lack of evidence for the theory of the Mirror Phase were not bad enough, Lacan's theory of the Symbolic Phase has an additional vulnerability: it is based on Freud's notion of the Oedipus complex, for which, it is now known, Freud obtained no independent evidence.[17] What little 'evidence' he adduced was extracted from patients (sometimes under duress) in whom he had implanted the idea of the Oedipus conflict in the first place. Lacan's notion of child development, central for the doctrines which he propounded and which are echoed by his non-medical disciples, is therefore a card castle built on quicksand. It is, however, enclosed in a bell jar, being entirely protected from exposure to empirical testing, though its form is that of an empirical theory.

Case 2: Derrida and Non-Facts

Jacques Derrida has made his reputation as a theorist of the human universe. His scope is enormous. His assertions regularly encompass 'Western philosophy', 'Western thought', etc., and he has much to say about (all of) 'writing', (all of) 'text'. In short, he feels able to speak with authority about the entire history of human discourse and

---

[17] The illusion that Freud amassed a huge body of evidence for the theory that he described as the cornerstone of psychoanalytical theory is just that. For full details see Allen Esterson, *Seductive Mirage: An Exploration of the Work of Sigmund Freud* (Chicago: Open Court Books, 1993); Richard Webster, *Why Freud was Wrong: Sex, Sin and Psycho-analysis* (London: HarperCollins, 1995); Robert Wilcocks, *Maelzel's Chess Player: Sigmund Freud and the Rhetoric of Deceit* (Lanham, Md.: Rowman & Littlefield, 1994). The fact that Lacan feels at liberty to displace the Oedipal stage by two years (taking it back from the age 3 to 5 that Freud claimed for it to his own 18 months to 3 years) without provoking any challenge from his Freudian followers testifies eloquently to the lack of empirical evidence for either version of this idea of psycho-sexual development.

declare that (for example) writing (in a very special sense) has primacy over speech; that Western metaphysics has certain distinctive characteristics, including a penchant for immediate presence, unmediated Being; that there is nothing outside of the text; etc. These positions—asserted in the teeth of Derrida's own professed and profound scepticism about our knowledge of the real world and his belief in the total indeterminacy of the meaning of texts—have been accepted without challenge by his very numerous disciples. Much of what he says is unsupported by evidence: he is the supreme contemporary master of the evidence-free assertion. Where he provides evidence, it is usually laughably insufficient to the position being argued.

His favoured technique is to discuss a handful of writers, or even a single writer, often approached from an egregious angle, and to use them as mighty synecdoches for the entirety of Western thought, Western consciousness, etc. In this regard, he is no worse than Lacan, Barthes, or, indeed, Alf Garnett—for whom a brief encounter in a Curry House will generate sufficient data to support a five-word summary of the Indian sub-continent. In another respect, however, he is less innocent. There is prima-facie evidence that his misrepresentation of thinkers key to propping up his cartoon account of 'Western thought' is not entirely accidental. Some of those who have chosen not to be his disciples have taken the trouble to check his sources and have found that they have been misquoted or misinterpreted in strategic ways.

Derrida's misrepresentations of thinkers and scholars initially escaped detection in the 'soft touch' world of interdisciplinary studies. Now, it seems that the game is up. The misrepresentations of Plato,[18] Saussure,[19] Peirce,[20] Husserl,[21] and E. R. Curtius[22] have been carefully documented. There is evidence that these errors are systematic rather than accidental not only because they serve the

---

[18] See Mary J. Devaney, *'Since at least Plato . . .' and Other Postmodernist Myths* (London: Macmillan, 1997).   [19] See Tallis, *Not Saussure*, 169–71, 211–13.

[20] See Brian Vickers, 'Derrida's Reading of C. S. Peirce', *Times Literary Supplement* (9 May 1997), 15; Tallis, *Not Saussure*, 213–14; Ann E. Berthoff, 'Why Peirce is Hard to Read', in *The Mysterious Barricades: Language and its Limits* (Toronto: Toronto UP, forthcoming).

[21] Tallis, *Not Saussure*, 189–202; Kevin Mulligan, 'How Not to Read: Derrida on Husserl', *Topoi*, 10 (1991), 199–208.

[22] James Drake, 'Derrida's Reading of E. R. Curtius', *Times Literary Supplement* (2 May 1997), 17.

ideas that Derrida wishes to foist upon the world—most notably that the meaning of discourse is indeterminate, that signs never reach a signified, and that human consciousness is absent from language—but also because some quotations with which Derrida supports his interpretations of the thinkers he suborns to his cause have been misedited with great care.

Take, for example, his misuse of E. R. Curtius's *European Literature and the Latin Middle Ages*, discussed by James Drake (see n. 22). Here, in order to make Curtius confirm Derrida's view that 'writing' means more than inscription and that this has been obscured by privileging speech over writing, he stitches together phrases from different parts of Curtius's book (so that their referent is displaced by 1,000 years!) and thereby forces the latter to say the opposite of what he manifestly intended. It is interesting to note that this distortion had to be pointed out by a non-academic and was published, not in a scholarly journal but in a literary weekly—*Times Literary Supplement*.

Peirce is a crucial witness in support of Derrida's absolutely central notion of 'the deconstruction of the transcendental signified'.[23] Earlier criticism of Derrida's mishandling of Peirce (e.g. in *Not Saussure*) was based upon the assumption that the errors were accidental. It is clear from Vickers's and others' investigations that the accidents have been too central to Derrida's purposes to be entirely accidental. In particular, Derrida's deliberate removal of reference to intelligent consciousness in Peirce's discussion of the chain of signs (*Of Grammatology*, 48–50) is obviously intended to make Peirce sound like Derrida, for whom intelligent consciousness must be left out of account.

4. Lack of Scandal: The Institutionalization of Fraud

The examples given above of evidence-bent theorizing could be multiplied many times over, especially if one were to include the vast following attracted by the *maîtres à penser*. After all, Derrideans number many thousands. What I have described is a scandal of the greatest magnitude. So why is no one scandalized? Had a scientist misrepresented data in the way that Derrida seems to have done, he

---

[23] Jacques Derrida, *Of Grammatology*, trans. Gayatri Chakravorty Spivak (Baltimore: Johns Hopkins UP, 1974), 49.

would have been the subject of a serious enquiry. Is it because, in the world of postmodern 'scholarship', where there is no such thing as truth (or even reference), anything goes?[24] This may be part of the story, combined with the fact that, as Drake has pointed out, people rarely check primary sources, and, as Vickers has noted, they frequently simply quote the passages others have quoted without reading the originating text. A second-order argument-from-authority— whereby truth is asserted by quoting an authority (e.g. Derrida) who quotes an authority (e.g. Peirce)—seems to be sufficient to secure assent.

In fact many academics *are* scandalized by what is happening. Serious and scrupulous scholars, such as Brian Vickers (see n. 3), have protested against the distortions and errors of the glamorous critics working in their fields. But matched against the promises irradiating from charismatic figures, the dissent of those who are wedded to factual truth may seem mere carping. To an outsider such as myself, it seems that a mighty work of scholarship such as Vickers's recent edition of Bacon, with its 300 pages of carefully argued footnotes drawing upon a huge knowledge of Renaissance political, social, and cultural history, of its literature, and a profound understanding of philology,[25] cannot possibly compete with an immediate understanding of the big picture based upon a few anecdotes and contrived readings which promises to be 'subversive'— both in overthrowing received ideas and supporting a fashionable Foucauldian paranoia about political power in the contemporary world. The competition is as unfair as that which George Steiner noted between science 'which amasses one grain after another in its storehouse only by hard, fatiguing, individual work' and knowledge acquisition by 'a spontaneous spiritual knowing, which would deliver truths about the outer as well as the inner world, without the trouble

---

[24] Just how far contempt for referential truth has trickled down from the commanding heights of Yale and the Collège de France is illustrated by a recent Open University collection on Representation. The introduction advises students that: 'We should perhaps learn to think of meaning less in terms of "accuracy" and "truth" and more in terms of effective exchange—a process of translation, which facilitates cultural communication while always recognising the persistence of difference and power between different "speakers" within the same cultural circuit.' Stuart Hall (ed.), *Representations: Cultural Representation and Signifying Practices* (London: Sage, in association with the Open University, 1997), 11.

[25] *Francis Bacon: A Critical Edition of the Major Works*, ed. Brian Vickers (Oxford: Oxford UP, 1996).

of recourse to mathematics or experiments'.[26] And yet, despite the unfairness of the competition, in medicine at least, the cautious clinical scientist has won against the omniscient witch doctor. Why has this not happened in literary studies? Why are the quacks—with their instant diagnoses and instant cures—in the ascendant? Why does being a rotten scholar peddling exciting ideas attract tenure rather than scandal?

There are many reasons for this. One possibility is that in the United States of America, and latterly in the United Kingdom, the pressure to maximize income from student fees encourages institutions to appoint 'big draw' teachers, and Big Ideas—even wrong or muddled or daft ones—are a bigger draw than rigorous scholarship, which is inescapably narrowly focused. This hypothesis would need to be tested by properly controlled case studies. An alternative—or contributory—explanation is the intrinsic methodological weakness of much literary studies. This weakness is evident not so much at the end of the spectrum where we find detailed scholarship relating to a small number of works—editing, glossing, footnoting—but at the other end, where literary history shades into wider cultural history. There is an aphorism among medical scientists (designed to puncture the pomposity of those who appeal to their clinical impressions or 'experience' to settle issues regarding the course or treatment of disease): *the plural of anecdote is not data*. Cultural history, in particular, is more often than not anecdote driven.[27]

5. The Sokal Hoax[28]

The methodological weakness of the higher reaches of cultural criticism and theory was exposed dramatically when the peer review system of one of the leading Theory journals, *Social Text*, was tested. A spoof paper—'Transgressing the Boundaries: Toward a Transformative Hermeneutics of Quantum Gravity'—was submitted

---

[26] George Steiner, *Real Presences: Is There Anything in What We Say?* (London: Faber, 1989).

[27] I owe this explanation to James Drake (in a personal communication).

[28] For a lucid account of the Sokal Hoax and of the lessons to be drawn from it, see Paul Boghossian, 'What the Sokal Hoax ought to teach us', *Times Literary Supplement*, 13 Dec. 1996. The pernicious impact of postmodernist Theory on academic standards and academic life is explored in Barbara Epstein's brief 'The Postmodernism Debate: More on the Sokal Parody' (*Z Magazine* (Oct. 1996), 57–9).

to this journal: it purported to relativize the claims of quantum mechanics to be in any objective sense true. The paper, written by a professional physicist, was deliberately planted with elementary errors in physics and was logically inconsistent in a very unsubtle way. Finally, it was peppered with totally incomprehensible phrases and assertions. The paper was accepted and published.

The success of the hoax gave powerful support to those who believed that there was now a complete breakdown of quality control in the field of cultural criticism and theory. A paper could be accepted, it seemed, if it appeared to be supporting the prejudices of the editorial board. As Paul Boghossian has written, the journal was prepared 'to let agreement with its ideological orientation trump every other criterion for publication, including something as basic as sheer intelligibility'.

There was a further element to this tale: the paper was written by a scientist who had been provoked to write it by the attacks upon science emanating from the postmodernist critics: the relativizers who pretended to believe that science had nothing to say about Nature, having only social power rather than objective truth to support its claims to be taken seriously; who pretended with equal hypocrisy to equate the scientists who have made modern technologically based society possible with the magicians whose technologies are singularly useless; those, in short, who regard science as being merely one among many competing discursive formations.

This hostility towards science[29] has a particular relevance to the issue of the disabling methodological weaknesses of some aspects of the humanities. It amounts to a pre-emptive strike on a superior rival. Moreover, as José Merquior suggested:

> In the age of cognitive growth and universal literacy, the humanist clerisy is a kind of antique. It no longer holds the monopoly on writing and knows that its expertise, verbal knowledge, is no match for the authority of science. One possible strategy, therefore, is to disparage this unfavourable setting by decrying modernity.[30]

Ernest Gellner has underlined this connection between 'the crisis-mongering of humanist intellectuals' and 'the archaism of their intellectual equipment'.[31]

---

[29] Discussed at length in Raymond Tallis, *Newton's Sleep: The Two Cultures and the Two Kingdoms* (London: Macmillan, 1995) and *Enemies of Hope*.

[30] J. G. Merquior, 'In Quest of Modern Culture: Hysterical or Historical Humanism', *Critical Review*, 5 (1991), 399–420.   [31] Quoted ibid. 409.

At any rate, the Sokal affair exposed the weakness of the peer review process in certain sectors of the humanities. Where there are no objective checks on the claims made in a piece of scholarship, the personal views of peers become all-important. Peers may be as bad as, as well as as good as, oneself. And this is the step by which fraud may move from the personal and individual to the institutional and collective. Moreover, where (as appears to be the case at present) post-Saussurians are in powerful positions in many humanities departments, the chances of publishing work hostile to post-Saussurian thought must be diminished.[32] In science, by contrast, there are numerous checks to prevent the domination of one school of thought over another simply on the basis of the powerful placement of its proponents: the most obvious of these is that the most junior researcher can test whether the results obtained by the Nobel prize winner are repeatable and whether the theory matches the data. No adoring herd of disciples can protect the eminent from scrutiny, from exposure to empirical checks.

In the absence of empirical tests, theoretical writings are liable to be selected for publication by their conformity to the received ideas which are favoured by the editorial boards of the journals to which they are submitted. Barthes's declaration in 1963 was an unconscious warning of the solipsist scholasticism to come:

the human sciences are losing some of their positivist obsession: structuralism, psychoanalysis, even Marxism prevail by the coherence of their system rather than by the 'proof' of their details: we are endeavouring to construct a science which includes itself within its object, and it is this infinite reflexiveness which constitutes, facing us, art itself: science and art both acknowledge an original relativity of object and enquiry.[33]

What the Sokal hoax has underlined is that, when an academic discipline loses its 'positivist obsession', fraud has an easier time; or something close to it: the editorial policy of journals 'prepared to let agreement with [their] ideological orientation trump every other criterion for publication, including something as basic as sheer intelligibility'.

---

[32] Where criticism is published, it is ignored. As Bruce Charlton points out (*Journal of Evaluation in Clinical Practice*, 3 (1997), 169–71), one can minimize the impact of valid dissent by denying it the publicity involved in rebuttal.

[33] Quoted in Vickers, *Appropriating Shakespeare*, 422.

6. *Beyond the Anecdote*

Let every student of nature take this as his rule: that whatever the mind seizes upon with particular satisfaction is to be held with suspicion.

(Francis Bacon, *Novum Organum*)

In his discussion of New Historicism, Vickers cites Jean Howard's objection to Stephen Greenblatt's 'anecdotal method'; namely, that it offers no way of determining whether the 'illustrative example' is 'representative, and if so, on what grounds, statistically, say, or just by one's own authority'.[34] This, in a nutshell, is why 'the plural of anecdote is not data' and why medical therapeutics remained pre-scientific and unreliable so long as it was based upon anecdotes— uncontrolled and isolated observations gathered at random. Reliance on anecdote, on impressions whose selection has been influenced by the hypothesis to be tested, becomes the royal road to untruth or at best half-truth as soon as literary studies raises its sights above scholarly attention to individual works or to a small corpus of work and attempts to become cultural criticism, cultural history or Theory. The stage is set for confirmatory bias to regulate scholarship and the critic becomes more like a lawyer making a case—focusing on supporting evidence, ignoring contrary facts—than a scientist trying to uncover robust general truths; or (to be a little kinder) more like a hypochondriac making a diagnosis ('Everything fits!') than to a clinician. If you then add in a little cross-disciplinary travel, so that one's audience is for the most part playing an away match, then the constraints are finally broken. The scene is set for global assertions, for glamorous opacity—in short for Theory.

I am uncomfortably aware that I am not above this process as I write the present chapter. Indeed, Trisha Greenhalgh's description of how one put together an overview in the bad old days before meta-analysis (see n. 8) fits my present procedure, which has been anecdote driven and dependent upon a selection of quotations from primary and secondary sources. However, so long as my comments are understood as the first word and not the last, this may be acceptable. Scientific medicine, after all, necessarily began with anecdotal clinical observations setting the agenda for systematic clinical enquiry.

The lack of appropriate quantitative methods to acquire the data

---

[34] Vickers, *Appropriating Shakespeare*, 229.

necessary to underpin descriptive general statements and to ensure the validity of causal explanations—such as those that purport to demonstrate the political, social, cultural, economic, and internal 'literary' influences on the structure and content of works of literature—lies at the heart of the present crisis in the humanities. In an age in which it is increasingly expected that general statements should be supported by robust evidence if they are to command credence, the humanities are in danger of being simply anachronistic, acceptable only to arts graduates who have known no better and are unacquainted with adequate methodological discipline. More specifically, by drifting further and further away from careful, evidence-based readings of individual texts and abandoning the traditional virtues of scholarship in favour of a *kulturkritik* of enormous scope, exponents of Theory are increasingly exposing 'the archaism of their intellectual equipment'. Theory shows the extent to which literary studies are still at the stage of clinical impression and personal charisma: the equivalent of the quackery of pre-scientific medicine.

Given that 'the plural of anecdote is not data', what new approach will protect the humanities from the kind of charlatanry that, much to the disgust of many honest scholars, threatens to overwhelm it? Huge collaborative effort would be necessary to acquire data adequate to support the kinds of claims that are routinely made in cultural history and criticism. In certain areas—for example the work that is being carried out in mining archives—something that resembles this is taking place. Otherwise, however, the tradition of the independent, isolated scholar predominates. This is in sharp contrast to the collaborative model of contemporary science—where collaboration is not merely explicit, as in the IST and other megatrials, but implicit and all-pervasive in the sense of building on others' methods, techniques, and findings.

Of course, mere data acquisition is not enough. In science, data are acquired in the context of a hypothesis being tested. The priority of hypotheses raises the danger, already alluded to, of confirmatory bias, particularly where one is dealing with the massive singularities of historical epochs; as Crews expressed it so eloquently, 'any thematic stencil will make its own pattern stand out'.[35] This is particularly likely in a discipline relatively new to the methods of empirical enquiry and where, as in the history of literature or cultural criticism,

[35] Quoted in Vickers, *Appropriating Shakespeare*, 430.

there are no checks available from independent tests and predictions on the basis of repeated run-throughs.

Avoiding confirmatory bias is central to the morality, as well as the methodology, of science. This is expressed with wonderful persuasiveness by the great physicist Richard Feynman in his moving commencement address to Caltech students in 1974:

> But there is one feature I notice that is generally missing in cargo cult science . . . It's a kind of scientific integrity, a principle of scientific thought that corresponds to a kind of utter honesty—a kind of leaning over backwards. For example, if you're doing an experiment, you should report everything that you think might make it invalid—not only what you think is right about it: other causes that could possibly explain your results; and things you thought of that you've eliminated by some other experiment, and how they worked—to make sure the other fellow can tell they have been eliminated.
>
> Details that could throw doubt on your interpretations must be given, if you know them. You must do the best you can—if you know anything at all wrong, or possibly wrong—to explain it. If you make a theory, for example, and advertise it, or put it out, then you must also put down all the facts that disagree with it, as well as those that agree with it . . . When you have put a lot of ideas together to make an elaborate theory, you want to make sure, when explaining what it fits, that those things it fits are not just the things that gave you the idea for the theory; but that the finished theory makes something else come out right in addition.[36]

Nothing could be further from this than the evidence-poor, evidence-free or evidence-faked theorizing of certain cultural critics and theorists, who, where they are not confabulating their data, are simply redrawing with highly selected fact the outlines of their thematic stencils or hobby horses.

In science, of course, Feynman's morality is not an optional extra: anyone transgressing will soon fall victim to public refutation. It is not that scientists are morally superior to humanist intellectuals but that there is no mileage in propounding untruths: you will very soon get found out, and whereas mistakes are allowed, faking is punished ruthlessly, and a scientist who sticks to his pet ideas in the teeth of refutation soon loses his reputation. In short, the institutional forces favour honesty; science fraud, while real and ever-present, is a minority pursuit. In the humanities, as James Drake has suggested to me

---

[36] 'Cargo Cult Science', in Richard P. Feynman, *'Surely You're Joking, Mr. Feynman!' Adventures of a Curious Character*, ed. Edward Hutchings (London: Unwin Paperbacks, 1986), 341.

(personal communication), the institutional forces work in precisely the opposite direction, and so it is very much down to personal morality. Rampant, unchecked theorizing not only adds to the quantity of falsehood in the world but is also counter-educational inasmuch as it teaches the opposite of the kind of scrupulousness that Feynman regarded as essential to science.

To establish large (or even large-ish) truths about cultural and literary history would require an enormous effort of data gathering which would in turn presuppose extensive co-operation and organization. While this effort is unquestionably worthwhile when one is evaluating a new treatment for a serious condition such as stroke, it may not be thought to be justified merely in order to establish some general truths of cultural history. Indeed, it may be deemed absurd to try to establish assertions about (say) 'the cult of sensibility in the eighteenth century' with the same level of certainty as that which should underlie clinical practice. Humanist academics often defend their data-poor assertions by suggesting that this would not only be difficult; it would also be inappropriate. And they cite Aristotle to the effect that one should apply to any given area of enquiry only the level of precision that is appropriate to it. Against this self-serving defence, I would argue that large-scale empirical statements—such as are made by many cultural theorists and historians—have to be underpinned by properly designed large-scale empirical enquiries. Without such an approach, one can have no guarantee that the body of higher-level 'knowledge' about cultural history is anything other than a reflection of the unsubstantiated opinions and prejudices of the most forceful and charismatic practitioners of the art—providing one of the few examples where intellectual activity actually does conform to the Foucauldian paradigm of the subordination of knowledge to power. If one does not have the means to acquire the data to support higher-level generalizations, one should avoid them. In short, if you can't substantiate statements, don't make them.

The bad examples of the *maîtres à penser* who have dominated literary theory and critical thought in recent years should be enough to encourage submission to such a self-denying ordinance. It cannot, surely, be a worthwhile use of one's life to add to the quantity of untruth in the world and thereby increase the contempt in which literary studies are sometimes held by those engaged in more exact disciplines. For this might lead to throwing out the baby of good literary scholarship with the bathwater of theorrhoea.

5

Science and the Self
Lacan's Doctrine of the Signifier

JACQUES BERTHOUD

I

Interpretations of Lacan's work vary enormously, but there seems to be some convergence on the view that it represents an attempt to raise psychoanalysis to the level of a science, along with other so-called human sciences such as linguistics, anthropology, sociology, even literary theory. It is well known that this project, which would variously occupy Lacan's energies for the rest of his life, first emerged in his address to the newly formed Société Française de Psychanalyse in Rome in September 1953.[1] It is equally agreed that it was in this 'Rome Discourse', as it is familiarly known, that Lacan registered for the first time, though somewhat covertly, the impact on himself of Lévi-Strauss's structural anthropology. What Lacan found in Lévi-Strauss was a radical claim: 'Like language, the social *is* an autonomous reality (in fact the same reality); symbols are more real than what they symbolise, the signifier precedes and determines the signified.'[2] These combative propositions reflected Lévi-Strauss's early decision to ground social meaning in symbolic codes understood as conditions of social meaning. As time passed, this decision hardened into an uncompromising rejection of anything outside the symbolic system, from social practice to individual purpose, to

---

[1] 'Fonction et champ de la parole et du langage', reprinted in the full collection of papers, *Écrits* (Paris: Seuil, 1966), 111–208; and trans. by Alan Sheridan in *Écrits: A Selection* (London: Tavistock, 1977), 30–113, as 'The Function and Field of Speech and Language in Psychoanalysis'. The first is cited hereafter as *Écrits* (Seuil), the second as *Écrits* (Sheridan).

[2] Claude Lévi-Strauss, 'Introduction' to Marcel Mauss, *Sociologie et anthropologie* (Paris: PUF, 1950), ix–lii (p. xxxii).

account for that system's signifying power. Thus, what gave an act of social exchange its meaning—for example, the giving away of a woman in marriage in an obligation of reciprocity—was not the gift itself, but the *system of representations* into which the 'act of giving' was inserted. As Lacan himself put it: '. . . these gifts are already symbols, in the sense that symbol means pact';[3] and, more portentously: 'The primordial Law is therefore that which in regulating marriage ties superimposes the kingdom of culture on that of a nature abandoned to the law of mating.'[4]

The intensity of Lacan's response to a 'scientific' analysis that dissolved away the contextual and the subjective in order to reveal the structural and objective was central to the 'Rome Discourse'. Indeed, he would soon join Lévi-Strauss in proclaiming the death of the subject, just as a little later Barthes and Foucault would declare the death of the author. These ideological executions were part of a more general mid-century repudiation by French intellectuals of conservative bourgeois individualism—cause of world wars, *mauvaise foi*, public morality, self-congratulatory patriotism, etc. More positively, they announced a scientific, or scientistic, programme. According to Lacan, 'this new order' signified 'nothing more than a return to a conception of true science'. What was this science? Certainly not 'experimental science', promoted by a positivism committed to measurement and proof, but what he called 'the conjectural sciences', which, he claimed, were 'forcing us to revise the classification of science we have inherited from the nineteenth century'. As a prime example of such a science Lacan singled out the structural linguistics of Saussure and Jakobson, especially the latter's phonological discoveries, which Lévi-Strauss had encountered and absorbed in New York during the Second World War. Lacan was particularly impressed by what he called the 'mathematicized form in which is inscribed the discovery of the *phoneme* as the function of pairs of oppositions formed by the smallest structure'. Saussure had thought that phonemes, or speech sounds considered in respect of their functional relations in a linguistic system, enabled a speaker to identify the words of a given language. Thus, because the phonemes [p], [b], [d], and [t] were functionally distinctive in English, they served to

---

[3] 'Function and Field', *Écrits* (Sheridan), 61.
[4] Ibid. 66. What is at issue here is the conversion of brute event into cultural action. Each of the following quotations is taken from 'Function and Field' (pp. 72 and 73).

distinguish the words 'pad', 'pat', bad', and 'bet'. Roman Jakobson, however, established that the phoneme was itself made up of micro-features which fell into oppositional pairs. For example, the phonemes [b] and [p] are the product of three sets of opposition (voicing, articulation, occlusion), only one of which (voiced/unvoiced) is positively active: thus [b] involves periodic vibration of the vocal chords while [p] does not, as a finger placed on the Adam's apple while sounding them will instantly reveal.⁵ In short, within the phoneme Jakobson discovered a binary system at work.

Lévi-Strauss immediately laid claim to this discovery as a model for his own very different anthropological system, devised, as we have noted, to distinguish a cultural act from a natural event. Where was such an a priori conceptual system to be found? Exactly where Jakobson's binary sets were held to operate: in the unconscious—or at least in some sort of generic unconscious. Be that as it may, my point is that for Lévi-Strauss Jakobson's structural phonology was never really more than an *analogy* for anthropological deep struc-tures, such as the structures of exchange; nor was his conception of the unconscious ('that category of collective thought', as he called it) much more than a *synonym* for the unknown. Lacan, however, per-haps because of the status of the 'talking cure' in psychoanalysis, went much further. He took language, as delivered by Jakobson, as the thing itself, and planted it in the unconscious, which he famously proclaimed to be 'structured *in the most radical way* [my italics] like a language'.⁶ As we shall see, what this means or might mean is far from evident. However, one thing is immediately sure: for Lacan, as for his contemporaries, subjective consciousness, regarded by some as being present in individual *parole* or speech, existed only as an effect of system, and had to be bracketed out if analysis of the psyche were to achieve scientific impersonality.

In what follows, I propose to test this claim by putting the phrase

---

⁵ Roman Jakobson, *Selected Writings*, i: *Phonological Studies* (Paris: Mouton, 1962), 58–64. The phonemes I cite as examples, [b] and [p], are, at the point of articulation, both bilabial (made with closed lips), and in the manner of articulation both occlusive (requiring the momentary closure of the vocal passage). According to Jakobson, 'the inherent distinctive features which have so far been discovered in the languages of the world and which . . . underlie their basic lexical and morphological stock, amount to twelve basic oppositions, out of which each language makes its own selection' (p. 41).

⁶ 'The Direction of the Treatment and the Principles of its Power' ('La Direction de la cure et les principes de son pouvoir'), *Écrits* (Sheridan), 284.

'structured like a language' under pressure. This will involve offering an analysis of Lacan's transformation of the Saussurian signifier.

II

In his 'Rome Discourse', Lacan writes: 'For it is still not enough to say that the concept is the thing itself, as any child can demonstrate against the pedant. It is the world of words that creates the world of things—the things originally confused in the *hic et nunc* of the all in the process of coming-into-being—by giving its concrete being to their essence, and its ubiquity to what has always been.'[7]

This fundamental proposition is less than pellucid. To be sure, in the original French the child is opposed to 'official teaching' (*contre l'école*)—that is, to the authority of common sense, rather than 'the pedant', as the translator has it. Moreover, Lacan confidently tells us what the child knows: that 'the concept is the thing itself'. But what does *that* mean? It cannot mean what that well-known schoolmaster Jonathan Swift meant—that words can be replaced by things, so that they can be dispensed with, like the sack-bearing Laputans in *Gulliver's Travels*. What then is Lacan's drift? He provides the answer in one of the elaborate verbal gestures that precede the quoted passage: 'Through the word . . . absence gives itself a name in that moment of recognition whose perpetual recreation Freud's genius detected in the play of the child.' For Lacan, children's make-believe is what summons reality to them. It is not by meeting Little Red Riding Hood, but by playing (or 'articulating') her, that they bring her to life. It is not words, it would appear, that can be replaced by things, but things that can be replaced by words. Lacan, however, would not accept this formulation, for it assumes that words and things are commensurable. He is much more radical than that: *things depend on words in that words create them.*

What does this process entail? Lacan tells us that words do not create things *ex nihilo*, but out of some sort of original plasma. The translation is slightly misleading here in that it implies that '*its* concrete being' and '*its* ubiquity' are language's. In the French it is clear that *son être concret* belongs to 'essence' (it is what the essence of things receives), and that *sa place partout* belongs to 'what has

---

[7] 'Function and Field', *Écrits* (Sheridan), 65.

always been' (the 'ubiquitous' essence out of which things are formed). Even so, the tone of Lacan's utterance remains vatic, for he is obliged to use language in order to describe a state of affairs that does not exist until language has had its say; he is also obliged to evoke a perpetual and omnipresent *noumenon* which only through words can be precipitated into time and place. Lacan's originating *world of words* supplants the Original *Word* which sat brooding on the vast abyss and made it pregnant.

In sum, for Lacan there is a wrong theory of the relationship between concept (the 'signified' of the Saussurian 'signifier') and referent—that words name things; and there is the correct theory— that words create things. We are in the presence of a creation myth. As we shall see, there is a very good reason why Lacan is forced to adopt so *unscientific* a posture. Meanwhile, two observations are in order. First, Lacan is surely right to claim that the naming theory, which assumes that things precede words, is naive. This theory only holds for those who are already language-users—that is to say, all of us, except perhaps Gargantua, whose very first post-natal cry was 'à boire!' Second, Lacan is surely wrong to think that once words have freed themselves from the tyranny of things to enter into their proper power they remain docile. By having them create things, Lacan's words retain an absolute power over their creation, disobedience on its part being not only intolerable but impossible. Lacan's signifier, which has long been notorious for its arbitrariness and instability, is in fact also totalitarian.

It would appear, then, that Lacan holds two incompatible ideas: that words create things, and that the relationship between language and the world is arbitrary. The first we have just analysed. With respect to the second, however, we should note that what is proposed is *not* the uncontroversial Saussurian principle that the link between the sound of a word and its meaning is arbitrary—which is no more than the generalization of the commonplace that different languages carry the same referent in different phonemic patterns (*girl, Mäd-chen, fille, ancilla*, etc.). It is the much more tendentious claim that the link between the signifier and the signified is insecure. This notion of arbitrariness, put into general circulation by Lévi-Strauss under the designation 'floating signifier',[8] assumes its most uncompromis-ing form in Lacan. Cut off from its referent (the world) and its use (a

---

[8] Lévi-Strauss, 'Introduction', xlix.

speech act) the Lacanian signifier enters into an independent pattern of relations with its fellow signifiers. In Lacan's view, 'it is in the chain of the signifier that the meaning "insists" but none of its elements "consists" of the signification of which it is at the moment capable'.[9] This we could readily understand if by 'elements' Lacan meant 'words', for as we all know it is not words themselves, but words in combinations and contexts, that achieve meaning. But what he means is 'signifiers' and 'signifieds'. Hence he must conclude: 'We are forced . . . to accept the notion of an incessant sliding of the signified under the signifier.' This version of arbitrariness, by means of which Lacan attempts to plug Lévi-Strauss into Freud, and psychoanalysis into science, has acquired such currency that any interrogation of it requires a return to basics.

III

In the course of a paper delivered in Vienna in 1955, Lacan told his audience of neuro-psychiatrists: 'If you want to know more, read Saussure . . . who can truly be said to be the founder of modern linguistics.'[10] Lacan may rail against *l'école*, but he too has been to school, in Geneva, where he would have learnt that human languages are codes whose elements are signs. This semiological story has often been told, but never better than by Vincent Descombes in *Grammaire d'objects en tous genres*,[11] as will emerge shortly.

Peirce has taught us to distinguish between a natural sign and a coded sign.[12] The first does no more than indicate something; its absence does not indicate at all. Thus the smoke I happen to see is a 'natural' sign of fire in that it is causally related to a fire; but if I do not see smoke it does not follow that there is no fire: all I can say is

[9] 'The Agency of the Letter in the Unconscious' ('L'Instance de la lettre dans l'inconscient'), *Écrits* (Sheridan), 153.
[10] 'The Freudian Thing, or the Meaning of the Return to Freud in Psychoanalysis' (La Chose freudienne, ou sens du retour à Freud en psychanalyse'), *Écrits* (Sheridan), 125.
[11] Vincent Descombes, *Grammaire d'objects en tous genres* (Paris: Éditions de Minuit, 1983), trans. Lorna Scott-Fox and Jeremy Harding as *Objects of All Sorts: A Philosophical Grammar* (Oxford: Basil Blackwell, 1986). This cornucopian text deserves to be widely known.
[12] The classic essay or compendium is 'Logic as Semiotic: The Theory of Signs', in *Philosophical Writings of Peirce*, selected and ed. Justus Buchler (New York: Dover, 1955), 98–119.

that the absence of smoke is the absence of any sign. Now let us imagine a different scenario.[13] You and I, still presumed to be language-users, sail to a desert island to look for treasure. Once disembarked, we divide the task, and agree that if we find what we are looking for we will send up a smoke signal. What we have done is to set up the most elementary code—a binary one. This means that, now, the absence of smoke is *itself* a signal, which says that the treasure has not been found. Thus the two signals 'smoke/no smoke' take their signifying power from each other. It is because the smoke, when it goes up, is *not* the absence of smoke that it means something. One could say that the difference between the two kinds of sign is that while the natural sign permits an induction, the instituted sign carries an intention—deliberate in the case of my example, but not necessarily so. In the case of the instituted sign, the code provides the conditions necessary to turn *things*—whether visible like smoke or auditory like coughs, etc.—into signs. We agree to call such signs 'signifiers' in order to distinguish them from merely symptomatic signs. Generally, signifiers can only function if they can be recognized as such within an expected range, often loosely called a system. All this is familiar enough.

What is not generally understood, however, is a crucial point that remained invisible until Descombes made it obvious:[14] that the signified of a coded signifier, as just defined, is not a *concept* but a *statement*. Thus, the appearance of smoke behind a headland does not mean the concept 'smoke', but the message 'I have found the treasure'. This is true of all so-called anthropological, sociological, and cultural signifiers so favoured by Lévi-Strauss and Roland Barthes. For instance, whenever Barthes detects a sociological signifier, he is identifying a statement. 'To wear a beret does not mean the same thing as wearing a bowler hat,' Descombes reports. True. I may of course wear a beret because it is cold, in which case the beret will be a natural sign of cold weather. But if I wear a beret because it is not a bowler hat, or a baseball cap, or a straw hat, or no hat at all—in short, if I treat it as a formal signifier within a rudimentary

[13] See Descombes, *Objects of All Sorts*, 'On Semiology and the Experience of Literature', 78–89.

[14] Ibid. 172–7. Descombes distinguishes between 'Brichot' and 'Norpois' signifiers, so called after the etymologist and the diplomat in Proust's *A la recherche du temps perdu*: the first studies words as such, the second uses in-words to declare status and profession. The 'beret' analogy (below) is cited on p. 174.

code—I emit a definite message. In France the beret will say: 'I believe in plain common sense and hate the trendy Left' (I was actually told this in Bordeaux in 1972). In England, on the other hand, it is more likely to mean: 'I am a Francophile.' A beret worn in the land of the *anciens combattants*, whose uniform it is, means something just as definite as a baseball cap on the head of the Conservative Party leader attending the Notting Hill Carnival on this side of the channel. Barthes's *Mythologies* remains so beguiling, when much of his pseudo-scientific work has fared less well, precisely because of the number of unperceived quotidian signals it uncovers. His talent is like that of the novelist who has learned to perceive and read the plenitude of ongoing social meanings generated by the community he inhabits. Barthes's power is the discovery of these meanings in an unsuspected range of determinate contexts: subsequent codification, which essentially remains a taxonomy, represents a more common-place achievement.

Why has the difference between a concept and a message not been recognized by semiological adepts? Saussure's famous *Cours de linguistique générale* distinguished between *langue* and *parole* in an attempt to analyse *langage* (real language), which it held to be both system *and* practice. Thus it did not privilege synchrony at the expense of diachrony; nor did it disregard whole categories of words such as prepositions, conjunctions, pronouns, etc. in favour of the megalomaniac noun; nor did it neglect that remarkably stable though not unchanging body of practices, known as grammatical rules, which govern the formation of intelligible sentences, and so function above the level of the signifier. Considered as a whole, the *Cours* may be incomplete and incoherent; but it remains the work of a man who has a professional interest in language rather than in anthropology or psychoanalysis. Nevertheless, Saussure's radical distinction between the synchronic and the diachronic dimensions of language, and within the synchronic his splitting the sign into a signifier and a signified, served to open up a logical gap between system and use. Hence his *langue*, a synchrony of signifier/signifieds, ended up by being some sort of ghost in the machine, like the Cartesian soul in the physical body. However hard Saussure might have tried to mend the rift—for example by insisting that signifier and signified (where the latter was necessarily defined not as a 'referent' but as a 'concept', that is to say the idea of a thing) were 'as undividable as the two sides of a single sheet of paper'—he remained trapped in categories of his own making. Thus individual agency was logically excluded from the linguistic picture, and *langage*, like a defeated colony, ceased to offer any resistance to the invasion of the human 'sciences'.

I have claimed that the reason why Saussurian linguistics has proved irresistible to ethnographers, semanticists, psychoanalysts, film theorists, and literary critics is that it appears to offer them the promise of depersonalization. To suggest, as Saussure did, that languages were codes, and linguistics a branch of semiology, has provided a model to legitimize the structuralist project. Consider the relationship between a code and the signals it permits. We have seen that a code precedes its messages, and is thus independent of both message and emitter. To revert to our example: the smoke signal I send over to you depends unconditionally on our prior institution of the binary code smoke/no smoke. Moreover, since the code is a condition of signalling, and not a grander or more basic signal in its own right, we cannot produce or abolish the code while we are using it. Again, we cannot produce a message that has not been foreseen by the code: all I as code-user can say is 'The treasure has been found', and 'The treasure has not been found'. Finally, the code selects in advance the situation that can be signalled. Were you, in your part of the island, to discover something as marvellous as a surviving family of dodos, you could not broadcast your discovery in the code. Indeed, from the point of view of the code, your discovery would not exist. In sum, what we have here is the gist of the structuralist credo of the 1960s and 1970s. We will now glance at the harvest it has reaped.

IV

Lacan has been called a post-structuralist. If this label implies, as it seems to, that he has left structuralism behind, it is misleading. To be sure, Lacan rejects the constituting principle of a code: that the link between the signifier and the signified be constant; but he remains a structuralist by virtue of the fact he can only overtake the structuralist project on its own terms.

To make this clear, we need to revisit structuralism's semiological premiss. A code is a closed system. What does that mean? Our exemplary code, so far, has been confined to two signifiers: a full signifier (smoke), and an apparently empty signifier (no-smoke) filled by the sole full signifier in the system. But only in a binary code can that empty slot, as it is called, be filled. Consider a slightly more elaborate code. Having reached our island we decide to survey it separately to see whether it can support human life, and we set up the following code: red smoke for 'fruit' (i.e. the statement 'I have found edible fruit'); blue smoke for 'water'; green smoke for 'herbs'. In this code, the sign is no longer opposed to the lack-of-sign but to the two other signs; hence the empty slot remains empty. The absence of any sign means only that the system we have instituted has not been put into operation; it neither affirms nor denies that I have found the coded items, or that I have found items outside the code, such as 'edible roots', or 'sucking pig', or 'eggs'. What it does do, in fact, is to mark the limit of a determinate range of signs. By virtue of the empty slot, all instituted codes, however elaborate, declare themselves to be closed systems.

This being the case, there is a necessary misfit between instituted codes, and natural languages. The latter cannot intelligibly be said to be in the required sense closed, and, unlike a code, are able to form the negation of the statements they produce. In short, a code is not a natural language in rudimentary form. Once this is understood, only two recourses are available: either to reject the code model out of hand on the grounds that a theory of language cannot be erected on the basis of one of the things language can do (e.g. the ability to set up a code); or else to alter the model to take account of some of the operations of language to which the model cannot do justice. The danger of the latter option is, of course, that such alterations may garble both the model and its applications. Lacan's commitment to a *science* of psychoanalysis tightens his grip, as it were, on a model that may deliver this science; yet his engagement, as a psychoanalyst and surrealist,[15] with the deregulated *paroles* exhibited in mental alienation on the one hand and avant-garde writing on the other, predisposes him to loosen the code and free up the play of its mechanisms. Indeed, in Lacan these twofold drives—towards scientific rigour and

[15] David Macey, *Lacan in Contexts* (London: Verso, 1988). This meticulous and comprehensive study situates Lacan's literary and rhetorical discourse in the Parisian culture of his formative years to reveal his affinity with avant-gardists and surrealists, including Breton, Bataille, Soupault, Duchamp, Tanguy, Tardieu, etc. Elizabeth Roudinesco's stylishly authoritative biography, *Jacques Lacan* (Paris: Fayard, 1993), trans. Barbara Bray (London: Polity Press, 1997), provides a very rich French context which downgrades the significance of Lacan's structuralist phase.

towards transgressive language—are forced into an unnatural alliance against a common foe (the reality of the subject); but this alliance also serves to disrupt and disable its constituting parties.

The French psychoanalyst François Roustang, who studied under Lacan for several years, has published a study of Lacan's scientific project which demonstrates that its function in his work is essentially rhetorical.[16] Roustang demonstrates that in the course of his career Lacan makes a number of attempts explicitly to align psychoanalytic theory and mathematical physics. As early as 1936, for example, Lacan invokes 'the vertiginous relativisms of contemporary physics and mathematics'[17] in order to deride appeals to the 'actual criteria of truth'—namely: 'simple conviction' (the test of 'mystical knowledge'), 'self-evidence' (the basis of 'philosophical speculation'), and 'non-contradiction' (the basis of 'empirico-rationalism'). 'Can it be said', he scornfully writes, 'that the scientist asks himself whether a rainbow . . . is real?' In his discussion of these remarks, Roustang notes that Lacan's definition of mathematical physics disregards its concern with quantification, ignores its quest for verification, and discounts its reliance on the 'use of deduction grounded on the identity principle', that is to say, on the principle of non-contradiction.[18] Lacan's appeal to physics reduces it to a purely mathematical practice designed, once again, to vaporize the individual subject. Thirty-nine years later, neither his rhetoric nor his polemic have changed. In his 1965 essay 'La Science et la vérité'[19] Lacan no longer summons Einstein's 'vertiginous' relativities to his defence; in their place we now find game theory—but used in exactly the same way. Game theory will have 'the advantage of the entirely calculable nature of a subject strictly reduced to a matrix of signifying combinations'.[20] In unadorned language: what game theory delivers is 'a disembodied and dehumanised subject without individuality . . . who, by all appearances, could be reduced to pure object—in this case, numbers'.[21]

[16] François Roustang, *Lacan, de l'équivoque à l'impasse* (Paris: Éditions de Minuit, 1986); trans. Greg Sims as *The Lacanian Delusion* (Oxford: Oxford UP, 1990), esp. 19–29 and 46–54.
[17] Jacques Lacan, 'Au-delà du "Principe de réalité"' (1936), repr. in *Écrits* (Seuil), 73–92. The quotation is from p. 79.
[18] See Roustang, *The Lacanian Delusion*, 20–2.
[19] *Écrits* (Seuil), 855–77.   [20] Ibid. 860.
[21] See Roustang, *The Lacanian Delusion*, 51–2 for a critique of Lacan's attempts to link psychoanalysis and science.

In alluding to such moments, my principal purpose is not to demonstrate that Lacan misrepresents mathematical physics or game theory; nor to argue that his own methods of enquiry bear scant resemblance to recognized scientific methods. Still less do I propose to elaborate my own theory of the self. All I wish to do is to draw attention to Lacan's actual, not professed, use of the scientific model. This use is essentially *analogical*, the purpose of the analogy being to eliminate once and for all the subjective self from any formula or equation proposing to map out the human psyche. In this use of science Lacan proves much more radical than his master Lévi-Strauss for whom the self, a product of social—that is, public— structures, retains some affiliation, however equivocal, with systems external to the self. Lacan, however, discards such external systems by dissolving them into the structures of the unconscious, converting the self into a mirage—that is to say, an illusion produced by the laws of optics.

V

Used analogically, science may define, but it will certainly not deliver, the Lacanian project. It may tell us where Lacan wants to get to; but to find out how he plans actually to get there we must return to the linguistic argument, which we recall is not analogical but substantial. Let us remind ourselves of Lacan's central formula. In his 1958 paper 'The Direction of the Treatment and the Principles of its Power', Lacan declares that 'interpretation [i.e. diagnosis] is based . . . on the fact that the unconscious is structured in the most radical way like a language, that a material operates in it according to certain laws, which are the same laws as those discovered in the study of actual languages'.[22]

Lacan's discovery that the laws of the unconscious are *identical* with the laws of language coincided, of course, with his discovery of Saussure. As we have seen, Saussure's separation of *langue* from *parole* is by no means unproblematic; but by insisting on the unity of signifier and signified he continued to cling to the notion that language belongs to individuals as members of a group. In the interest of the structural unconscious, Lacan severs that unity. The now liberated signifier, 'by its very nature', says Lacan (unblush-ingly adopting the diction of an essentialist), 'anticipates meaning by unfolding its dimension before it'.[23] This formulation resists exegesis but incites *amplificatio*. Breaking the bondage of mono-gamy (its attachment to a single signified) this new figure now 'unfolds' its machismo before a whole seraglio of signifieds. Else-where, with its 'defiles' and 'batteries' it seizes military power. Everywhere it proclaims its mastery. Much later, before a Yale University audience, Lacan was more affable: 'I have substituted for the word *word*, the word *signifier*. This means that it is prone to ambiguity, that is to several possible significations.'[24] This substitution, for all its sheep's clothing, is once again an *auto-nomy*: if you remove a word from its context (its use) and from its position in a sentence (its grammar), what else can it do but become prone to ambiguity?

The three major landmarks of Lacan's elaboration of the linguistic model, 'Agency of the Letter in the Unconscious' (1957), 'Function and Field of Speech and Language' (1963), and 'Science and Truth' (1965), all confirm that he regards the unconscious as a combinatory system of signifiers.[25] How is this system to be understood? Accord-ing to Lacan: 'Now the structure of the signifier is . . . that it should be articulated. This means . . . that these units [i.e. the signifiers] are subjected to the double condition of being reducible to ultimate differential elements, and of combining them according to the laws of a closed order.'[26] But this is a very tricky sentence, which slides surreptitiously from a passive construction ('of being reducible') to an active one ('of combining them'). I can understand a condition of reducibility: for example, if a Meccano model were not reducible to its component parts, it would cease to possess one of the necessary conditions of being Meccano. But I can make little sense of a condi-tion of *combining*: I cannot understand how, to continue with our example, how the Meccano pieces can *combine themselves* into this or that model.

---

[23] *Écrits* (Sheridan), 'Agency', 153.
[24] Jacques Lacan, 'Yale Declaration', *Scilicet*, 6–7 (1976), quoted Descombes, *Objects of All Sorts*, 180. *Scilicet* was the journal of the École Freudienne de Paris, founded by Lacan on 21 June 1964, following his condemnation by the International Psychoanalytical Association, which he compared, *mirabile dictu*, to Spinoza's expul-sion from the synagogue.
[25] For a discussion of Lacan's use and abuse of the combinatory, see Roustang, *The Lacanian Delusion*, 55–8.   [26] *Écrits* (Sheridan), 'Agency', 152–3.

More generally, to give assent to Lacan's invocation of the combinatory system, we are required to swallow two indigestible assumptions. The first is that the Lacanian language system should remain entirely independent of any act of mind, whether conscious or unconscious; for Lacan the mind's function must not extend a whit further than receiving and containing the system, i.e. it can only perform the function of a box. It is as if I were to place a set of clothes—socks, shoes, undergarments, shirt, trousers, tie—in a drawer and expect them to put themselves on themselves. The second assumption is that the Lacanian system should consist of elements—signifiers—that remain completely formal. Here I have to ask how the system 'knows' what combinations to form, if the signifier remains vacant. Such assertion gets no support from Jakobson. Let us recall Jakobson's construction of the phoneme, described in Section I above, which involved binary pairs of micro-elements combinable in terms of resemblance and contrast. Such a combination is not yet a signifier, empty or otherwise. Why? Consider how phonemes combine into signifiers proper. For example, the differentiated consonants 'p', 'd', and vowels 'o', 'i', can be combined to produce the aural units 'pod' and 'dip', which are indeed signifiers in the English language. But how can these *English* combinations be formed if we are denied access to criteria of intelligibility? How are we to distinguish, for example, signifiers like 'pod' and 'dip' from non-signifiers like 'pid' and 'dop' on purely formal grounds? Lacan gestures towards this problem by asserting that 'combining according to the laws of a closed order' requires what he calls a 'topographical substratum' or—more familiarly—a 'signifying chain'; yet all he can tell us about this substratum is that it takes the form of 'rings of a necklace that is a ring in another necklace made of rings'.[27] Is this mere doodling? Lacan does not even leave us the means of deciding.

In general, the problem of how the Lacanian combinatory system, whatever it may be, is able to *function* remains unresolved. To be sure, Lacan tries to map it over Freud's dynamic unconscious, with its drives, its dreams, its repressions, its libido. He attempts to convert psychic forces into linguistic categories—for example rewriting Freud's 'condensation' and 'displacement' (respectively, the compression of a profusion of dream thoughts into a laconic dream, and the

[27] Ibid. 153.

108   JACQUES BERTHOUD

divergence of the 'central point' of the dream images from dream thoughts)[28] as Jakobson's 'metaphor' and 'metonymy'.[29] But this effort cannot bring the combinatory system into activity, for all it does is to transmute, piece by piece, Freud's active unconscious into the static synchronic system. Calling metaphor 'condensation' does not produce any alteration in the Lacanian notion of metaphor, hence all it can do is to strip condensation of its Freudian meaning.

How does the subject survive the Lacanian treatment? As we know, the traditional subject is defined in relation to the object, i.e. the object of perception. Freud, who is concerned with the development of the libido, converts this object into the part-object—specifically, those parts of the body—whatever they are—invested with erotic interest. Lacan reduces the part-object to the *objet-a* (the *objet-autre*), so-called because in Lacanian psychology the object of desire is always already absent. In other words, Lacan severs the object from the world, as he has severed the signifier from its signified, to relocate it in an 'unconscious' understood as a system of pure signifiers. We are back where we started from: with the subject as an effect of system, except that now the status of the 'system' has become completely mysterious.

VI

Seán Burke, who has produced an elegant diagnosis of the contradictions inherent in any attack on the idea of authorship, has highlighted the '*folie circulaire* of *authoring* and *authorising* the disappearance of the subject, of *declaring* that no-one speaks'.[30] If Lacan succeeds in persuading us that speech (*parole*) is impossible, he has successfully falsified his demonstration; alternatively, if we are led to accept that speech is invariably symptomatic, rather than also intentional, then all language, including Lacan's, is reduced to 'lalangue' (as it were, 'bibabble'), which, in his self-parodying theorizing gloss, comes out as follows: 'A minimal composition of the battery of

[28] Sigmund Freud, *The Interpretation of Dreams*, trans. James Strachey (Harmondsworth: Penguin Books, 1967), 183–6, 414–17.
[29] Even here Lacan is over-casual: Jakobson identified displacement with metonymy but condensation with *synecdoche*.
[30] Seán Burke, *The Death and Return of the Author* (Edinburgh: Edinburgh UP, 1992), 99.

signifiers suffices to install in the signifying chain a duplicity which overlaps with its reduplication of the subject.'[31] It would appear, then, that Lacan's theoretical project can only be realized through self-contradiction. I say 'appear', because, philosophically considered, the issue is not quite so clear-cut. For example, if we were to subscribe to Burke's diagnosis of a *folie circulaire*, what would we make of such sentences as 'All rules have an exception'? Does this sentence include itself in its generalization? If so, should it be regarded as unintelligible? Or is it telling us something about language, truth, and logic?—All I can do here is to avert my gaze and ask what Lacan's project means in practice.

To answer that question, we must begin by measuring the full extent of Lacan's demotion of the speaking subject. His promotion of the signifier at the expense of the signified completes the transfer of agency from *parole* to *langue*. It has often been noticed that Lacan is very cavalier in his use of the terms *langue* and *langage*. Macey, for example, notes that his exposition of Saussure in 'La Chose freudienne' seems to confuse the *langue–parole* distinction with his own *langage–parole* version.[32] The reason is, of course, that for Lacan *langue* is indeed *langage*, that is to say that the differential system which Saussure more or less confines to phonology is applied by Lacan to the whole of language, including semantics and discourse. It follows that *parole* even at its most motivated (that is, at its most innovative) must remain the slave of system; for, in Lacan, even here, 'it is in the substitution of signifier for signifier that an *effect* of significance is produced that is creative or poetic'.[33]

The essay which contains this statement also contains an illustration which has been endlessly cited as definitive in establishing the coherence of Lacan's repositioning of the signifier. Saussure illustrates the dual identity of the sign by writing the word 'TREE' over a bar below which he draws the image of a tree. Lacan replaces this illustration with another consisting, below the bar, of the drawing of two identical doors above which he distributes the words 'LADIES' and 'GENTLEMEN'. This revision is designed 'to show how the signifier enters the signified'. The signifieds are identical; the signifiers, on the other hand, separated from their signifieds by a bar which is now a

[31] *Écrits* (Seuil), 'A la mémoire d'Ernest Jones: sur sa théorie du symbolisme', 687–717 (p. 711). Quoted in Macey, *Lacan in Contexts*, 285.
[32] 'The Freudian Thing', *Écrits* (Sheridan), 114–145. Quoted in Macey, *Lacan in Contexts*, 131.   [33] 'Agency', *Écrits* (Sheridan), 164.

barrier, assume their full authority, segregating the 'double and solemn procession' of biological humans through each entrance.[34]

Unsurprisingly, this intervention has earned the plaudits of converts. Elizabeth Wright, for example, hails it as 'an example where what appears to be the same signified can be marked with two different signifiers'.[35] We must, however, distinguish between rhetorical brio and conceptual sophistication. The example is alleged to show that if we relocate the signified in the real world (that is to say, if we relate it to its referent), we discover that only the originating signifier, protected by its barrier, remains intact. As Wright puts it: 'The Saussurian security is here renewed: a hidden gap opens up between signifier and signified.'[36] But does Lacan's parable sustain this? Not in the least. If we recall Descombes's crucial distinction, which he applies to Lacan's parable, it instantly becomes evident that Lacan's 'Ladies' and 'Gentlemen' are no longer signifiers, as was 'Tree' in Saussure's illustration, but *messages*, which of course belongs to *parole*, not *langue*. Saussure's illustration is offered as an illustration of the sign, compound of signifier and signified. He could have used any other, such as 'horse', or 'door', or 'man', or 'woman', with identical effect. Lacan, on the other hand, is presenting us with examples of two *communications*: 'This door is only for ladies', 'This door is only for gentlemen'. Moreover, like all communications, they function in a context within which all competent language- and lavatory-users naturally slot into what Lacan calls 'the laws of urinary segregation'. What has happened is devastatingly simple: in revising Saussure's illustration, Lacan has switched from *langue* to *parole*. In this, however, he is excusable, for, as we have seen, it is only in discourse (speech or writing) that discourse can be abolished. Individual speech, as we know only too well, can be gagged; but discourse as such is confirmed by the very arguments that proclaim its overthrow.

VII

Lacan, along with Lévi-Strauss, Deleuze, Barthes, Todorov, etc., may ostensibly reject the communication code as a model for language. Yet since they all subscribe uncritically to Saussure's semiological

[34] 'Agency', *Écrits* (Sheridan), 151.
[35] Elizabeth Wright, *Psychoanalytic Criticism: Theory in Practice* (Lonodn: Methuen, 1984), 109.   [36] Ibid. 109.

assumptions, they are obliged to account for new or original or creative meanings in terms of transgression. The Saussurian sign fuses signifier and signified; the Lacanian sign is a defused signifier which relates to other signifiers to form a structure not unlike that of Roget's *Thesaurus* which distributes words into binary slots (orthodoxy/ heterodoxy, peace/war, master/servant, etc.) and assembles them in interchangeable slots (existence, relation, quantity, order, number, time, change, causation, etc.). We should not, however, overlook the little fact that this structure is a taxonomy, not a combinatory system. A taxonomy, of course, is well adapted to the Lacanian doctrine that novel linguistic effects are the product of substitution. '*One word for another*: that is the formula for metaphor.' The 'poetic spark' (Lacan's phrase) is produced as the substitution takes place, at the point at which the old signifier expires into the new one. In Lacan's formulation: 'We see, then, that metaphor occurs at the precise point at which sense emerges from nonsense.'[37]

What can this mean at the level of the unconscious structured like a language? In order to get a grip on this problem, one is tempted to treat Lacan's 'substitution' as a synonym of Freud's. In Freud, substitution is a mechanism of repression which entails (to oversimplify) the replacement of an unauthorized idea or representation by one acceptable to the ego. Confronted by the manifest symptom (which is a message, for Freud antedates the kingdom of the signifier) his task is to recover, with his patient's collaboration, the occluded thought. The significance of what is represented (for example, Hamlet's love for his father) is what has been repressed (Hamlet's hate for his father, that is, his love for his mother). But for Lacan this is not the case: the substitution of one signifier for another releases a *new* meaning.

I have no difficulty in following Freud because his model is the censored text, with which we are all familiar. If a text is to pass the censor (particularly if that censor is the self) it must have two equally intelligible meanings, one acceptable to the censor, and one directed at the inner audience, which receives the real or subversive sense. The excitement in Freud's conception comes from the fact that two contrary intentions are active in a single mind. But I have great difficulty in following Lacan's conception, because his inner 'text' is *langue*, the outer *parole* being accountable only to that covert grid. Consider his

37 'Agency', *Écrits* (Sheridan), 157.

treatment of a line from Victor Hugo's famous poem 'Booz endormi', which has become a *locus classicus* of Lacanian exegesis: 'Sa gerbe n'était point avare ni haineuse' ('His sheaf was neither miserly nor spiteful').[38] According to Lacan, 'sheaf' is metaphorical for 'Booz': that is to say, one signifier, 'Booz', has been replaced by another signifier, 'sheaf', and the law of substitution that produces the poetic effect has been satisfied.[39] However, a question has been begged: how did Lacan know what substitution had taken place? How did he discover that 'sheaf' means 'Booz'? To an English reader who has never heard of the poem, and has access only to the quoted line, this attribution will appear entirely arbitrary. To a French reader, however, for whom 'Booz endormi', which dramatizes the central episode in the Book of Ruth, is perhaps the most familiar poem in the French anthology, it will be evident. Several years later, referring to this example, Lacan wrote: 'Of all poems, I have taken the one that, in French, may be said to echo in more people's memories than any other. Who did not learn when a child to recite "Booz endormi"?'[40] The reason why Lacan obtains his audience's instant assent is that he is able to rely on their familiarity with the poem *as discourse*. In short, without access to *parole*, the metaphor could never be recognized. To be more exact, the immediate verbal context of the line certainly warrants a less expansive metaphorical sense than Lacan's: the biblical Booz, in harvesting the plenitude of nature, repeats nature's generosity by allowing the poor to gather the surplus wheat for themselves. However, Lacan rightly is more ambitious, for the context for the line is also the whole poem. Lacan, of course, does not quite say this. The sheaf, he informs us, does indeed refer us to Booz himself 'because it has replaced him in the signifying chain at the very place where he was to be exalted by the sweeping away of greed and spite. But now Booz himself has been swept away by . . . the munificence of the sheaf . . . But if in this profusion the giver has disappeared . . . it is only to rise again in what surrounds the figure of speech in which he was annihilated. For it is the figure of the burgeoning of fecundity.' Indeed, it is this figure that 'announces *the surprise that the poem celebrates*: . . . the promise of paternity'.[41] No clearer

[38] 'Agency', *Écrits* (Sheridan), 156. [39] Ibid 164.

[40] Jacques Lacan, *Les Quatre Concepts fondamentaux de la psychanalyse* (Paris: Seuil, 1964) (transcript of Séminaire XI); trans. Alan Sheridan as *The Four Fundamental Concepts of Psychoanalysis* (Harmondsworth: Penguin Books, 1979), 247.

[41] 'Agency', *Écrits* (Sheridan), 157–8.

give-away could be found than the italicized lines, in which Lacan himself tells us that he relies on the poem, on the poem as *parole*, indeed on that *parole* as interpreted, for his theme of paternity. However much he may insist, it is impossible even for him to derive the 'electricity' of that figure of speech (the sheaf as paternity) from the crossover of sinking and rising signifiers. The attraction of the spark-plug theory of metaphor (no spark without a gap) should not blind us to the fact that Hugo's 'Booz endormi' does indeed *celebrate* (Lacan's not insensitive term) paternity exactly where one would expect to find it: in discursive language, here offered as a verbal structure of extraordinary semantic richness, available to all who care to look, and which gathers into itself a 'harvest' of meanings that are at once agrarian, moral, sexual, and supernatural.

I have no quarrel with Lacan's desire to account for the old shock of the new in terms of metaphor. What I cannot accept is a substitution theory that finds a poem and leaves it a bomb-site. Does metaphor have to be theorized thus? I will apply Lacan's formula for metaphor ('one word [*sic*] for another') to an English example— D. H. Lawrence's evocation of a sunlit early spring morning in the South of France, when 'the wind is polished with snow'. What word does 'polished' replace? 'Cold'? 'Clean'? 'Translucent'? 'Luminous'? There is in fact no hidden substitute, only a novel linguistic precision—which, we are bound to notice, is also a perceptual one. It would be much more accurate to say that the metaphorical consists in finding a *new use for a familiar word*. Of course, in invoking 'use' I remain in the realm of *parole*—which enables me to account not just for the new, but the intelligibly new. That this matters is shown by an unusual incident connected with W. H. Auden's well-known line 'And ports have names for the sea'. Auden had written 'And poets have names for the sea', but the typesetter made a slip which Auden, a true poet, retained in the proofs. Here we do have 'one word for another', but this has nothing to do with the new meaning. Auden would not have passed 'epots', or 'teops', for instance—though Joyce might, because he sought to create a speech that had never been spoken—a project, however, that wholly relied on an extraordinary mastery of languages that are most certainly spoken.

VIII

The commitment of structuralism to science as a knowledge founded on the objectification of the subject (though not of course of the scientist) ensured that it would espouse the code model; but it also ensured that it would dissolve the code's instituted premiss (the bonding of signifier and signified). The philosophical explanation of this is that the definition of the signified as the *concept* of the thing reintroduced the notion of the subject (objects, unlike human heads, do not contain concepts), but did so unnecessarily since the definition had already cut off the signified from the world (I can see Margaret Thatcher, but not the concept of Margaret Thatcher, across the street). Thus language became a free-standing system composed of signifiers as empty as algebraic symbols, identified only in relation to each other, and linked only by virtue of the alleged substitutive-combinatory functions. And so we found ourselves installed in the Lacanian unconscious. There remained one little difficulty, however: we could no longer move.

What then is human language? Whatever method we choose in our quest for an answer, we will make no progress if we continue to assume that language is (like God's originating *fiat* or Lacan's re-originating 'world of words that creates the world of things') *in apposition to the world*. Like the linguistic community that uses it, language is part of the world. The act of naming, whether instituted positively, as with the Saussurian signifier, or negatively, as with the Lacanian signifier, should not be construed in terms of a correspondence theory of truth. That act is only one of the immense range of operations that language empowers us to perform.

Part II

Criticism and the Aesthetic

6

Poetry as Literary Criticism

MICHAEL O'NEILL

In early October 1979, Stephen Spender sat in a classroom, reading to himself from an anthology as he prepared to teach poetry to some would-be poets. The next day, in Lynchburg, Virginia, he wrote in his journal: 'The Wild Swans at Coole, Book IX of *Paradise Lost*, some William Carlos Williams which made me revise my opinion of him. What incredible language, how edible, how delectable, why, I wonder, do I ever read anything but poetry?' 'The Bishop Orders his Tomb!', he went on to exclaim, warming to his theme.[1] It is a revealing poem on which to alight since Browning's lapis-loving prelate, who insists for his epitaph on 'Choice Latin, picked phrase, Tully's every word',[2] arouses divided feelings. The Bishop is corruptly but magnificently worldly, embodying the contradictions of the Renaissance; the poem half-allegorizes the tug between ethics and aesthetics and might be said to show that poems are not merely epicurean verbal feasts. But Spender's joyous savouring reminds us that, in Wallace Stevens's phrase, 'It must give pleasure', even if that 'pleasure' often derives, as Harold Bloom suggests, from the way a poet masters 'the unpleasure of a dangerous situation'.[3]

In fact, Spender's pleasure was such that he found himself hoping his students would not turn up to interrupt his reading. Before he confesses to this unprofessional wish, though, a reply to his question

[1] Stephen Spender, *Journals 1939–1983*, ed. John Goldsmith (London: Faber & Faber, 1985), 375–6.

[2] 'The Bishop Orders his Tomb at Saint Praxed's Church', line 77, in *Robert Browning*, ed. Adam Roberts, introd. Daniel Karlin, Oxford Authors (Oxford: Oxford UP, 1997).

[3] The Stevens phrase is the title of the final section of *Notes towards a Supreme Fiction*, in *The Collected Poems of Wallace Stevens* (London: Faber & Faber, 1971); Harold Bloom is quoted from his *The Anxiety of Influence: A Theory of Poetry* (1973; London: Oxford UP, 1975), 58.

has already arrived: 'The answer is that poetry has become a kind of battle of critics . . . disturbing the pure springs. One comes to think of poems as the objects of abstractly prose commentaries.'[4] It is an old complaint, suggesting the persistence inside readers of a voice that desires to respond to poems as other than 'the objects of abstractly prose commentaries'. Such a voice, demanding a critical language answerable in its intelligence and imaginativeness to what is read, will not be silenced and is often best appeased, I shall argue, by other poems.

This essay reopens the question of aesthetic knowing that Patricia Waugh raises in her contribution to the present volume. How and what does a poem know? Does it know in a different way from the way literary criticism, or literary theory, or philosophy knows? Does poetry know at all, or does it, as Paul H. Fry suggests, suspend truth-claims (for Fry, poetry is 'that characteristic of utterance, defined as "ostension" . . . which temporarily releases consciousness from its dependence on the signifying process')?[5] Fry celebrates poetry as a releasing from what Keats calls 'any irritable reaching after fact & reason', as making readers a kind of gift of being by means of a 'literary letting-be' that 'constructs nothing' but serves 'only to disclose that aspect of existence which is—apparently—in and for itself'. There, however, 'apparently' indicates that the contrast between 'construction' and 'disclosure' may not hold water; for all its many valuable aspects, Fry's 'extreme form of anti-intellectualism' (his own description) risks at times an emptying-out of poetry's inventive power and cognitive capacity.[6]

In his poem 'The Bitter World of Spring' William Carlos Williams writes: 'And, as usual, | the fight as to the nature of poetry | —Shall the philosophers capture it?— | is on.'[7] In some moods I find these lines talismanic. Williams's determination that 'the philosophers' will not 'capture' poetry is one with which I can sympathize. This is a response that should not be confused with dislike of or disrespect for philosophy. It is, rather, to register the sense that philosophical dis-

<hr/>

[4] Spender, *Journals*, 376.
[5] Paul H. Fry, *A Defense of Poetry: Reflections on the Occasion of Writing* (Stanford, Calif.: Stanford UP, 1995), 4. For a fuller discussion of this important book, see my review in *Criticism*, 38/4 (1996), 642–4.
[6] *The Letters of John Keats 1814–1821*, ed. Hyder Edward Rollins, 2 vols. (Cambridge, Mass.: Harvard UP, 1958), i. 193; Fry, *A Defense of Poetry*, 43, 111.
[7] Quoted from *The Collected Later Poems of William Carlos Williams* (rev. edn. New York: New Directions, 1963).

course, which can, as in Plato or Nietzsche, be poetic in its mode of working, is sometimes—especially when setting up supposedly generalizable categories—left floundering in the wake of poetic rhythms, images, and diction. In so doing such discourse, when applied to poetry, is in danger of succumbing to the second of two modes of critical insufficiency sketched by Harold Bloom: 'tautology—in which the poem is and means itself—and reduction—in which the poem means something that is not itself a poem'.

Bloom's solution—an 'antithetical criticism' in which 'the meaning of a poem can only be a poem, but *another poem—a poem not itself*'—must await further consideration.[8] But for an example of 'reduction', one might consider a possible collocation of Friedrich Schlegel and William Wordsworth. Take Schlegel's axiom 'The romantic kind of poetry is still in the state of becoming; that, in fact, is its real essence: that it should forever be becoming and never be perfected.'[9] Now consider Wordsworth's glimpse of 'something evermore about to be' as the unreachable goal of his imaginative quest in *The Prelude*.[10] Schlegel, an inventive generalizer, nevertheless generalizes; for all the witty play that identifies 'essence' with 'becoming', and despite his desire to 'unite' 'poetry and philosophy',[11] his mode of discourse cannot carry over to us what it feels like to experience the interplay between intuition and descriptive detail in *The Prelude*, book vi. Wordsworth brings together, as only poetry can, rootedness in particular experience (the fact that he has discovered that he has crossed the Alps while thinking he still had to cross them) and an unparaphrasable emotional state. Though 'something evermore about to be' affirms, it does so in rhythms that are yearningly aware that only they can corroborate the poetry's desire. Schlegel has been described by Samuel Weber as attempting (with Novalis) to conceive of criticism as 'an integral and essential part of the artistic process', and his critical practice does involve a view of

---

[8] *The Anxiety of Influence*, 70.
[9] Friedrich Schlegel, *Athenäum Fragments*, 116; quoted from David Simpson (ed.), *The Origins of Modern Critical Thought: German Aesthetic and Literary Criticism from Lessing to Hegel* (Cambridge: Cambridge UP, 1988), 193.
[10] *The Prelude* (1850), vi. 608; quoted, as are subsequent quotations from Wordsworth's poetry, from *Wordsworth: Poetical Works*, ed. Thomas Hutchinson, new edn. rev. Ernest de Selincourt, Oxford Standard Authors (1936; London: Oxford UP, 1967).
[11] *Ideas*, 108; quoted from Simpson (ed.), *The Origins of Modern Critical Thought*, 199.

criticism as, in Weber's words (glossing Walter Benjamin on Novalis), 'the completion or consummation of the work and . . . its [the work's] consumption or dissolution in the discourse of criticism'.[12] To this extent, Schlegel is a forerunner of any vision of criticism as creative; yet his theoretical bias leads him to adopt a perspective from which criticism risks setting itself up as in some ways superior to the work that prompts it into existence.

In 'The Bitter World of Spring' Williams may identify a problem, the quarrel between 'poetry' and 'philosophy'. But his solution here and elsewhere—a return to 'things'—risks selling poetry short.[13] It is to Shelley in *A Defence of Poetry* that we might go back for an account of poetry that is neither subservient to nor afraid of 'philosophy'. Shelley's prose poem teems with images and cadences that make it untranslatable, irreducible even to the very positions it defends with such passion; it brims over with keen, humane, and eloquent arguments, and yet, finally, it begins to matter more for what it is than for what it can be paraphrased as saying. Partly making and partly illustrating this point, Shelley writes: 'Poetry is a sword of lightning, ever unsheathed, which consumes the scabbard that would contain it.'[14] Language ceases to serve instrumental ends; the medium becomes the message. *A Defence of Poetry* suggests that poetry depends for its value on a unique, 'vitally metaphorical'[15] mode of existence bestowed on (or recovered for) language. The same *can* be claimed for literary criticism; at its finest it can be as well as be about. My personal canon includes T. S. Eliot whenever he quotes and comments on his quotations; William Empson in *Seven Types of Ambiguity*; admiring analyses in F. R. Leavis; gnomic meditations by Wallace Stevens; jagged, angst-ridden sentences in John Berryman; velvety expositions by Helen Vendler; and sumptuous metaphors in Seamus Heaney. What these dissimilar critics have in common is a recognition that the language used by the critic is the means by which we re-experience his or her imaginative response. Too often, however, the interpretative

---

[12] Samuel Weber, 'Criticism Underway: Walter Benjamin's *Romantic Concept of Criticism*', in Kenneth R. Johnston et al. (eds.), *Romantic Revolutions: Criticism and Theory* (Bloomington, Ind.: Indiana UP, 1990), 309.

[13] 'The Bitter World of Spring' turns from abstractions to description of 'shad', 'their bodies | red-finned in the dark | water headed, unrelenting, upstream'.

[14] Quoted from *Shelley's Poetry and Prose: Authoritative Texts, Criticism*, ed. Donald H. Reiman and Sharon B. Powers, Norton Critical Edition (New York: Norton, 1977), 491. Unless indicated otherwise, all quotations from Shelley's prose and poetry are taken from this edition.   [15] Ibid. 482.

lust of literary criticism breeds a language in which there is a worry-ing gap between the poem and the critical performance.

The major claim that deconstructive readings of literature have on the reader interested in imaginative achievement is their awareness of this gap. For instance, J. Hillis Miller's piece on Shelley's *The Triumph of Life* concludes a dizzying reading of the poem's images with this reflection:

At the end of all my commentary, I find myself where I began. As a reader of 'The Triumph of Life' I am the next in a chain of repetitions without beginning or end. I find myself again enfolded in a fold, asleep under a caverned mountain beside a brook, watching a sequence of shapes all light, projecting in my turn figures over those shapes, figures that fade even as they are traced, to be replaced by others, in an unending production of signs over signs. . . .[16]

Hillis Miller finds himself undone by his attempt to outdo the text, condemned like a schoolboy writing out lines to repeat the scenarios of the original. Yet the prose has about it a ghostly fire of rekindled creativity; it re-enacts the compulsive echoing and irresolution of the master-text as it rhymes 'traced' and 'replaced', and gazes forwards with its own hopeless desire in that final run of ellipses. Confessing failure, the essay's shift of awareness is a critical triumph. Hillis Miller awakens a fresh sense of the strange power of Shelley's well-nigh uninterpretable poem. The essay grants the language of the original something close to its full authority: something close because Hillis Miller is still fixated—as 'production of signs over signs' reveals—on reading the poem as allegorizing the signifying process.

Jorge Luis Borges, in 'Pierre Menard, Author of the *Quixote*', is more dazzlingly exercised by the problem of adequate response. In this work the critic does indeed become author as, in Seán Burke's words, Borges turns 'essay into story, story into essay'.[17] Pierre Menard in Borges's fable is a twentieth-century 'Symbolist from Nîmes, essentially a devoté of Poe', who seeks to compose '*the Quixote itself*'. This is to be a consciously belated act of recreation; Menard 'never contemplated a mechanical transcription of the

[16] J. Hillis Miller, *The Linguistic Moment: From Wordsworth to Stevens* (Princeton; Princeton UP, 1985); repr. in Michael O'Neill (ed. and introd.), *Shelley*, Longman Critical Readers (London: Longman, 1993), 239.
[17] Seán Burke, *Authorship: From Plato to the Postmodern: A Reader* (Edinburgh: Edinburgh UP, 1995), 307.

original'. The narrator marvels over the difference between versions of passages from the book produced by Cervantes and Menard, despite the fact that they are exactly the same, word for word:

> It is a revelation to compare Menard's *Don Quixote* with Cervantes's. The latter, for example, wrote (part one, chapter nine):

> . . . truth, whose mother is history, rival of time, depository of deeds, witness of the past, exemplar and adviser to the present, and the future's counsellor.

Written in the seventeenth century, written by the 'lay genius' Cervantes, this enumeration is a mere rhetorical praise of history. Menard, on the other, writes:

> . . . truth, whose mother is history, rival of time, depository of deeds, witness of the past, exemplar and adviser to the present, and the future's counsellor.

History, the *mother* of truth: the idea is astounding. Menard, a contemporary of William James, does not define history as an inquiry into reality but as its origin.

This excerpt characterizes a parable that bears with exquisite irony and some poignancy on the predicament of the reader who would recreate, from a position of unignorable historical distance, the impact of a masterpiece. Pierre Menard knowingly 'set himself to an undertaking which was exceedingly complex and, from the very beginning, futile'; he acts as a figure for the tragi-comically defeated reader. But Borges is also alive to the creative possibilities of reading demonstrated by works of art. As he puts it in 'Kafka and his Precursors', 'every writer *creates* his own precursors'. Harold Bloom alludes to this topsy-turvy assertion in *The Anxiety of Influence* in order to point up the difference between his troubled view of 'influence' and that of Borges. For Bloom, the Borgesian idea of cleaning the word precursor of 'all connotation of polemics or rivalry'[18] yields to a fraught notion that strong poets give the impression that they 'are being *imitated by their ancestors*'. From Bloom's perspective, engagement by strong poets with the work of their predecessors 'reduces', in his finely contradictory phrase, to 'the mystery of narcissism'. Bloom's account of poets' relations with their precursors compels admiration by virtue of its daring and frequent assent by dint of its insight. Yet his own antithetical criticism cannot wholly escape

---

[18] Jorge Luis Borges, *Labyrinths: Selected Stories and Other Writings*, ed. Donald A. Yates and James E. Irby, preface by André Maurois (1964; Harmondsworth: Penguin, 1970), 67, 65, 69, 70, 236.

the danger of simplifying dogmatism. My own departure from Bloom arises from a quarrel with the post-Freudian pessimism of his insistence that 'Every poem is a misinterpretation of a parent poem.'[19]

One example must suffice. In *The Anxiety of Influence* and *Poetry and Repression* Bloom analyses the beautiful, enigmatic account in *The Triumph of Life* of Rousseau's encounter with the 'shape all light' (line 352). This encounter is suffused with echoes of Wordsworth's 'Ode: Intimations of Immortality'. Disappointingly Bloom 'reduces' Shelley's response to Wordsworth in these melodramatic ways: 'Here, at his end, Shelley is open again to the terror of Wordsworth's "Intimations" ode, and yields to his precursor's "light of common day"'; 'After seven years of struggle with Wordsworth's poetry, Shelley's work still battled to keep itself from being flooded out by the precursor's.'[20] These assertions wantonly rule out a reading that does justice to Shelley's deep understanding of Wordsworth's poem. For *The Triumph of Life* sees that Wordsworth's poem needs to construct a coherent fiction of origins and ends. It knows that Wordsworth's questions at the end of stanza IV—'Whither is fled the visionary gleam? | Where is it now, the glory and the dream?' (lines 56–7)—overwhelmingly demand to be answered. Wordsworth comes up with a notion of pre-existence which explains how we came into the world 'trailing clouds of glory' (line 64). The light this bequeaths fades, but our recollections of it are valuable for their own sake and for the promise they offer of eternal life. *The Triumph of Life*, by contrast, lets the questions multiply, questions provoked by the vanishing of lights into other lights and culminating in the narrator's 'what is Life?' (line 544).

Unlike Bloom, then, for whom all readings are misreadings, I would reassert the value of poetry as a mode of knowing when the object of knowledge is literature itself. Few critical accounts of W. H. Auden's early poetry convey the impact of that jauntily menacing body of work as powerfully as the bracketed third section in Stephen Spender's 'Auden's Funeral'. The section concludes with three lines from a section of an untitled sequence that Spender set up, when printing Auden's *Poems* (1928), on his own 'five-pound printing press':

---

[19] *The Anxiety of Influence*, 141, 146, 94.
[20] Ibid. 140; id., *Poetry and Repression: Revisionism from Blake to Stevens* (New Haven: Yale UP, 1976), 109.

> 'An evening like a coloured photograph
> A music stultified across the water
> The heel upon the finishing blade of grass.')[21]

The cold brilliance that shone off Auden's clipped syllables and mesmerized his contemporaries is recaptured by the play of the italicized lines against the white of the page: a white that mimics the wordless stun of admiration and the silence that has come upon the elegized poet. Spender asserts quietly an intimacy with the dead poet by quoting the original version of that last line, 'The heel upon the finishing blade of grass', a version with 'upon' rather than 'on' (the reading in revised versions). If Auden's revision gives the line a snaky, gliding effect, the earlier, more metrically regular line is suited to the elegiac, 'finishing' mood of Spender's poem. Spender quotes out of context, as if to imply the hypnotic effect of individual lines 'whose letters bit | Ink-deep into my fingers' ('Auden's Funeral', III) and far more than inch-deep into his mind. But when the context is recovered one can see why the lines made such an impact on Spender. In the version printed in *Poems* (1928), Auden refers to those 'Less clinically-minded' who will admire 'An evening like a coloured photograph, | A music stultified across the water', eating his cake and having it too.[22] The poem continues with hints of a relationship that appears to have been 'clinically' ended. Yet the finished relationship is said to leave 'Sporadic heartburn' in its wake. By alluding to the poem in *Poems* (1928), Spender reminds us of the admiring yet conflict-ridden personal and poetic dialogue he conducted over the years with Auden, a poet more 'clinically-minded' than Spender, yet able, as Spender's tribute sees, to anatomize the romantic impulse with a frozen intensity that is itself not entirely unromantic.

Auden himself appears at his aphoristic best in section 2 of 'In Memory of W. B. Yeats':

> You were silly like us; your gift survived it all;
> The parish of rich women, physical decay,
> Yourself; mad Ireland hurt you into poetry.

---

[21] Quoted from Stephen Spender, *Collected Poems: 1928–1985* (London: Faber & Faber, 1985).

[22] The revised version occurs in section 4 of 'It was Easter as I walked in the public gardens', in *The English Auden: Poems, Essays and Dramatic Writings, 1927–1939*, ed. Edward Mendelson (London: Faber & Faber, 1977); lines from the earlier version (*Poems*, 1928) are quoted from *The English Auden*, 438.

Now Ireland has her madness and her weather still,
For poetry makes nothing happen: it survives
In the valley of its saying where executives
Would never want to tamper; it flows south
From ranches of isolation and the busy griefs,
Raw towns that we believe and die in; it survives,
A way of happening, a mouth.[23]

Though tomes on Yeats's life and art are upstaged by these stylish lines, the lines are not merely content with stylishness. They lie close to the heart of an uneasy, amusing, and serious poetic act of literary criticism. Yeats's magnificent but bothersome career 'hurts' Auden, to use his own verb, into a complicated defence of the older poet's poetry. In this section Auden debunks the life ('You were silly like us') and the context ('mad Ireland') in order to salvage the surviving 'gift'. The passage is the more persuasive for anticipating our own discomfort with its deflations; so 'You were silly like us' purposefully strikes a flippantly trite note. One thing that can be said of Yeats's silliness is how fabulously unlike our own it was. Immediately Auden takes a different tack, as if prompted by the desire to make amends, piercing to the heart of Yeats's achievement: 'your gift survived it all.' Auden takes the long view here, his gaze sweeping across Yeats's adulation of Lady Gregory and Coole Park, obsession with 'dull decrepitude',[24] and arcane concern with the complex nature of identity, to celebrate the fact that the poet's 'gift' has emerged unscathed from its encounters with circumstance. Circumstance, briefly, is a necessary dross. But only briefly is it so, because having in this section extracted poetry from a world of weather and executives Auden will in the third section find a role for poetry at a time of historical crisis.

Elegies for dead poets have an in-built tendency to turn into meditations on the nature of poetry. To this tendency *Lycidas*, *Adonais*, and 'North Haven' (Elizabeth Bishop's elegy for Robert Lowell), among many other poems, bear witness. Auden's poem is no exception. At the centre of the second section is the famous

---

[23] Quoted from the earlier version in *The English Auden*. Subsequently Auden made a number of revisions, including the alteration of 'valley of its saying' to 'valley of its making'.

[24] Section III, line 67 of 'The Tower', quoted from W. B. Yeats, *The Poems*, ed. Daniel Albright (1990; London: Dent, 1994); this edition is used for quotations from Yeats's poetry.

assertion,'poetry makes nothing happen'. Here Auden turns on his own poetic generation's ideological suspicions of art for art's sake. Poetry, his poem begins to argue, is not an agent of history. Yet this emphasis is itself quick to see its own one-sidedness, as if Auden makes, in Yeatsian fashion, a poem out of a quarrel with himself. (Auden's prose work 'The Public v. the Late Mr. William Butler Yeats' shows how the wish to accommodate the mind's arguments with itself led him to create a particularly lively critical mode: the essay as trial transcript.) As one rereads the lines from the elegy's second section, 'nothing' seems to turn into something: poetry makes nothing happen, the no thing that is poetic experience. This is because it is 'A way of happening', a mode of being in the world, 'a mouth' suggesting that this mode of being is both reduced and unsilenceable. Granted a geographical habitation and a name ('the valley of its saying'), poetry begins river-like to flow from—a duplicitous preposition here—'ranches of isolation'. By the end of the section 'survival' is accorded to poetry, not just to one poet's 'gift', even as that 'gift' is the means by which poetry 'survives'. In the final section Auden adopts a more Yeatsian manner as he suggests why poetry's 'way of happening' is of value 'In the nightmare of the dark': 'With your unconstraining voice | Still persuade us to rejoice', Auden urges in incantatory but thought-prompting trochaics, picking up a key word—'rejoice'—in late Yeats.

Though Auden ends 'In Memory of W. B. Yeats' on a positive chord, his elegy is the more valuable for making us think hard about the claims of poetry. Compared with prose literary criticism, poems are at once privileged and vulnerable when it comes to weighing in their scales why it is that the art of poetry matters. They are more intimate with all that 'poetry' means; at the same time they are fighting for their life: 'Feeling clumsy as I do. | Every poem my Waterloo', Spender notes ruefully in a bit of journal doggerel.[25] The stakes are high. When in his poem 'The Mystery of the Charity of Charles Péguy' Geoffrey Hill meditates on 'one of the great souls, one of the great prophetic intelligences, of our century', praise and irony wrestle intently.[26] Péguy's possible responsibility for the assassination of the socialist deputy Jean Jaurès leads Hill to ask:

[25] Entry for 17 Oct., 1979, in *Journals*, 381.
[26] Quoted from Geoffrey Hill, *Collected Poems* (Harmondsworth: Penguin, 1985), 207; quotations from Hill's poetry are taken from this edition.

Did Péguy kill Jaurès? Did he incite
the assassin? Must men stand by what they write
as by their camp-beds or their weaponry
or shell-shocked comrades while they sag and cry?

Hill masks yet reveals his own personal involvement through the concision and force with which he asks more general questions about the writer's role. The best criticism of this questioning occurs in a pair of intertextually linked poems: in 'Man and the Echo' Yeats wonders about the relationship between words and deeds: 'Did that play of mine send out | Certain men the English shot?'; Paul Muldoon hears a note of arrogance in Yeats's question and debunks it in his '7, Middagh Street' where his 'Wystan' says, 'As for his crass rhetorical ‖ posturing, "Did that play of mine | send out certain men (*certain* men?) ‖ the English shot. . . ? | the answer is "Certainly not".'[27] Pointing up as either unintended or over-intended Yeats's word-play in 'certain' (meaning 'some' and 'committed'), this is not Muldoon's last word, though it may be his poem's most memorable passage. Indeed, the poem, with an elegant, bitter frivolity, dramatizes the mind's dialogue with itself. Later, Muldoon's 'Louis'—Louis MacNeice—with Lorca in mind, says, 'For poetry *can* make things happen— | not only can, but *must.*'

In Hill's lines rhyme turns its interrogator's light on the issue worrying the poet; 'write' and 'incite' are handcuffed together. At the same time 'The Mystery of the Charity of Charles Péguy' affirms poetry's capacity to achieve a temporary breathing-space in which it is possible to resist history's script: 'History commands the stage wielding a toy gun, | rehearsing another scene,' Hill writes dismissively. That said, Hill's language makes us aware that if history can be resisted, mocked, analysed, and taken issue with, it cannot, in the end, be sent packing; its meanings inhabit every word that Hill chooses with such care. The poem becomes an evocation and a critique of the way that a poet's life is inseparable from its time, and from the dreams and longings that took it out of that time. It concludes by restating the impulse to commemorate at the heart of poetry: '"in memory of those things these words were born".' Péguy's words and Hill's words about Péguy are enfolded by the line, an adaptation—so Hill's note informs us—of a sentence from Marcel

---

[27] Paul Muldoon, *Meeting the British* (London: Faber & Faber, 1987).

Raymond's *From Baudelaire to Surrealism*.[28] Critical work and poem
find a common cause; yet it is the poem that has suffered as well as
thought about Péguy's career.

Poems can harness prose criticism to their own purposes of understanding. Amy Clampitt's 'Voyages: A Homage to John Keats' co-
operates harmoniously with its biographical and critical sources,
work by Walter Jackson Bate and Helen Vendler, to enact, in the
words of Clampitt's note, 'The powerful way in which literature can
become a link with times and places, and with minds, otherwise
remote'.[29] Yet the poem's juxtapositions, musical pathos, and intense
compressions move beyond the reach of biography and critical essay.
Clampitt's counter-response to the life of Keats's poetry and the life
out of which it came culminates in the final lines:

> Untaken voyages, Lethean cold, O all but unendured
>
> arrivals! Keats's starved stare before the actual,
> so long imagined Bay of Naples. The mind's extinction.
> Nightlong, sleepless beside the Spanish Steps, the prattle
> of poured water. Letters no one will ever open.

The steadfast phrases balance the 'actual' and the 'imagined'; the
poetry itself endures in the double sense of 'undergo' and 'last', and
pays tribute to Keats the suffering man and extinguished creative
mind.[30]

Literary criticism of the kind found in poetry seeks to make of past
literature what George Steiner calls 'a present presence'.[31] To capture
this sense of 'present presence' it may be necessary for a poem to
convey its awareness of the strange otherness of the past writing or
writer. When in the first Pisan canto (LXXIV) Pound writes 'By no
means an orderly Dantescan rising | but as the winds veer' he suggests
how his poem is at the mercy of and made possible by historical,
cultural, and personal 'winds' at odds with 'an orderly Dantescan
rising'.[32] The problem of distance is formulated and, in being for-

[28] *Collected Poems*, 205.
[29] Amy Clampitt, *What the Light Was Like* (1985; London: Faber & Faber, 1986),
107. Clampitt's poetry is quoted from this volume.
[30] For a fuller reading of Clampitt's poem, see Michael O'Neill, *Romanticism and
the Self-Conscious Poem* (Oxford: Clarendon Press, 1997), 271–89.
[31] George Steiner, *Real Presences: Is There Anything in What We Say?* (1989;
London: Faber, 1991), 13.
[32] All quotations from *The Cantos* are taken from Ezra Pound, *The Cantos* (London: Faber & Faber, 1975).

mulated, partly answered by Charles Tomlinson in his 'In Memoriam Thomas Hardy':

> How to speak with the dead
> so that not only
> our but their
> words are valid?

That subdued off-rhyme between 'dead' and 'valid' defines the poem's tentative trust that it can speak validly with the dead. Tomlinson invites us in this poem to remember that 'His besetting word | was "afterwards".'[33] 'Besetting' meaning 'assailing with difficulties' is a word applicable to Hardy's attempt to speak to his dead wife in, say, 'The Voice'. It is applicable, moreover, to Tomlinson's effort to speak to Hardy—or, rather, to speak about speaking with Hardy partly so that Hardy can speak with us, where 'with' rather than 'to' is significantly un-buttonholing. Through the unegotistical admission of difficulties, however, Tomlinson's poem is, to use its own word, 'released' into communion with the possibilities of communication.

Literary criticism in poems is, above all, linguistic and relational in its way of knowing, a way that frequently supports George Steiner's contention that 'The best readings of art are art.'[34] Yet in seeking to speak with the dead, poets as critics are tomb-haunters. Hart Crane's 'At Melville's Tomb' detects in Melville's writing a frustrated religious longing: 'Frosted eyes there were that lifted altars; | And silent answers crept across the stars.'[35] As the image of eyes lifting altars brings out, to say nothing of the subsequent 'silent answers', the poem knows that Crane may, finally, only project his own longing onto *Moby Dick*, that most hospitable of texts. In, and especially at the end of, 'Le Tombeau de Charles Baudelaire' Mallarmé suggests how dead writers affect us permanently yet will not abide our questions. Throughout the sonnet there is an intricate mingling of opposites, 'mud and rubies', as the second line has it, a mingling accentuated by the poem's fluid punctuation. The poem builds itself through a series of images that suggest the nature of Baudelaire's

[33] Quoted from Charles Tomlinson, *Collected Poems* (1985; Oxford: Oxford UP, 1987).

[34] *Real Presences*, 17. Many of my own surmises about poetry as criticism find heartening confirmation in Steiner's magisterial assertion and illustration of the view that 'All serious art, music and literature is a *critical* act', ibid. 11.

[35] Quoted from Hart Crane, *Complete Poems*, ed. Brom Weber (Newcastle upon Tyne: Bloodaxe, 1984).

inspiration and legacy. Ambivalences run through both, yet for all the emphasis on absence the poem senses that Baudelaire has changed for ever what poetry can do, and it concludes with the poet's tomb guarded by a muse-like Wraith that is, in Henry Weinfeld's translation, 'A tutelary poison . . . | We breathe in always though it bring us death'.[36]

The Mallarméan sonnet reads as a sombre variation on Shelley's comment that 'one great poet is a masterpiece of nature which another not only ought to study but must study'.[37] Virgil's reworking of Homer's techniques and matter is the archetypal instance of one great poet studying another to write his own masterpiece—and in the process pointing up why the predecessor poet was worth studying. Dido's tragic plight can still affect because *The Aeneid* is attuned to what Homer does and does not do, with, say, epic similes:

> Unlucky Dido, burning, in her madness
> Roamed through all the city, like a doe
> Hit by an arrow shot from far away
> By a shepherd hunting in the Cretan woods—
> Hit by surprise, nor could the hunter see
> His flying steel had fixed itself in her;
> But though she runs for life through copse and glade
> The fatal shaft clings to her side.[38]

Elaboration informed by empathy is everything here. The doe hit by an arrow may seem ordinary. The unknowingness of the archer ('Nescius' in the original) does not, nor does the fact that Dido's fate is precisely forecast by the painful irony of the doe running for life while 'the fatal shaft' clings to her side. Virgil imparts to the simile a ruthless pathos. Whereas Homer accepts in, for instance, the grim image of Odysseus' maidservants hanged in a way that brings to mind Second World War collaborators—'like thrushes, who have spread their wings, or pigeons, who have | flown into a snare set up for them in a thicket, trying | to find a resting place, but the sleep

[36] English translation quoted from Stéphane Mallarmé, *Collected Poems*, trans. with commentary Henry Weinfeld (Berkeley and Los Angeles: University of California Press, 1994).

[37] *Shelley: Poetical Works*, ed. Thomas Hutchinson, rev. ed. G. M. Matthews (London: Oxford UP, 1970), 206.

[38] 4. 95–102 (4. 68–73 in original), in Virgil, *The Aeneid*, trans. Robert Fitzgerald (1983; Harmondsworth: Penguin, 1985). George Steiner remarks that 'Virgil reads, guides our reading of, Homer as no external critic can', *Real Presences*, 12.

given them was hateful'[39]—Virgil unsentimentally laments. But the note of lament so individual to Virgil illuminates Homer's starker epic inflections. Later in the same book, in the process of describing the Trojans loading their ships prior to leaving, Virgil will address Dido directly: 'At that sight, what were your emotions, Dido?'[40] Virgil's involvement with his heroine takes the form of speaking to her as if she were real, not fictional. A rhetorical effect that is also a comment on our need to identify with the emotions of fictional characters, the line is a creative moment that is its own best gloss.

Again, Robert Henryson's *The Testament of Cresseid* is unequalled as a creative response to Chaucer's *Troilus and Criseyde*. In Henryson's 'drypoint version'—the phrase is used of Henryson's poem by the contemporary poet Jamie McKendrick in 'Mermaid', a poem about the gradual destruction of a sculpture of a mermaid—the story picks up where Chaucer leaves it: with Cresseid's desertion of Troilus in favour of Diomeid.[41] Henryson wrings a harsh yet cathartic tragedy out of 'the fatall destinie | Of fair Cresseid, that endit wretchitlie' (lines 62–3). 'Nane but myself as now I will accuse' (line 574), she says close to her death, finally taking the blame for her fate. Yet if the ambiguities of response towards Criseyde adroitly crafted by Chaucer are resolved by Henryson, they are also brought to mind. An early weather description serves to describe Henryson's response to Chaucer: 'The northin wind had purifyit the air, | And shed the mistie cloudis fra the sky' (lines 17–18).[42] But it recalls Chaucer's readiness to dwell for much of his poem—clear-sightedly yet compassionately—in the misty clouds created by complex human relations and situations.

Poems are the more valuable as witnesses to the achievements of previous poets because the notion of objective judgement is foreign to them. We take it as read that Heaney's poem on Larkin, 'The Journey Back', in *Seeing Things* has licence to interest us in, and as, Heaney's response to Larkin. When Larkin's shade is made to quote Dante in translation in this poem, 'The Journey Back', one can imagine that shade snorting with some incredulity. But then one is

[39] 22. 467–9 (in translation); quoted from *The Odyssey of Homer*, trans. Richmond Lattimore (1965; New York: Harper & Row, 1975).
[40] 4. 567 (4. 408 in original) in *The Aeneid*, trans. Fitzgerald.
[41] Jamie McKendrick, *The Sirocco Room* (Oxford: Oxford UP, 1991).
[42] Quoted from Robert Henryson, *Poems*, selected and ed. with introd., notes, and glossary Charles Elliott (2nd edn. Oxford: Clarendon Press, 1974).

meant to. 'Larkin's shade surprised me' is Heaney's way of surprising Larkin's shade—and of surprising us into recognizing the affinities between the exiled Florentine visionary responding to the quotidian and the Hull-based poet discontentedly content to come to terms with the toad work. Heaney's own ambitions to link the ordinary with the strange also find a voice. Larkin's shade is made to speak of 'the forewarned journey back | Into the heartland of the ordinary'— which soothingly mutes the terror of death evident in the poet's 'Aubade'. Heaney's final line—in which Larkin's ghost is said to describe himself as 'A nine-to five-man who had seen poetry'—allows, with equal generosity, for Larkin's matter-of-fact anti-Romanticism and for the manifest fact that he had 'seen poetry', even if that seeing only, and yet at its most sharp-eyed, made possible a glimpse of what 'High Windows' calls 'the deep blue air, that shows | Nothing, and is nowhere, and is endless'.[43]

From Horace's *Ars Poetica* to Czeslaw Milosz's 'Ars Poetica?' the poem about poetry has been a genre containing an awareness of risk, of what is at stake in the composition of verse. Urbane, witty, apparently un- or even anti-theoretical, Horace's poem adopts the tone of conversational musings (it is a verse epistle, *Epistula ad Pisones*). It offers itself as shavings from the workshop, tips, practical criticism—sometimes tongue in cheek, as when the aspiring writer is advised to show to discerning judges his attempts, 'then put the papers away and keep them for nine years'. What follows is more serious: 'You can always destroy what you have not published, but once you have let your words go they cannot be taken back.' This fear that words cannot be 'taken back' is partly overcome in the poem by its conversational manner, as it conceals the art with which it presents its reflections on art. But Horace's fear accompanies a perfectionist pride evident in an earlier passage: 'only in certain walks of

---

[43] 'The Journey Back' is quoted from Seamus Heaney, *Seeing Things* (London: Faber & Faber, 1991); 'High Windows' is quoted from Philip Larkin, *Collected Poems*, ed. with introd. Anthony Thwaite (London: The Marvell Press and Faber & Faber, 1988). One might note that Heaney's critical essay 'Englands of the Mind' finds a responsive and attuned way of discussing Larkin's procedures, as in the following sentences where the adverbs in the first sentence mime in their syntactical movement the process they describe and where the interplay between 'rational light' and 'luminous beauty' in the second sentence indicates the inclusiveness of the poetry's achievement: 'His tongue moves hesitantly, precisely, honestly, among ironies and negatives. He is the poet of rational light, a light that has its own luminous beauty but which has also the effect of exposing clearly the truths which it touches', *Preoccupations: Selected Prose 1968–1978* (London: Faber & Faber, 1980), 164.

life does the second-rate pass muster. An advocate or barrister of mediocre capacity . . . is not without his value; on the other hand, neither gods nor men—nor, for that matter, booksellers—can put up with mediocrity in poets.' Interpreters, commentators, reviewers are rather like the advocates or barristers in this passage: they can all be of use, we can bear with their, with our, mediocrity; but poetry (by which as throughout this essay I mean the question-begging but necessary category 'great poetry') always rebukes 'mediocrity'. This is what great poems that incorporate within themselves literary criticism are able to communicate: an intuition that poetry cannot afford to fail, nor can it afford to avoid taking risks that might result in failure. Reading Horace's poem, for all its slippered case, can seem to be like watching a tightrope walker. In the following lines he balances deftly on the high wire in the process of describing his fallings-off: 'I try my hardest to be succinct, and merely succeed in being obscure.' The thought of failure inspires the poem's finest successes:

Just as at a pleasant dinner-party music that is out of tune, a coarse perfume, or poppy-seeds served with bitter Sardinian honey give offence, for the meal could just as well have been given without them, so is it with a poem, which is begotten and created for the soul's delight; if it falls short of the top by ever so little, it sinks right down to the bottom.[44]

For all the laid-back way that Horace's simile unfolds, there is an uncompromising awareness here that poetry is written for 'the soul's delight'.

In *An Essay on Criticism* Pope writes that '*Horace* still charms with graceful Negligence, | And without Method *talks* us into Sense' (lines 653–4): a compliment clinched by the rhyme of 'negligence' and 'sense' that enacts Pope's sense of the coexistence of apparently opposite qualities in Horace.[45] Pope himself is a major literary critic in prose, as his notes to his translation of Homer's *Iliad* reveal; they are full of precise observations about his author's 'poetical beauties' and of critical good sense, as in this grand put-down at the expense of critics straining to be original: 'it is generally the fate of such people who will never say what was said before, to say what will never be

---

[44] Horace, *On the Art of Poetry*, in *Classical Literary Criticism: Aristotle, Horace, Longinus*, trans. with introd. T. S. Dorsch (1965; Harmondsworth: Penguin, 1967), 92, 79, 92.
[45] All quotations from *An Essay on Criticism* are taken from *The Poems of Alexander Pope: A One-Volume Edition of the Twickenham Text with Selected Annotations*, ed. John Butt (London: Methuen, 1963).

said after them.'[46] He is also a multifaceted critic in his poetry: whether defending his own satiric practice in ways that inventively rework Horace or describing the ideal literary critic in *An Essay on Criticism* as one 'Blest with a *Taste* exact, yet unconfin'd; | A *Knowledge* both of *Books* and *Humankind*' (lines 639–40). This couplet avoids platitude because of its verbal imitation of a difficult balance and inclusiveness. Generally, it is fascinating to watch Pope's alertness to the large issues provoked by thinking about details of style. For instance, he mocks with great ingenuity those who '*Equal Syllables* alone require, | Tho' oft the Ear the *open Vowels* tire' (lines 344–5). There, the suavely bad second line succinctly makes the point that a poet's control over language has to operate on many levels simultaneously and is nothing without some expressive end. If expression is the dress of thought, then Pope can be said to possess, critically, a superb clothes sense.

The violet in the crucible—Shelley's image in *A Defence of Poetry* for the poem that is translated—is the fate of all poetry once we start to talk about it. Yet the thing itself bristles with a power to which sometimes only another poem, even one in translation, can do justice. The Polish poet Czeslaw Milosz's 'Ars Poetica?' captures the violation of decorum that poetry often involves. Milosz alludes to Horace but tags on a question mark since his poem is disturbed by the art it seeks to define:

> In the very essence of poetry there is something indecent:
> a thing is brought forth which we didn't know we had in us,
> so we blink our eyes, as if a tiger had sprung out
> and stood in the light, lashing his tail.

Milosz's lines evoke the power of that tiger-like emergence and the 'shame' it leaves in its wake. The poem is anti-confessional and anti-ironic, yet it is also confessional and ironic; 'It's true', he continues, 'that what is morbid is highly valued today, | and so you may think that I am only joking | or that I've devised just one more means | of praising Art with the help of irony.' This stanza seeks to exonerate itself from 'irony', but, self-incriminatingly, the poem knows that it has, in part, hit on 'just one more means | of praising Art'.

---

[46] Quoted from *The Iliad of Homer, Translated by Alexander Pope*, ed. Steven Shankman (Harmondsworth: Penguin, 1996), 46, 47.

Like all fine poems it recognizes the kinship between authentic utterance and respect for silence, concluding with the following stanzas:

And yet the world is different from what it seems to be
and we are other than how we see ourselves in our ravings.
People therefore preserve silent integrity
thus earning the respect of their relatives and neighbors.

The purpose of poetry is to remind us
how difficult it is to remain just one person,
for our house is open, there are no keys in the doors,
and invisible guests come in and out at will.

What I'm saying here is not, I agree, poetry,
as poems should be written rarely and reluctantly,
under unbearable duress and only with the hope
that good spirits, not evil ones, choose us for their instruments.[47]

The modest disclaimer should not fool us, even though it is Milosz's attempt to preserve the strangeness of the art which, in a sense, his poem has demystified: this *is* a poem, and it unfussily bears witness to the 'duress' involved in writing poetry. The poem insists on poetry's ethical obligations—poets 'must hope that good spirits, not evil ones, choose us for their instruments'—yet sees that poetry may lie beyond good and evil, a house open to invisible guests. '*Je* est un autre' becomes in Milosz an ashamed, even appalled admission.[48] But in his confrontation with the demands of poetry he suggests that, so far as poetry as literary criticism is concerned, much depends, in Pound's lines from the Pisan Cantos (LXXVI), on 'the quality | of the affection— | . . . that has carved the trace in the mind'. Given the terms of this essay's argument, it is appropriate that Pound's hard-won trust in 'the quality | of the affection' should spring from his poetic response to Guido Cavalcanti's poetry. Immediately following the lines just quoted from Canto LXXVI occurs the phrase 'dove sta memoria' from Cavalcanti's 'Canzone', translated by Pound in Canto XXXVI as 'Where memory liveth'. Thus, Pound not only recommends the critical (and experiential) virtue of 'affection'; he also

---

[47] Quoted from Czeslaw Milosz, *Bells in Winter*, trans. the author and Lillian Vallee (1980; Manchester: Carcanet, 1982).

[48] The words are Arthur Rimbaud's, in a letter to Georges Izambard of 13 May 1871, *Rimbaud: Complete Works, Selected Letters*, trans., introd., and notes Wallace Fowlie (Chicago: University of Chicago Press, 1966), 304.

shows the workings within his lines, through the quotation from Cavalcanti, of creative 'memory': an exemplary instance of a poem making a general critical recommendation and revealing 'affection' for a particular work.[49]

[49] Elsewhere, Pound translates the lines containing the phrase from Cavalcanti as follows: 'In memory's locus taketh he his state | Formed there in manner as a mist of light', *The Translations of Ezra Pound*, introd. Hugh Kenner (1953; London: Faber & Faber, 1970), 135.

7

Literary Criticism and Literary Creation

DAVID LODGE

The word 'criticism' covers a great many types of reflection on literature, from the most private and casual to the most public and systematic. It includes the activity of reading itself, inasmuch as reading a literary text is a process of continuous interpretation and evaluation. The mere decision to go on reading a novel or poem to its end is a kind of critical act, since you will suffer no material loss or practical inconvenience by abandoning it. In this large sense, criticism is, as T. S. Eliot observed, 'as inevitable as breathing'.[1] But for the most part I shall be concerned with criticism as the written articulation of the reading process in the form of reviews, essays, books, which may themselves take many different forms and have many different objectives: descriptive, prescriptive, polemical, theoretical, and so on. Criticism covers a huge variety of discourses, and when generalizations are made about the relation between it and creative writing, or between it and scientific discourse, it is usually a particular type of criticism that is being referred to, implicitly or explicitly.

There are, I suggest, four main ways in which the relationship between creative writing and criticism has been perceived:

1. criticism as *complementary* to creative writing;
2. criticism as *opposed* to creative writing;
3. criticism as a *kind* of creative writing;
4. criticism as a *part* of creative writing.

---

[1] T. S. Eliot, 'Tradition and the Individual Talent', in *Selected Essays* (1932; 3rd edn. London: Faber, 1951), 13.

The first of these perspectives—criticism as complementary to creative writing—is the classical, commonsense view of the matter. It may be expounded as follows. There are writers and there are critics. Each group has its task, its priorities, its privileges. Writers produce original works of imagination. Critics classify, evaluate, interpret, and analyse them. This model usually accords priority to literary creation. The conventional bibliographical distinction between primary and secondary sources implies that creative writers could do without critics—indeed, they seemed to manage very well without them until the Renaissance—but that critics are axiomatically dependent on creative writers for something to criticize. Subscribing to this hierarchical distinction does not however necessarily make critics humble.

The absence of anything much resembling literary criticism before the Renaissance, apart from a few treatises on rhetoric and general poetics, does not imply that the critical activity, 'something as inevitable as breathing', did not go on then. Of course it did. But when the production of manuscript books was slow, costly, and laborious, few people felt it was worth while recording their responses to literary texts in permanent form. The invention of printing, and its development into a very cost-effective industrial process, encouraged the publication and circulation of literary criticism on a vast scale. Much of it has been trivial and ephemeral. But the invention of printing also encouraged the production of much trivial and ephemeral creative writing. In this situation good criticism is seen to have a vital cultural function, namely, filtering out the good literature from the bad, defining and preserving the literary canon. This has been the traditional view of the function of criticism in the academy.

Matthew Arnold was perhaps the first English writer to formulate in an influential way the idea of criticism having this high cultural mission. But he was not just concerned with policing the canon. He stressed the value of criticism in creating a climate conducive to the production of good new writing. In his essay 'The Function of Criticism at the Present Time' he says: 'Life and the world being in modern times very complex things, the creation of a modern poet, to be worth much, implies a great critical effort behind it.'[2] And he goes so far as to say that in a period of creative sterility or mediocrity,

---

[2] Matthew Arnold, 'The Function of Criticism at the Present Time', in *Essays in Criticism: First Series* (1865; London: Macmillan, 1911), 6.

such as he perceived the second half of the nineteenth century to be in English literature, it might be more useful to be a critic than to be a creative writer. For Arnold criticism was more or less synonymous with the pursuit of humane knowledge. It was, he said 'a disinterested endeavour to learn and propagate the best that is known and thought in the world'.[3] T. S. Eliot, writing his own 'Function of Criticism' essay with Arnold's very much in mind, used criticism in a more restricted and more familiar sense, to mean 'the elucidation of works of art and the correction of taste'.[4] Speaking of his experience of teaching adult education classes he says, 'I have found only two ways of leading any pupils to like anything with the right liking: to present them with a selection of the simpler kind of facts about a work—its conditions, its setting, its genesis—or else to spring the work on them in such a way that they were not prepared to be prejudiced against it.'[5] Eliot thus gave his blessing to two very different schools of academic criticism which have often been at war with each other—on the one hand, traditional historical scholarship, and on the other hand, the close reading of unattributed poems pioneered by I. A. Richards at Cambridge under the name of Practical Criticism, from which evolved the so-called New Criticism in England and America. Both these schools claimed to be trying to make criticism more 'scientific': historical scholarship by focusing on hard empirical facts about the literary text, and the New Criticism by focusing on the verbal structure of the literary text itself. What Eliot most distrusted was what he called 'interpretation': 'for every success in this type of writing there are thousands of impostures. Instead of insight, you get a fiction.'[6] This is a slightly puzzling observation—what were his students supposed to do with the poems he sprang on them except interpret them? To read a poem is to interpret its meaning. By interpretation Eliot seems to mean something more personal and assertive: the effort to explain an author or a work in terms provided by the critic, criticism that offers itself as a kind of key that unlocks a mystery.

The theorists of the New Criticism were always struggling with the problem of how to define the limits of legitimate interpretation. Wimsatt and Beardsley's 1946 article 'The Intentional Fallacy' is a classic case in point.[7] They assert: 'Judging a poem is like judging a

---

[3] Ibid. 38.   [4] *Selected Essays*, 24.   [5] Ibid. 32.   [6] Ibid.
[7] W. K. Wimsatt, Jr., and Monroe C. Beardsley, 'The Intentional Fallacy', in W. K. Wimsatt, Jr., *The Verbal Icon: Studies in the Meaning of Poetry* (1954; London: Methuen, 1970), 3–20 (quotations from pp. 4 and 5).

pudding or a machine. One demands that it work.' One can see in this analogy the desire to put criticism on a quasi-scientific footing, to make its judgements objective by viewing the literary text in terms of functions. But clearly a poem is not like a pudding or a machine in many important respects. It is a verbal discourse not a material object, and discourses have complex and multiple meanings. The meaning of a pudding or a machine (a clock, say) is inseparable from its utilitarian function, but a poem does not have a utilitarian function. You could discover how a clock was made by taking it apart, and with this knowledge make yourself another clock which was just as useful; but if you take a poem apart, you may learn something about how it was made but you cannot infer a set of instructions for making a poem equally good—unless it is a replica of the poem you started with.

Wimsatt and Beardsley continue: 'It is only because an artifact works that we infer the intention of an artificer.' True enough. Literary texts are obviously intentional objects—they do not come into existence by accident. The critics then quote Archibald MacLeish's famous line, 'A poem should not mean but be,' and comment: 'A poem can *be* only through its *meaning*—since its medium is words—yet it *is*, simply *is*, in the sense that we have no excuse for inquiring what part is intended or meant. Poetry is a feat of style by which a complex of meaning is handled all at once.' Some lyric poems may give that illusion, but we know that they were produced in time, and we certainly experience a poem's meaning in time, not 'all at once'—and differently every time we reread it. This is even more obviously true of long, complex works like novels.

Wimsatt and Beardsley's article was a brave and salutary, if ultimately unconvincing, attempt to situate the literary text in some public space unconditioned either by its creative origins or by its individual readers:

The poem is not the critic's own and not the author's (it is detached from the author at birth and goes about the world beyond his power to intend about it or control it). The poem belongs to the public. It is embodied in language, the peculiar possession of the public, and it is about the human being, an object of public knowledge.

This is a more abstract formulation of the idea of the impersonality of artistic creation which Eliot expounded in his enormously influential 1919 essay 'Tradition and the Individual Talent', in which he said that 'the more perfect the artist, the more completely separate in him will be the man who suffers and the mind which creates,' and that 'honest criticism and sensitive appreciation is directed not upon the poet but upon the poetry'.[8] Eliot's cultivation of the idea of 'impersonality', however, like his attack on 'interpretation', was in part a manœuvre designed to conceal the very personal sources of his own poetry from inquisitive critics.

Here we begin to touch on the second view of the relation between creation and criticism: that they are not complementary but opposed, even antagonistic. As the case of Eliot reveals, it is quite possible for one writer to hold both views, according to what kind of criticism is in question; or to hold both at different times, with different hats on. I must admit to this inconsistency—one might almost call it schizophrenia—myself. For instance, I generally avoid reading criticism about my own work, especially academic criticism of the kind I used to write myself, and taught students to write, because I find it hinders rather than helps creation.

Academic criticism is the demonstration of a professional mastery. It cannot help trying to say the last word on its subject; it cannot help giving the impression that it operates on a higher plane of truth than the texts it discusses. The author of those texts therefore tends to feel reduced, diminished by such discourse, however well meant it is. In a way, the more approving such criticism is in its own terms, the more threatening and unsettling it can seem to the writer who is its object. As Graham Greene said, there comes a time when an established writer 'is more afraid to read his favourable critics than his unfavourable, for with terrible patience they unroll before his eyes the unchanging pattern of the carpet'.[9]

Academic criticism may pretend, may even deceive itself, that its relation to a creative work is purely complementary. But it also has its own hidden agenda: the demonstration of a professional skill, the refutation of competing peers, the claim to be making an addition to knowledge. The pursuit of these ends entails a degree of selection, manipulation, and re-presentation of the original text so drastic that its author will sometimes have difficulty in recognizing his creative work in the critical account of it. But it is not only in relation to

---

[8] *Selected Essays*, 18 and 17.
[9] Graham Greene, *Ways of Escape* (London: Bodley Head, 1980), 134. The allusion is to a short story by Henry James, *The Figure in the Carpet*.

criticism of their own work that creative writers often feel alienated by academic criticism. Inasmuch as it aspires to a scientific, or at least systematic, knowledge of its subject it can be seen as hostile to creativity itself. D. H. Lawrence took this view of the matter:

Criticism can never be a science: it is, in the first place, much too personal, and in the second, it is concerned with values which science ignores. The touchstone is emotion, not reason . . . All the critical twiddle-twaddle about style and form, all this pseudo-scientific classifying and analysing of books in imitation-botanical fashion, is mere impertinence and usually dull jargon.[10]

On such grounds it is sometimes argued that it is a bad idea for an aspirant writer to do a university degree in literary studies. I came across a remark to this effect recently in a newspaper interview with the Irish film-maker and novelist Neil Jordan (director of *Michael Collins*). Jordan went to University College Dublin because he wanted to write, the interviewer reported, but quotes Jordan as saying: 'I found the academic study of English very depressing, and strange that something so personal could be analysed so coherently.' It is interesting that whereas Lawrence was scornfully dismissive of the pretensions of academic criticism, it was the very *power* of the critical process, its analytical coherence, that Jordan found intimidating. He accordingly switched to medieval Irish history which he found more conducive to creativity, since almost nothing for certain is known about it. 'You're studying a society where history is invention, a kind of fiction really.'

This issue has been raised in a new form by the proliferation, first in America, and increasingly in Britain, of creative writing courses in universities, often pursued in tandem with courses in literary criticism. Is this healthy, is this wise, is it likely to nourish the production of quality writing? I can only say that it all depends what kind of writer you are or want to be. I have certainly never regretted reading English at university and making an academic career in that field. There were sometimes problems in reconciling the social roles or personae of professor and novelist, but I never found any intellectual or psychological incompatibility between the two activities. If I had done, I should have retired much sooner from academic life. Neil Jordan undoubtedly made the right decision for him. It would not be the right one for everybody.

[10] D. H. Lawrence, 'John Galsworthy', in *Selected Literary Criticism*, ed. Anthony Beale (London: Mercury Books, 1961), 118.

I have been talking so far about academic criticism, but tension is just as likely, perhaps more likely, to occur between the creative writer and his *journalistic* critics, since they have a more direct impact on the writer's career—his status, his financial prospects, and his self-esteem. Reviews are the first independent feedback the writer gets to his work, as distinct from the reactions of friends, family, agent, and publisher. But of course they are not totally objective, totally disinterested. Reviewers, like scholars, have their own hidden agenda, which explains why their judgements are often so extreme. Extravagant praise, especially of some obscure or exotic work, is often a means by which the literary journalist asserts his professional mastery, attempts to steal a march on his peers, and draws attention to his own eloquence. Extravagant dispraise can have the same effect when directed at a well-established reputation. When the reviewer himself is a practising or aspiring writer there may be a political motive—political in the literary sense—one generation of writers seeking to oust its seniors, as in the speculative anthropology of Freud. The reviewing by the Angry Young Men writers of the 1950s, for instance—Kingsley Amis, John Wain, and others—had behind it a determined effort to displace the existing literary establishment, the faded remnants of pre-war Bloomsbury and cosmopolitan modernism.

There has always been this Oedipal drama played out on the review pages of newspapers and magazines; but today—at least in Britain—its tone seems particularly spiteful. Salman Rushdie—who has, of course, been subjected to a much more lethal form of criticism—has described the public discussion of contemporary literature in Britain as 'the culture of denigration'. I think this has something to do with the extent to which the literary novel has recently become big business and the object of intense interest to the mass media. This did not seem to be the case earlier in the century. It is clear from Virginia Woolf's wonderful diaries, for instance, that she never expected to make much money out of her novels, and that she cared more about her standing among her peer group than about her success or failure with the reading public. 'I have made up my mind that I am not going to be popular,'[11] she says at one point. But she is plunged into deep depression and loses faith in her novel in progress because at a party

[11] Virginia Woolf, *A Writer's Diary*, ed. Leonard Woolf (London: Hogarth Press, 1953), 51.

T. S. Eliot seemed to neglect her claims as a writer and raved all the evening about James Joyce. In those days literary reputations were made first among a small élite, and through the medium of small-circulation literary magazines. Structural changes in the economics of publishing and the insatiable appetite of the mass media for information have made it possible in our own day for a gifted literary writer to become rich and famous quite quickly. This then provokes a backlash of envy and spite in the media against the very figure they created, which can be an uncomfortable experience for the subject. While post-structuralism has asserted the impersonality of creative writing in the most extreme theoretical terms—the so-called 'death of the author'—literary journalism has never been so obsessed with the personality and private life of the author.

'The worst of writing', Virginia Woolf observed in her diary, quoting a friend, 'is that one depends so much upon praise.'[12] Which is to say that a writer, like any other artist, is continually offering his or her work for public assessment, and it is only human to want to be praised for one's efforts rather than blamed. Virginia Woolf's diaries give a wonderfully vivid account of this side of a writer's life, the way her spirits go up and down, in spite of her efforts to remain detached, as favourable and unfavourable verdicts on a new book are received from friends, colleagues, and reviewers. She notes that George Eliot 'would not read reviews, since talk of her books hampered her writing', and Woolf sounds envious of such self-control. But one cannot help wondering whether George Eliot's partner George Henry Lewes did not make sure she saw or knew about the favourable reviews.

My own ideal review was exemplified when a former publicity director of my publishers reviewed one of my books under the simple headline 'Literary Genius Writes Masterpiece'. Unfortunately it was published in an English-language Hong Kong newspaper of very small circulation.

I turn now to the third of my perspectives on the relation between creation and criticism: that criticism is itself creative, or that there is essentially no difference between the two activities. T. S. Eliot considers this idea only to dismiss it. 'No exponent of criticism . . . has I presume ever made the preposterous assumption that criticism is an autotelic activity,' he wrote in 'The Function of Criticism'.[13] But of course the preposterous assumption has often been made—by, for

[12] Virginia Woolf, *A Writer's Diary*, 24.   [13] *Selected Essays*, 24.

instance, Gilbert, the speaker in Oscar Wilde's dialogue 'The Critic as Artist', who seems to be a mouthpiece for Wilde himself: 'Criticism is in fact both creative and independent. . . . The critic occupies the same relation to the work of art that he criticizes as the artist does to the visible world of form and colour, or the unseen world of passion and of thought.'[14] This view is antithetical to the view of criticism as complementary to creative writing, aiming at objectivity, striving 'to see the object as it really is', as Matthew Arnold urged, or discovering its hidden meaning by what Eliot disapprovingly called 'interpretation'. Criticism, Wilde's Gilbert says, is 'in its essence purely subjective, and seeks to reveal its own secret and not the secret of another'.[15]

Criticism as the expression of subjective response is of course an essentially romantic idea and implies a romantic theory of literary creation as self-expression. It is often associated with the lyrical and impressionistic, musing-in-the-library style of critical discourse which I. A. Richards and F. R. Leavis, and the American New Critics, sought to discredit and expunge from academic criticism from the 1920s to the 1950s. But more recently the idea that there is no essential difference between creation and criticism has been given a new academic respectability, and a new sophistication, under the aegis of post-structuralism, and especially the theory of deconstruction, which questions the very distinction between subjective and objective.

A fundamental tenet of deconstruction is that the nature of language is such that any discourse, including a literary text, can be shown under analysis to be full of gaps and contradictions which undermine its claim to have a determinate meaning. If poems and novels have no fixed, stable, recuperable meaning, then clearly criticism cannot pretend to have a duty or responsibility of truth-telling towards them, but is inevitably involved in *producing* their meaning by a process to which Jacques Derrida gives the name 'play'.[16] In this perspective, criticism is not complementary to creative writing, but supplementary to it, using supplement in a double sense to denote

---

[14] *The Works of Oscar Wilde*, ed. G. F. Maine (London: Collins, 1948), 966.
[15] Ibid. 967.
[16] See Jacques Derrida, 'Structure, Sign and Play in the Discourse of the Human Sciences', in Richard Macksey and Eugenio Donato (eds.), *The Languages of Criticism and the Sciences of Man: The Structuralist Controversy* (Baltimore: Johns Hopkins UP, 1970).

that which replaces what is missing, and that which adds something to what is already there. The absence criticism fills up is precisely the illusory fixed stable meaning of traditional criticism, and what it adds is the product of the critic's own ingenuity, wit, and resourcefulness in the exercise of semantic freeplay. It is not surprising that Derrida has admitted to being a creative writer *manqué*. His work is a kind of avant-garde literary discourse—punning, allusive, exhibitionistic, and teasingly provocative to those who are not simply baffled and bored by it. Professor Harold Bloom has developed his own idiosyncratic version of creative criticism based on the idea that the apparent misreading of texts by 'strong' critics (like himself) replicates the process by which strong poets struggle with the intimidating example of their precursors and liberate themselves from the anxiety of influence. No wonder that in reading Bloom we are so often reminded of Wilde, to whom he refers in *The Western Canon* as 'the sublime Oscar Wilde, who was right about everything'.[17]

It is, I think, possible to concede that there is a creative element in criticism without collapsing the distinction between creative and critical writing entirely. A good critical essay should have a kind of plot. Some of T. S. Eliot's most celebrated essays were critical who-dunnits which investigated such mysteries as 'Who murdered English poetic diction?' (The culprit turned out to be Milton.[18]) Modern critics of the anti-foundationalist school, like Paul de Man or Stanley Fish, are masters of the critical peripeteia, by which the conclusion of the essay turns upon and undermines its own arguments. And there is no reason why criticism should not be written with elegance and eloquence. I try to do so myself. But when I write criticism I feel that I am involved in a different kind of activity from when I write fiction, and part of that difference is that everything in writing a novel has to be decided, nothing is given, whereas in the case of criticism the prior existence of the work or works to be criticized, and the prior existence of other critical opinion about them, places limits on the development of the critical discourse, and makes it on the whole an easier and less anxiety-making process.

Roland Barthes suggested in a pregnant little essay called 'Criticism as Language', published in 1963, that:

---

[17] Harold Bloom, *The Western Canon: The Books and School of the Ages* (New York: Harcourt Brace, 1994), 16.
[18] See 'Milton' in T. S. Eliot, *On Poetry and Poets* (London: Faber, 1957), 138–45. Originally published as 'A Note on the Verse of John Milton' in 1936.

the task of criticism . . . does not consist in 'discovering' in the work of the author under consideration something 'hidden' or 'profound' or 'secret' which has so far escaped notice . . . but only in *fitting together* . . . the language of the day (Existentialism, Marxism or psychoanalysis) and the language of the author . . . If there is such a thing as critical proof it lies not in the ability to *discover* the work under consideration, but on the contrary, to *cover* it as completely as possible with one's own language.[19]

Criticism must face the fact that it can only be 'true' by being tautological—that is, by repeating what the text says in the text's own words; and it can only escape from tautology by representing the text in other words, and therefore *mis*representing it. As Professor Morris Zapp says, in my novel *Small World*, 'every decoding is another encoding'. But this need not entail surrendering all responsibility to the original text. Criticism can be a useful, as well as a merely playful activity. For reasons I have already suggested, creative writers are apt to find the experience of having their language covered by somebody else's language rather unsettling, and would prefer not to know about it; but for readers, especially of classic texts, it can do for literature what literature does for the world—defamiliarizing it, enabling us to see its beauty and value afresh.

Finally I come to criticism as a part of creation. This is something well known to creative writers who are also critics. Wilde's Gilbert, for instance, says: 'Without the critical faculty, there is no artistic creation at all worthy of the name.'[20] Graham Greene said, 'An author of talent is his own best critic—an ability to criticise his own work is inseparably bound up with his talent: it *is* his talent.'[21] T. S. Eliot said:

Probably. . . the larger part of the labour of an author in composing his work is critical labour; the labour of sifting, combining, constructing, expunging, correcting, testing: this frightful toil is as much critical as creative. I maintain even that the criticism employed by a trained and skilled writer on his own work is the most vital, the highest kind of criticism; and . . . that some creative writers are superior to others solely because their critical faculty is superior.[22]

Like so many of Eliot's critical pronouncements, this one puzzles as well as illuminates. Did he mean by 'the criticism employed by a

[19] *The Critical Moment: Essays on the Nature of Literature* (London: Faber, 1964), 123–9 (quotation from pp. 127–8). [20] *The Works of Oscar Wilde*, 959.
[21] Graham Greene, *Reflections: 1923–88*, ed. Judith Adamson (London: Reinhardt, 1990), p. xii. [22] 'The Function of Criticism', 30.

trained and skilled writer on his own work' *published* criticism of this kind, such as Henry James's prefaces to his collected novels? If so, Eliot gave us remarkably little of such criticism himself. If he meant the 'critical labour' involved in creation then it would seem that the 'most vital, the highest kind of criticism' is for the most part only experienced by writers themselves. Perhaps that is why, as readers, as critics, we are so interested in the genesis of works of literature, in authors' notebooks and draft manuscripts, and in their comments on their own work—it is a way of reconstructing and sharing the 'critical labour' that is part of creation.

But Eliot's main point seems to me entirely right. Most of the time spent nominally writing a creative work is actually spent reading it— reading and rereading the words one has already written, trying to improve on them or using them as a kind of springboard from which to propel oneself into the as yet unwritten part of one's text. There are exceptional writers who seem able to produce quality work very quickly, with hardly any hesitations or revisions, but for most of us writing is an absurdly labour-intensive activity. Few modern novels, for example, take more than ten hours to read, but the novelist will work for hundreds, perhaps thousands of hours to make that experience enjoyable and profitable, and most of those hundreds or thousands of hours will be taken up with work that is essentially critical, as Eliot describes it. It is not work that necessarily goes on at the writer's desk, but at all times and places: in bed, at table, while shaving or ironing, or walking the dog.

Does this mean that writers are always the best critics of their own work in a public sense? No, of course it does not. They are far too involved to assess the value of their work, or to generalize about its meaning and significance. Where the writer has an advantage over his critics is in explaining how a book came to be written, what its sources were, and why it took the form that it did. But few writers are eager to use this privilege. Even Henry James, in his famous prefaces, conceals much more than he reveals, as does Graham Greene in the introductions to his books gathered together in *Ways of Escape*. Eliot always politely declined to reveal the sources and describe the genesis of his notoriously obscure poems. Personally, I rather enjoy explaining how I write my novels, and have published a number of essays describing the problems, choices, revisions, and discoveries involved. But I would not claim that this is the most vital, the highest kind of criticism I or anyone else could write, nor would I claim that the picture of composition it gives bears more than a highly selective and artificially tidy resemblance to the actual process. There are many facts about the composition of my work that I could never recover and many that I would never divulge.

There are several reasons why writers are generally reluctant to engage publicly in analytical criticism of their own work. They may fear they will lose their gift if they analyse it too closely. They may be reluctant to restrict the reader's response by imposing an 'authorized' interpretation on the text, knowing that sometimes works of literature mean more than their authors were conscious of. Very often, I believe, the motive for silence is that the writer has tried to give his work the effect of an effortless inevitability, and is understandably reluctant to destroy that illusion by revealing too much about the choices, hesitations and second thoughts involved in composition. As W. B. Yeats put it:

> A line will take us hours maybe
> Yet if it does not seem a moment's thought
> Our stitching and unstitching has been naught.[23]

The paradox is not confined to poetry. The American short story-writer Patricia Hampl has written: 'Every story has a story. This secret story, which has little chance of getting told, is the history of its creation. Maybe the "story of the story" *can* never be told, for a finished work consumes its own history, renders it obsolete, a husk.'[24]

One reason why literary creation continues to fascinate us and elude our attempts to explain it is that it is impossible to, as it were, catch oneself in the act of creation. It is not as if one has an idea for a poem, say, and then puts it into words. The idea, however vague and provisional, is already a verbal concept, and expressing it in more precise, specific words makes it different from what it was. Every revision is not a reformulation of the same meaning but a slightly (or very) different meaning. This was one reason why Wimsatt and Beardsley questioned the idea that a work of literature is the realization of an intention that exists prior to it.

There is a sense in which an author, by revision, may better achieve his original intention. But it is a very abstract sense. He intended to write a

---

[23] 'Adam's Curse', in *Collected Poems* (2nd edn. London: Macmillan, 1950), 88.
[24] Quoted in Daniel C. Dennett, *Consciousness Explained* (London: Allen Lane, 1991), 245.

better work, or a better work of a certain kind, and now has done it. But it follows that his former concrete intention was not his intention. 'He's the man we were in search of, that's true' says Hardy's rustic constable, 'and yet he's not the man we were in search of. For the man we were in search of was not the man we wanted.'[25]

Writers discover what it is they want to say in the process of saying it, and their explanations of why they wrote something in a particular way are therefore always retrospective extrapolations, working back from effect to cause, wisdom after the event. It is this inevitable deferral of meaning in discourse that the deconstructionists seized on to destabilize the whole concept of meaning.

The difficulty of understanding the nature of literary creation is part of the larger problem of understanding the nature of consciousness, which is currently preoccupying specialists in a wide range of disciplines—philosophers, linguisticians, cognitive scientists, sociobiologists, neurologists, zoologists, and many others. It is said that consciousness is the last great challenge to scientific enquiry. If you browse through the more accessible literature in this field it is interesting to note how often it touches on questions and phenomena that concern literary critics and literary theorists. For example, I came across that suggestive quotation from Patricia Hampl in a book by the philosopher and cognitive scientist Daniel C. Dennett, *Consciousness Explained*. Dennett relies heavily on the analogy of literary creation for his model of consciousness. He used to believe, he tells us, that there had to be 'an awareness line separating the preconscious fixation of communicative intentions from their subsequent execution',[26] but he came to reject this idea on grounds similar to those on which Wimsatt and Beardsley rejected the intentional fallacy. In its place he formulated the 'multiple draft' model of consciousness, which proposes that all thought is produced through a process of expansion, editing, and revision, like a literary text, though unlike literary creation it is so fast that it seems experientially to be instantaneous. To Dennett the mind is like a hugely powerful parallel-processing computer that operates itself, and this is his description of how a particular thought or utterance is produced:

Instead of a determinate content in a particular functional place [in the brain], waiting to be Englished by subroutines, there is a still-incompletely-determined mind-set distributed around in the brain and constraining a

[25] 'The Intentional Fallacy', 5.   [26] *Consciousness Explained*, 236.

composition process which in the course of time can actually feed back to make adjustments or revisions, further determining the expressive task that sets the composition process in motion in the first place . . . It is just as possible for the content-to-be-expressed to be adjusted in the direction of some candidate expression, as for the candidate expression to be replaced or edited so as better to accommodate the content-to-be-expressed.[27]

This is a phenomenon familiar to anyone who has tried to write regular verse: the search for a rhyming word, or a phrase with the required metrical structure (the 'candidate expression'), will condition the semantic content of a poem, and since this happens many times the final draft of a poem may as a result be almost unrecognizable from the first draft. It is rather unsettling to imagine that this may be equally true of every utterance we make, and yet the more you think about it the more intuitively plausible it seems.

Dennett pursues the analogy between consciousness and literary creation even further. The very idea of the individual self, he argues, is constructed, like a novel. Unlike other animals we are almost continually engaged in presenting ourselves to others, and to ourselves, in language and gesture, external and internal. 'Our fundamental tactic of self-protection, self-control and self-definition is not spinning webs [like a spider] or building dams [like a beaver] but telling stories—especially the story of who we are.'[28]

There are many different competing theories of consciousness, and Dennett's is only one of them. He is a Darwinian materialist, albeit a remarkably subtle, intelligent, and cultured one. Basically, if I understand him correctly, he thinks that consciousness is the accidental consequence of *Homo sapiens* developing through natural selection a huge brain and vocal organs which allowed the species to acquire language, and making selves is what we do with this equipment, which is surplus to the needs of mere survival. At the opposite pole we find religious theories of consciousness which identify the self with the individual immortal soul which derives from God. Philosophically this is regarded as dualism, the fallacy of the Ghost in the Machine, though the idea of an immaterial self is so deeply engrained in our language and our habits of thought, whether we are religious believers or not, that it is doubtful whether it will ever be completely expunged. Somewhere between the two poles are those thinkers who reject the Ghost in the Machine but deny that the concept of mind

[27] Ibid. 241, 247.   [28] Ibid. 416–17.

can be equated with neurological brain activity, and suggest that consciousness will always be ultimately a mystery, or at least not explainable or reducible to scientific laws. The distinguished neuro-biologist Gerald Edelman, in his book *Bright Air, Brilliant Fire*, says : 'We cannot construct a phenomenal psychology that can be shared in the same way that physics can be shared'—because 'consciousness is a first person matter',[29] because it exists in and is conditioned by history and therefore every individual's consciousness is unique, because linguistically based consciousness is 'never self-sufficient, it is always in dialogue with some other, even if that interlocutor is not present'. These observations will ring all kinds of bells with anyone who is familiar with modern literary criticism, notably the work of Mikhail Bakhtin. It is not surprising to find Edelman saying, towards the end of his book: 'what is perhaps most extraordinary about conscious human beings is their art.' Humanists have always main-tained that literature contains real knowledge about man, even if it is not empirically testable and falsifiable. Now it seems we need no longer feel defensive in the face of science. The contemporary debate about consciousness offers a real prospect of convergence and colla-boration between the two cultures.

[29] Gerald M. Edelman, *Bright Air, Brilliant Fire: On the Matter of the Mind* (London: Allen Lane, 1992), 114.

8

Writing Autobiography

At the very end of his life Goethe said that he had only just learned how to read. He was the most distinguished man of letters in Europe, one of a galaxy of literary eminences, so he wasn't talking about his ABC. So what was this very old man talking about, when he said he had only just learned how to read?

I have put this at the beginning of my essay because it illustrates what a long time it sometimes takes to learn things. Writing volume I of my autobiography I learned a good deal I didn't expect, and I was amazed at myself because it had taken so long. You always learn when writing a book. It is a fact as yet unknown to science that when you tackle a new subject then suddenly it is everywhere, on the television, in the newspapers, on the radio, people start talking about it, an overheard conversation on a bus—there it is again, and a book falls open at just that relevant place. This is a quite astonishing phenomenon, but, like many others, we take it for granted. I am not however talking about that kind of learning, but what happens when you say, 'Good God, how was it I didn't see that before! It's perfectly obvious!' I have been reading biographies and autobiographies all my life, yet I have never actually sat down to think about the differences between them, nor the differences between them and novels. Yet the very moment I began to think seriously, the problem began to bristle with difficulties.

One reason I didn't expect anything different *in kind* was that I had written autobiographical pieces before, for instance, *In Pursuit of the English*. That little book has a good deal in common with a novel. Not that it isn't true—it is true enough except for some things changed for libel purposes. It is more a question of a tone, a pace. It has the feel of a novel. And this raises such questions that I shall have to leave it right there. The tone, or 'voice' of a novel—what it is, why it is—is probably the most important thing you can say about it. Certainly the book has a shape like a novel. I'll come back to shape.

The fact is, novels, autobiographies, and biographies have a lot in common. One thing is something we take for granted: they are all written down. What we take for granted is often the most important thing and we don't examine it. We take for granted that novels, autobiographies, and biographies are sitting up there on a shelf, tidy, self-contained books, complete—*written down*. The truth.

For many thousands of years we—the human race—told stories to one another: tales told, or sung. Not written down. Fluid. Biography of our kind is quite new; I suppose Boswell's *Life of Johnson* is the first. Autobiography of our kind? Cellini, Casanova were the first, I think: fixed and permanent records, something you can lift from a shelf, and quote from. Extracts that appear in think-pieces and theses, and then travel to other theses and books: immutable—the Truth.

The reason why people feel uneasy and disturbed when their lives are put into biographies is precisely because something that is experienced as fluid, fleeting, evanescent, has become fixed, and therefore lifeless, without movement. You can't appeal against the written word, except by more written words, and then you are committed to polemic. Memory isn't fixed: it slips and slides about. It is hard to match one's memories of one's life with the solid fixed account of it that is written down. Virginia Woolf said that living was like being inside a kind of luminous envelope. I would add to that 'inside a moving, flickering luminous envelope, like a candle flame in a draught'.

Our own views of our lives change all the time, different at different ages. If I had written an account of myself aged 20 it would have been a belligerent and combative document. At 30—confident and optimistic. At 40—full of guilt and self-justification. At 50—confused, self-doubting. But at 60 and after something else has appeared: you begin to see your early self from a great distance. While you can put yourself back inside the 10-year-old, the 20-year-old, any time you want, you are seeing that child, that young woman, as—almost—someone else. You float away from the personal. You have received that great gift of getting older—detachment, impersonality.

Once I read autobiography as what the writer thought about her or his life. Now I think, 'That is what they thought *at that time*.' An interim report—that is what an autobiography is. Would Cellini, would Casanova, would even Rousseau, later have agreed with what they said about themselves in those books that we assume is the fixed truth about what they thought?

It was much easier when the talk about each other or about ourselves was oral. For thousands of years, when story-telling was oral, there was autobiography, but very different from ours, just as biography was different. Here is a fragment of autobiography from just over a thousand years ago.

Egil Skalla Grimsson wrote the poem which will be found in his saga, an old man, lonely, despondent, after all the activity of his life. His sons were dead, his god had betrayed him. Poetry, he said, wasn't easily drawn any more 'from the hiding-place of thought' but he composes, he mourns, and can say for himself, and for others, in conclusion:

> It is bad with me
> now, the Wolf, Death's
> sister, stands on the headland,
> but gladly, without fear
> and steadfast shall
> I wait for Hel,
> goddess of death.[1]

This little verse, part of a long saga, must have been told or sung by dozens of story-tellers or singers, in the halls of queens, kings, chieftains, or in gatherings of robbers in the forests. They felt no need to stick to an exact pattern of words. Between those story-tellers and us is a great gulf, and that *is* the gulf. Many different kinds of men and women were described by that verse. The man whose words I read is strongly characterized. He is stoic, brave, full of self-respect. Now let us imagine a different kind of man—nervous, fearful. The people listening will have known the saga by heart, and while they listen their brains are doing two different things, checking for the familiar, but delightedly anticipating the new—what this teller will do with the old words, on this occasion.

> Oh dear, I don't feel well,
> I saw the wolf today,
> We all know what that means,
> I have bad dreams.
> I am afraid of the goddess of death.

[1] Quoted from Geoffrey Grigson, *A Private Art: A Poetry Notebook* (London: Allison & Busby, 1982), 82.

I am a child of our culture, which has depended for some hundreds of years on print, and so I feel guilty when I change sacred print. I have to set aside guilt to do what story-tellers and singers did as a matter of course. Let us try another kind of person.

> Guess what!
> I saw the wolf today.
> You don't have to tell me what *that* means.
> So what! I'm not scared of that old bag
> the goddess of death.

These old people depicted themselves in broad bold strokes. They didn't go in for our kind of psychologizing—no subtlety, no complexity. That would not have suited the sweep of the saga, the epic, the kind of story that had to hold the attention of listening serfs and soldiers and servants as well as the lords and ladies who were more educated, though probably not much more.

Psychology came in with print, with the explosion of the written word: Proust, Mann, Woolf, Joyce were the products of the print revolution.

There must have been a great change in the structure—the physical structure—of our brains when print was invented. Suddenly books were being printed by the thousand all over Europe by printing presses we now think of as primitive, yet they made some of the most beautiful books ever created. We haven't yet come to terms, I think, with that revolution. Have we ever asked *what* changes took place in our brains then, when people began to read instead of to listen? It was a process that went on in stages. People did not just pick up a book and begin reading in the way we do. St Augustine describes how he was reading, and suddenly thought, 'but I don't have to mouth the words as I read, I can read silently'. Monks read aloud, as did anyone who actually owned books. Then they read silently but mouthed the words. Then they realized they did not have to shape the words with their lips. The process was complete.

We are on the verge of another revolution as powerful—we are living through it in fact—the electronic revolution. This is evidently affecting our brains. I can observe the process in myself: my attention span is shortening. Probably it is because of television, the way we constantly switch attention from one channel to another, but we don't really know the reason. We have no idea what the end of it all will be, any more than the people knew who lived through the print revolution. We can say either that we are a very careless species, recklessly undertaking great changes without asking what the result will be, or that we are helpless in the face of our own inventions. To return to the immediate problems of novels, autobiographies, biographies. There is one way autobiographies have to differ from novels. Novels don't have to be the truth. Autobiographies do have to be. At least the attempt must be made. And this brings us to Memory. What memories can we trust? Only the slightest of thoughts on the subject show that memories are about as dependable as soap bubbles. I think there are two kinds of memory that we can rely on.

One. You are very small. You are looking up at enormously tall people. The doorhandle is out of reach. Chairs and sofas are great cumbersome obstacles. A cat is almost as big as you are. The dog is much bigger. The ceiling is almost out of sight. Everything is an assault on your senses. Smells are very strong. Every surface has a different texture, a different world. Sounds are so various you spend a lot of your time trying to understand them. You are so various you spend a lot of your time trying to understand them. You are inside a whirlpool of sense impressions, an assault. This is the world of a small child. No adult lives in that world. We have blocked most of it out long ago. No adult could live in that world: they wouldn't be able to do anything else but try to remain steady while sounds, scents, sights, insist on being understood. These are reliable memories: the hot slippery surface of a horse's neck, the strong smell of the horse. The sharp cutting edges of stone steps, where you descend, as if going down a mountain side.

Two. The other class of memory I think you can rely on is events that have happened repeatedly, day after day.

The memories that are not reliable are probably most of those about our older childish selves. Parents create memories for their children. 'See this photo? That's you, there. Do you remember, we went down every weekend to the park, and you fed the ducks, and then we had a picnic under the trees. Do you remember?' And the child remembers, the memory has been made for him or her.

The moment I was suddenly informed how utterly unreliable memories can be was when I met, after years, someone with whom I had been on a trip to Russia, early in the 1950s. This was two weeks of intense experience, and I have strong memories of it. But when I said to this woman, 'Do you remember—this or that', she didn't. She remembered quite different things. We might have been on two quite different trips. Or when I met my brother after many years, and he did not remember things we did together that are among the most powerful memories I have.

Now, in a novel, it doesn't matter: memories true and false become part of the fabric of the story and for a while you become one with the psychotherapists and psychiatrists who say that it doesn't matter if your fantasies are not true: they are diagnostic of your condition. They are the product of your psyche. They are valid. If you are writing autobiography that won't do at all. So you sit there for hours, wondering. Is that true, Did I make it up? What is the truth? Immediately other questions come up and you have to deal with them before getting on with your task, which is writing your autobiography. And not sitting brooding about all these ideas, for it is not getting the work done.

Why do you remember this and not that? You might remember a weekend, or an hour, or a month in the greatest possible detail, and then there are weeks or months of blank. What you remember so clearly might easily be unimportant. The experts say you remember a certain event or time because something very important was going on. They also say the opposite, that if you forget something—a person or event—it is because it was all very important, but stressful: it is repressed. I think that what makes you remember something, important or unimportant, is that you were particularly awake at the time, paying attention. Most of the time we are in a sort of trance, not noticing much. We are probably thinking about what we will have for our supper or that we must buy medicine for the cat.

If memory is identity then we are indeed in a bad way. Can you remember what you did yesterday? perhaps yesterday, yes. Three days ago? This time last week? This time last month? Very hard to remember: most of it has gone.

This business of identity I wrote about in my book *Briefing for a Descent into Hell*. A young woman, a friend of mind, was in the psychiatric ward of the local hospital where I was visiting her. Very late one night, she told me, a man was brought in who had been found wandering on the embankment. He had lost his memory. But so much 'together' was he that the doctors at first thought he was putting on an act, was pretending. He was well dressed and clean. He was obviously educated. He engaged in long conversations about literature and art. If you hadn't been told, you would never have known he had lost his memory. Yet he had. He had no idea who he was, and it took something like six weeks before he remembered. During those six weeks he was all there, a strong, intact presence. Yet he had no memory.

In any case it is such a flickering, fleeting record. Sometimes I feel I could wipe it all away with one sweep of my hand, like brushing away a kind of highly coloured veil or thin rainbow . . . and there still sits the autobiographer, uneasy about her memories, about the truth, and the book is not being written.

Why a book at all? Why do we have this need to bear witness? We could dance our stories, couldn't we?

In Binga on the shores of Lake Kariba is a shop where you can buy highly carved sticks on which are carved the histories of the local tribe. There have been cultures that wove stories and histories and information into carpets.

But we tell stories, we have to.

Why? why a story? We must have a pattern in our minds, and we tell stories because we have to conform to that pattern. We need a shape for the tale. A beginning, a middle, and an end. What is the template for that pattern? Only one that we can immediately see: we are born, we grow older, and then we die. Perhaps that is the template. Perhaps that is why we need to know what will happen next when we read or hear a story. This is so strong that even if you are in, let's say, a dentist's waiting room, and you are reading some truly rubbishy tale, you still need to know the end and hope it will not be time to be called in to the dentist until you have finished it. Yet you don't care at all for the actual tale: you have to know what is going to happen next.

So, when you are shaping an autobiography, just as when you shape a novel, you have to decide what to leave out. Novels are given shape by leaving out. Autobiographies have to have a shape, and they can't be too long. Just as with a novel, you have choice: you have to choose. Things have to be left out. I had far too much material for the autobiography. Yet it should be like life, sprawling, big, baggy, full of false starts, loose ends, people you meet once and never think of again, groups of people you meet for an evening or a week and never see again. And so as you write your autobiography it has to have a good deal in common with a novel. It has a shape: the need to make choices dictates that. In short, we have a story. What doesn't fit in to the story, the theme, gets cut out.

I wrote a novel once called *The Marriages between Zones Three, Four and Five*. I had the material for that novel for years, but could not find the way to do it. Suddenly I found it. The solution was simple, as solutions usually are. I decided I had to use the story-teller's voice. The story-teller is in everyone and we tell stories all the time. When we come back from the supermarket and say to whoever is here, 'You'll never guess what I saw. Bridget was in the supermarket, and she wasn't with her husband, she was with that young fellow from the hotel . . .', and you're off, and your listener wants to know what happens next, even if she or he cares nothing about Bridget, nor about the young fellow from the hotel. The story-teller is sexless, ageless, timeless, is thousands of years old, and not culture-bound. Folk tales and jokes travel across frontiers, always have, always will.

There is another interesting little paradox when you think about novels and autobiographies. We are now familiar with the idea that in each one of us live several personalities. This is easier to see in other people than in ourselves. The extreme case was Sybil, about whom there was written a book, and there was a film and television. She had, it seems, up to thirty-odd separate personalities. I am not talking about roles. A man is a brother, husband, son, father, etc. A woman is a sister, wife, daughter, mother, and so on. Roles are not personalities.

One of the ways one can use novels is to see the different personalities in novelists. Dickens is very useful for this. You can see the same personalities appearing in novel after novel, perhaps different sexes, different ages, but obviously the same. These are the personalities that make up Dickens. You are looking at a map of Dickens— what he is. And the same with other novelists. Now here is the paradox. It is easier to see this map of a person in their novels than in the autobiography. That is because an autobiography is written in one voice, by one person, and this person smoothes out the roughness of the different personalities. This is an elderly, judicious, calm person, and this calmness of judgement imposes a unity. The novelist doesn't necessarily know about her own personalities. But when the same character keeps popping up in novel after novel, then you have to think. In me somewhere is a delinquent girl or boy, or at least defective in some way, if not young, a non-coper, and clearly this creature is lurking or latent. 'Oh there you are again', I say, as there is yet another appearance, and you have to be somewhat fearful: under what circumstances would this inadequate person appear in life, come off the page into reality? And you think, 'well, I wouldn't like *you* very much, if I met you'.

An autobiography—or for that matter a biography—uses a lot of novelist's tricks. These are not necessarily used consciously—if you have been at it for decades, you have learned the tricks so thoroughly the material demands them and you use them, and only afterwards, reading what you've written, think: 'Oh, that was what I was doing, was I!'

For instance, in *Under my Skin* I have a piece about a small girl—me—lying down in the afternoon, and her mother—my mother. It is about time, the different ways children, young people, middle-aged people, old people, experience time. I sometimes say 'I, me', and sometimes say, 'the child'. I say 'my mother', but sometimes 'she'. And there is a point where I suddenly change tone, and say 'the woman'. My mother is writing a letter home to England, as, at that time, the wives of farmers did: when they wrote letters to England they were writing *home*. And I say, 'the woman who'—and when I did that I made it general: she becomes all the farmers' wives writing letters home. This whole section could be a novel, one of the big loose novels, like Dreiser's or Thomas Woolfe's (the old one, not the journalist), some of Christina Stead's, Faulkner's.

There is another problem, a major one. It is a question of the first person, and the third person—when to use what. The first person, autobiography, the 'I', in fact holds the reader at a distance, and this is strange, since on the face of it 'I' should be—surely—an invitation to the reader: 'Come on, nothing is being held back, here I am, no disguises.' But really it is much harder to identify with an 'I' than with 'he', or 'she'.

Let us go back to that little verse.

> Things don't go well with me now.
> The wolf, death's sister,
> stands on the headland,
> But bravely and with a stout heart
> I am waiting for the goddess of death.

I wouldn't find it all that easy to be familiar with that 'I': a self-contained and dignified man. But let us make it 'he'.

> Things aren't too good for him now.
> The wolf, death's sister,
> stands on the headland,
> but bravely and with a stout heart
> he waits for the goddess of death.

This man is much easier to approach. The 'I' distances you, insists on a sort of privacy. 'He' could be you.

And when you change it to 'she', then suddenly you are in a most contended-for area.

> It's not too good for her now . . .
> bravely and with a stout heart
> she waits for the goddess of death.

At once we are in a quite different kind of story. As soon as you use the word 'she' the associations crowd in, in this case, probably a wise woman with her herbs and friendly attendant crow, or a woman warrior, or some beautiful but ageing queen. And from each of these spring all kinds of ideas that have nothing to do with the situation of an old person waiting for death.

Suppose it went:

> I, an old woman, find life hard,
> The wolf—

That 'I' defines, excludes, makes exact.

A quotation from Goethe—Goethe again—seems to me to go to the heart of the problem, of how we judge, how we read. It is from his autobiography.

Hence it is everybody's duty to inquire into what is internal and peculiar in a book which particularly interests us, and at the same time, above all things, to weigh in what relation it stands to our own inner nature, and how far, by that vitality, our own is excited and rendered fruitful. On the other hand, everything external that is ineffective with respect to ourselves, or is subject to a doubt, is to be consigned over to criticism, which, even if it should be able to dislocate and dismember the whole, would never succeed in depriving us of the only ground to which we hold fast, nor even in perplexing us for a moment with respect to our once-formed confidence.

This conviction, sprung from faith and sight, which in all cases that we recognise as the most important, is applicable and strengthening, lies at the fountain of the moral as well as the literary edifice of my life, and . . .[2]

And, with Goethe, back to the beginning of this essay, when he said he was an old man and had only just learned how to read. What did he mean? I think, that he had learned a certain passivity in reading, taking what the author is offering, and not what the reader thinks he

[2] *Poetry and Truth: From my Own Life*, part III, bk. XII, trans. John Oxenford, 2 vols. (London: H. G. Bonn, 1848–9), ii. 131–2.

should be offering, not imposing himself (herself) between the author and what should be emanating from the author. That is to say, not reading the book through a screen of theories, ideas, political correctness, and so forth. This kind of reading is indeed difficult, but one can learn this sort of passive reading, and then the real essence and pith of the author is open to you. I am sure everyone has had the experience of reading a book and finding it vibrating with aliveness, with colour and immediacy. And then, perhaps some weeks later, reading it again and finding it flat and empty. Well, the book hasn't changed: you have.

9

Beneath Interpretation
Intention and the Experience of Literature

PAUL H. FRY

Literary theory is for the most part a thing of the past. To be sure, if
we allow that all of today's approaches to literature that have already
been grounded in social identity are 'theoretical', then certainly a
great deal of theory is still being written concerning the identification, interpretation, and criticism of literature. And indeed, although
it seems to me that no single one of these 'discourses', as they are
called, entails a power of generalization strong enough to support
either a foundational or an antifoundational account of the human
science we call literary, it is true none the less that all of them taken
together (all the race, class, gender, and historicist theories) do continue to reflect a paradigm conflict of general purport in the antifoundational tradition. The pioneering version of this conflict was
Jacques Derrida's 'Structure, Sign, and Play in the Discourse of the
Human Sciences', where the system of binary oppositions central to
structuralism, from Saussure to Lévi-Strauss, was subjected to
critique under the general notion of 'freeplay'. On this view, the
'signified' yoked to the 'signifier' in the Saussurian formula stands
revealed as itself a signifier in an indeterminate chain of implication,
such that there can be no governing signifier or god-term standing
outside a given structure with respect to any signified taken to be that
structure.[1] (Wittgenstein's deconstruction—if I may—of objectivist
accounts of the part–whole relation in paragraphs 47–67 of the
Philosophical Investigations is a similar landmark along the sep-

[1] See J. Derrida (1966), in Richard Macksey and Eugenio Donato (eds.), *The
Languages of Criticism and the Sciences of Man: The Structuralist Controversy,* (Baltimore: Johns Hopkins UP, 1970), esp. 248–9. Derrida goes on to level this argument
against various occasions on which Lévi-Strauss fails to avoid placing the interpreter
outside the interpreted system.

arate path that led to neo-pragmatist appropriations of speech-act philosophy.)

Nothing strikingly new has happened in antifoundational discourse theory since that moment. Each new race, class, gender, and historicist theory has ontogenetically recapitulated the philogeny of the Lévi-Strauss/Derrida encounter. Certain more or less naive but empowering notions dialectically interconnecting Them and Us give way to certain more or less sophisticated but in the long run disempowering notions revealing the apparent binarism of Them and Us to be a skein of inter-identifications that is much too complex—and too clearly subject to extra-systemic factors—to unravel. It happens during the course of each new identity-politics 'debate': an alleged structure of oppression gives way to an alleged *jouissance* of postcoloniality without anything having happened in the real world (or even in fiction) that could be said very strictly to correspond to either view.

An understandable feeling of repletion in response to this state of affairs gave rise to the two most important literary-theoretical position papers of the early 1980s, Paul de Man's 'The Resistance to Theory', which argues that no one has yet proved capable of being theoretical, and 'Against Theory', by Steven Knapp and Walter Benn Michaels, which argues that everyone should stop being theoretical.[2] If nothing new has happened in antifoundational discourse theory since the Derrida paper of 1966, it is also the case that nothing has happened since these papers of 1982 in what is at once more broadly and more narrowly to be understood as literary theory—more narrowly for obvious reasons, more broadly because both these more recent accounts openly or implicitly acknowledge the philosophy of speech acts in the course of showing (perhaps with limited success) that literature is one sort of discourse among others and not just a modality of a unified field known as 'discourse'.

Both these arguments too, like Derrida's, are antifoundational, and I suppose that that happenstance exposes my bias as a chronicler of

[2] See P. de Man (1982), in *The Resistance to Theory*, foreword Wlad Godzich (Minneapolis: University of Minnesota Press, 1986), 3–20; and Knapp and Michaels (1982), in W. J. T. Mitchell (ed.), *Against Theory: Literary Studies and the New Pragmatism* (Chicago: University of Chicago Press, 1985), 11–30. This book includes responses to Knapp and Michaels, together with two subsequent responses of theirs, all of which appeared, as did the original article, in *Critical Inquiry* between 1982 and 1985.

significant events. The foundationalist is likely to say, rather, that the last important hermeneutic news appeared when E. D. Hirsch published *Validity in Interpretation* in 1967—the year that also witnessed Derrida's *Of Grammatology*, which argues that the Western philosophical tradition lays too much stress on the full presence of voice and not enough on the displacements of writing, together with Father Walter Ong's *The Presence of the Word*, which argues to the contrary that the Western philosphical tradition values the letter that killeth rather than the living *Logos*. Hirsch, for his part, drawing on sources as diverse as Husserl, Strawson, and Emilio Betti, did more than any other theorist to ground (to 'found') the writing of meaning in the voice of intention, and he shall not be ignored in what follows.

In this essay, I want to express both my agreement and my disagreement, in each case, with the arguments of de Man and of Knapp and Michaels, laying special emphasis on the issues raised by Knapp and Michaels and their critics and drawing where necessary on points raised by the speech-act philosophers, all with the aim of reaching conclusions about theory and interpretation that I believe to be new, and to show that literature itself is nothing other than a critique of discourse studies. I shall agree with Knapp and Michaels that, with due acknowledgement of certain qualifiers and terministic confusions, no distinction can or should be made between intention and meaning, but disagree with their contention, when criticizing de Man, that there is no language which is not a speech act. I shall agree with de Man (*The Resistance to Theory*, 11, 19) that the determination of meaning we bring to bear on speech acts is ideologically constrained in contrast with our potentially unconstrained encounter ('reading', 'theory') with the language of which speech acts (*paroles*) are comprised and to which they appear identical, but disagree that this 'language' (*langue*) is that virtual semiotic system inferred by Saussure from the sum of speech acts (*langage*) and preserved intact in de Man's argument. I shall claim rather that what remains in literature, and only in literature, when interpretation has exhausted meaning is an underdetermination of predication (I have elsewhere called it the ostensive moment of the literary[3]) which not only defies interpretation but constitutes its critique.

---

[3] See Paul H. Fry, *A Defense of Poetry: Reflections on the Occasion of Writing* (Stanford, Calif.: Stanford UP, 1995), esp. 1–69.

I

Steven Mailloux has usefully summarized the Knapp and Michaels argument as follows: 'They demonstrate how typical theorists base their methodological prescriptions on the prior separation of entities that are in fact logically inseparable (intention and meaning, language and speech acts, knowledge and true belief)' (*Against Theory*, 68). Or again, as Adena Rosmarin paraphrases the authors, 'The "mistake" of ontology is to imagine an intentionless language, the "mistake" of epistemology to imagine a beliefless knowledge' (ibid. 80). That the latter imagining is a mistake will go without saying for our present purposes because it seems to me inconsequential. Objectivist arguments from falsification etc. are not really inconsistent in practice, after all, with the insistence that the groundless hypothesis which made the object visible *as* an object and as that particular object (Wittgenstein's 'seeing *as*', Heidegger's 'Vorhaben' ('fore-having'), Gadamer's 'Vorurteil' (prejudice)) can never be grounded *a posteriori*. As long as we can show that a thing is true for all the intents and purposes we have brought to bear, and undoubtedly we can do so, the scientific method will have served its turn, and no special consequences need follow from our then choosing to say, respectively, that we know the thing or that we believe it. The classical argument against scepticism (you (appear to, or claim to) know that nothing can be known) is a terministic return on the accuser that one can simply refuse to accept, like a gambit in chess: no, I just believe it unqualifiedly.

For the sake of the present argument, it is the former imagining— that there is such a thing as an intentionless language—that deserves attention. This claim is not unrelated to, and is perhaps even finally the same as, the prior issue concerning the relation of intention to meaning. Many critics have argued that Knapp and Michaels fail to distinguish between an author's original intention, which remains a thing apart (Hirsch had definitively called meaning 'an affair of consciousness, not of words'),[4] and the intentionality or purposiveness of a text, which, everyone agrees, is just continuous with the meaning of the text.[5] In other words, the argument goes, the authors

[4] E. D. Hirsch, *Validity in Interpretation* (New Haven: Yale UP, 1967), 4 ff.
[5] For versions of this argument in *Against Theory*, see E. D. Hirsch, 50–4; Adena Rosmarin, 82; and William Dowling, 92.

must either grant that they have failed to eliminate the need for a justified hermeneutic hypothesis (for a theory that grounds the search for intention and the derivation of meaning from intention), or admit that they have reduced the issue to the New Critical insistence, already fully pronounced in Wimsatt and Beardsley's 'The Intentional Fallacy', that meaning is intrinsic to the text.[6]

Now, Knapp and Michaels have several ways of responding to these objections. First, they would argue that language is not language (but only resembles language) unless the premiss of having been intended is present in a text to authorize its intrinsic intentionality. If marks identical to the second stanza of 'A Slumber Did my Spirit Seal' wash up on the sand, the wave having washed away the first stanza (which the beachcomber could hitherto have supposed some person to have scrawled there), then the apparent stanza is not language and has no meaning (see *Against Theory*, 15–18). In Kantian terms, but in opposition to Kant's—proto-New Critical—view of the aesthetic manifold (purposiveness without a purpose: *Zweckmässigkeit ohne Zweck*), for Knapp and Michaels an object is not purposive unless it is purposeful. To interpret the marks, which of course one can easily do, is just *ipso facto* to suppose an author: God, the genius of the shore, homunculi in a tiny submarine, or even 'chance'.

This argument, however, does not dispose of the objection that to interpret an author's intention as it is conferred upon a sentence and to construe the conventional meaning of that sentence may yield differing, even conflicting, results. Harking back to Frege's influential distinction between *Sinn* (the sense denoted by the words of an utterance) and *Bedeutung* (the meaning conferred on the words in a communicative context), this position can be put as follows: for any given utterance, the utterer confers upon it a certain intended meaning, but at the same time the utterance conforms to a certain type, recognizable as a sentence in the utterer's language, part of which, or at least something in relation to which, can in all likelihood—but not necessarily—be inferred as the utterer's meaning. Knapp and Michaels dispose of this problem as follows. It is mistaken, they claim, to distinguish between the particular, unconventional intention of an utterer and the socially determined conventions embedded in lexicography, the rules of syntax, etc. This latter entity looks like

---

[6] See W. K. Wimsatt and Monroe Beardsley, 'The Intentional Fallacy' (1946), in W. K. Wimsatt, *The Verbal Icon* (1954; New York: Noonday, 1964).

Saussure's *langue*, and its sheer undecoded material presence in dictionaries, grammars, and metalanguage (like poetry) is what every writer in the Saussurian tradition, not just de Man, considers to be intentionless language—the language that we do not speak but that speaks us. But for the linguistic pragmatist, everything encoded and codifiable in language is nothing other than the compilation of what Knapp and Michaels call 'normal intentions', which are 'just frequent particular ones' (*Against Theory*, 142). A word in the dictionary would not have a certain meaning (it would have no meaning at all) unless many individuals in concert had intended that meaning. Hence there is no logical distinction to be made between *Sinn* and *Bedeutung* but only a single composite intentional meaning to be construed for every sentence—which is always perforce an uttered sentence. To utter metalanguage ('The cat is on the mat') or fiction ('It was a dark and stormy night') is just to mean that a certain type of referential meaning belongs to a certain type of sentence while appearing to mean that one's utterance has illocutionary force. The philosopher or the novelist, that is, becomes the utterer of a sentence in visible or invisible quotes which only pretends to be illocutionary[7] but is still a sentence because one can and does utter such a sentence. To pretend is still to intend. To some extent Knapp and Michaels would agree, then, that something speaks through us when we speak; but for them what speaks is not language. It is the conjoined force, rather, of the communities whose language we speak.

It would be tempting for anyone just wanting to get on with the business of interpretation to pause here, having taken a side. Most people do. But it still needs to be said, for all the breadth and sophistication of both arguments, that both are still undergirded by the *naïveté* of the child who wants to tell us decisively, having thought hard about the matter, that the chicken or the egg came first. (Perhaps one could administer the same rebuke to Hegel and Marx, but at least they were pioneers; and in any case they both inherited from Rousseau, Vico, and others the healthy willingness to admit that

---

[7] It was something of an embarrassment to the ordinary language philosophers that J. L. Austin, invoking the criterion of seriousness, had dismissed fictional literature with a wave of the hand ('I must not be joking, for example, nor writing a poem') in *How to Do Things with Words*, ed. J. O. Urmson (New York: Oxford Galaxy, 1965), 9, until John R. Searle addressed the problem squarely by arguing that fiction pretends to be an illocutionary utterance in *Expression and Meaning: Studies in the Theory of Speech Acts* (Cambridge: Cambridge UP, 1979), 58–75.

the first stages of their historical schemes were sheer conjecture: Master–Slave, prehistoric communism, etc.)

It is perhaps too easy just lately to notice the peculiar animism with which the Saussurian—or Lacanian—invests 'language', among other things covertly reintroducing not just intentionality but intention to its workings, making the 'materiality of the letter' itself a force as though that force did not require acceleration. Thus when Shelley's Earth pronounces, in the fourth act of *Prometheus Unbound*, that:

> Language is a perpetual Orphic song,
> Which rules with Daedal harmony a throng
> Of thoughts and forms, which else senseless and shapeless were,

he seems inadvertently, as a clumsy ally, to be exposing the fancifulness of the structuralist premiss that language precedes thought and the post-structuralist premiss that language and thought are indistinguishable (Asia had stated earlier in the poem that the priority of language to thought was a gift conferred on man by Prometheus). Obviously it is all just a myth; and, what is worse, Shelley's version of it seems to call attention to the tendency toward the aestheticization of language that many critics have found, rightly or wrongly, in de Man especially:[8] diacritical marks and suprasegmental aporias on this view constitute a totality, a complete form, whereas poems and novels are just ideologemes offered up to the interpreter by that wilful process of mystification which goes by the honoured name of intention in the opposed camp.

With the opposed camp now the ascendant faction, pragmatist and historicist accounts of the origin and function of language have come to seem the most natural ones, making it less easy, but all the more important, to show that they are just as exuberantly mythological as their discredited counterparts. It just seems natural to suppose that language is a tool which came into being for the purpose of transmitting messages, hence that every tagmeme is as much the product of an undivided collective will, or 'normal intention', as every semanteme is. But as speculative anthropology this is an extremely dubious claim. Tools have a purpose, yes, and once their crude prototypes are in existence there is no doubt that they are brought into being and refined in order to fulfil that purpose and perhaps to fulfil new

---

[8] Wrongly, I think. See *The Resistance to Theory*, 19.

purposes. But what of the crude prototypes? Archetypal tools are discovered, not invented. That is, familiar objects, hitherto ignored or feared or valued perhaps for impractical reasons, are found by accident to have a practical value and thenceforth modified to suit their new purpose. What burns also turns out to cook, and one is tempted to say that language is no more intended for communication than fire is intended for cooking. If it be objected, though, that language ought to be compared not with fire but with the opposable thumb, one can finally rest one's case, perhaps, on the simple hypothesis that is at the heart of evolutionary theory: the thumb, like all things, just happened; that it turned out to be useful for survival accounts for its continued existence, and this is obviously also the reason why the 'hard-wiring' for language has not atrophied or been pushed into a corner by improved hard-wiring for, say, olfactory discrimination. Things survive for a reason, but they do not exist for a reason. No one can doubt, or ever would doubt, that language survives and flourishes because it is good for communication. Frequently, perhaps almost inevitably, proponents of an intentionless language fall into the trap of saying that this language communicates (if only to impart the theme of its own undecidability); but the only thing they need properly to have said about intentionless language, in order to rest their case, is that it exists.

Now, the pragmatist may still appear to have a response for this: humanity must always have communicated, in that in some sense every living organism does, and whatever tool was ready to hand for the purpose of communication was the tool we call language—or better, semiosis, given that 'language' is a word that just means 'action of the tongue'. If at some point one could imagine hand gestures, or whatever, to have been used to communicate and articulate grunts reserved for some solipsistic occasion (or better, used on occasion at random, like birdsong), then it was the hand gestures and not the grunts that were 'language', even though from the modern observer's standpoint it was the grunts which, like 'No motion has she now, no force' materializing in the sand, resembled language (see *Against Theory*, 16). This response drives the issue still further back into the recesses of mythological time, but I do not think it meets the objection, which is that the intention to communicate is an attribute of survival, not of existence. Any conceivable speculation about the purpose of language must take its point of departure from mythological time (where Rousseau's savage sitting under his uncontested tree had no need to communicate but may well have purred like a cat), and this very fact serves to show how unwary we become when a prevailing paradigm starts to seem like common sense. I hope the pragmatist will now be prepared to concede that believing language (as opposed to speech acts) to be intentional is not pragmatism but theism.

II

Despite having protested at what I take to be the presupposition behind the notion that there is no intentionless language, I have in fact conceded a great deal of ground, indeed perhaps virtually all of it, to the pragmatist cause. Even though I would go so far as to say that the essence of language, like the essence of a stone, is intentionless, I would not know where to look for this essence (or, indeed, for any other). That there is tension, not harmony, between an existing language and any author's attempt to get something said in that language probably no one would deny, and the existence of such a tension suggests on the face of it that there is also a tension between conventional and individual intentions; but that both sorts of intention are logically continuous and not distinct, with the meaning of any utterance being always a single composite intention, has I think been pretty convincingly demonstrated by Knapp and Michaels (ibid. 142) among others. That at this point the argument is stretched to its extreme limit is signalled by the evident strain of saying that a 'normal intention' is the sum of 'frequent particular intentions', but the move seems only relatively less successful for being a breach of scale.

Still, the very existence of the strain may be instructive. If a dictionary definition seems somehow to entail more than just 'normal intention' (of two kinds, the metalingual and the collective), that is because it is in the case of definition that the synonymity, in ordinary language, of 'meaning' and 'intention' breaks down. As Stanley Cavell says, 'I know how to give the meaning of a word, but not how to give the intention of a word.'[9] Here two qualifiers obtrude themselves. First, and quite obviously (this is just a reminder), our tendency to feel comfortable thinking of language as intentional action is linked to the semantic unit (or 'gross constituent unit', as

---

[9] Quoted from 'The Division of Talent' by W. J. T. Mitchell in his introduction to *Against Theory*, 8. On this issue see also Stanley Cavell, *Must We Mean What We Say? A Book of Essays* (1969; Cambridge: Cambridge UP, 1976), 38–9, 235–7.

Lévi-Strauss called it[10]) on which we normally focus. If we think of language as sentences, we are squarely in the domain of speech acts because for a sentence we take some communicative context for granted. If our focus is words, we feel torn, even if we are not in fact torn, between intention and meaning. And if our focus is the smallest constitutive units of language, finally (phonemes, diacriticals, etc.), the still demonstrable relevance of intention seems completely counter-intuitive.

It is further interesting that the difficulty of proving that intention has determinate force moves in just the opposite direction. The larger the semantic unit, the more it is that various factors—fiendish complexity of intention, 'conflicting intention', failure to clarify, and even 'noise' (unintentional, if not quite intentionless)—are likely to undermine our confidence in the construal of meaning. Reading a poem by Mallarmé or an essay by a remedial prose student makes us wonder whether it is not at best merely trivial to say that intention and meaning are the same. From this point of view it suddenly seems that it is language that is clearly intentional after all (for whatever that is worth), and speech acts rather less so. Cavell's remark reminds us also, finally, that an ordinary language account of the relation between intention and meaning will vary from language to language. *Sinn* and *Bedeutung* I have mentioned, but the German also harbours the—for an anglophone—elusive word *Meinung*, or intention. Hence in German we have: 'Sense' (*Sinn*), for which there is no verb, hence it seems scarcely agent-specific; 'meaning/reference' (*Bedeutung*), for which the verb is frequently governed by an inhuman agent (*das bedeutet=das heißt*), as though meaning were an infratextual matter; and 'intention' (*Meinung*), for which the verb is always governed by a human agent and never means 'mean' except where 'mean' means 'intend' ('I mean business'). How could Knapp and Michaels have negotiated such straits as these?

III

Perhaps, though, they could have won their way through, because their argument, to do it credit, has ontological rather than terministic

---

[10] Claude Lévi-Strauss, *Structural Anthropology*, trans. Claire Jacobson and Brooke Grundfest Schoepf (1963; Garden City, NY: Doubleday Anchor, 1967), 207.

174   PAUL H. FRY

force. Let us concede the point, as indeed, again, we have, and
concentrate on the question that lingers because one finds that in
so many ways it strikes one as implausible, the question that has
moved the Saussurian tradition, for example, to believe that there
must be something else and to posit that something else, 'language',
as a kind of virtual reality. Although for my part I admit freely that I
cannot put hands on the intentionless essence of language (I know I
cannot even though I have not perhaps looked very hard), I shall want
to argue now that this essence is residually present as a 'moment' in
certain features of language that remain in themselves intentional. In
a more or less mystical vein, my whole argument is of course present
in an extraordinary pair of essays by the young Walter Benjamin, 'On
Language as Such and the Language of Man' and 'The Task of the
Translator', where the speculative anthropology I outlined above is
simply taken for granted as a Judeao-Christian parable of man's Fall
from true logocentrism (for which language is simultaneously reality
and its name, hence has no referential component) into pragmatism
(which adapts language to the belated and estranged task of reference).[11] But I have no wish to be mystical (having said that the
pragmatist is more theistic than I!), and confess that I know of no
language other than intentional language, claiming only that in
certain moments this intentional language seems nevertheless to
evince nostalgia for a purer self, intentional but less intention-driven.
Such moments I define, always in relative terms, as 'literary'.

    There is an interpretation-compulsion on the part of the (trained)
reader that corresponds to meaning-compulsion on the part of an
author. For neither participant is it just self-evident that meaning and
interpretation, respectively, are what the experience of language, and
in particular literary language, necessarily takes place to accomplish.
The casual reader will be almost too eager to agree here, I realize,
hoping to applaud a display of anti-professionalism from within the
ranks; and I do wish to appeal in passing to the casual reader's
experience. Even though of course the silent work of parsing goes
forward incessantly in the experience of culinary or passive reading,
this experience is much closer to that of Rousseau's savage under the
tree than we normally recall. What we receive, and indeed crave, in

---

[11] Both essays are widely available in English. For the former, see W. Benjamin,
Reflections, ed. Peter Demetz, trans. Edmund Jephcott (New York: Harvest, 1978),
314–32. For the latter, see Walter Benjamin, *Illuminations*, ed. Hannah Arendt, trans.
Harry Zohn (New York: Schocken, 1969), 69–82.

the suspension of the active interpretative process, is what Roland Barthes calls the effect of the real.[12] Even though it is certainly the case that every sentence has a meaning, readers unobsessed with meaning will also recognize a degree to which the reference component of a sentence is irrelevant or, as we say, 'beside the point'.

A Homeric catalogue of ships undoubtedly refers with great purposefulness to the locales and peoples mentioned, but the auratic sonorousness of Milton's roll-calls (burdened certainly with even greater semantic complexity than Homer's), alerts us to the importance of evocation as such: not the phenomenon of this or that place or name but rather the phenomenology, the romance, that revels in the simple having-been-named of the exotic. And this perceived sufficiency of designation as its own end makes us reflect back on Homer's encyclopedic intent and recognize beneath it an important source of the rhapsode's power of enchantment. We say that we recite 'Thirty days hath September' or 'Righty tighty lefty loosey' as we would use a database, and we refer to these mnemonics as the last modern vestiges of Homeric practice, pointing out that at least some of us have to recite 'Thirty days' in order to 'access' the number of days in June. And yet it is possible to recite even these scraps of formulaic encyclopedism, as children often do, without attending at all to their content, taking satisfaction in the lulling verbal assurance of factuality itself.

'Beside the point', I have said. Is it not still the case, then, that there is, after all, a point? Should we not stand warned that the sensuous place-experience of Miltonic naming is an allurement of fallen language (the Son in *Paradise Regained* scrupulously avoids 'the palpability of the sign')? Yes, that is probably Milton's intention, but it is an intention from which one can confidently stand aloof (there is no felt compulsion to read the names under censure), unlike the intention to 'assert Eternal Providence, | And justify the ways of God to men'. This underdetermination of meaning is what I call the ostensive moment of the literary text, and I claim that it is what defines literature, as opposed to other modes of discourse, in so far as it is—to use the Russian formalist notion—the dominant feature of a given text.

One could also speak here of the residually unparaphrasable,

[12] R. Barthes, *The Rustle of Language*, trans. Richard Howard (Oxford: Basil Blackwell, 1986), esp. 146–8.

without quite meaning what Frost meant in saying that poetry is what gets lost in translation. Joyce's *Ulysses*, for example, invites the rigours and excitements of interpretation, volume upon volume of it, yet the very vividness and diversity of the detail to be interpreted evokes a powerful sensation of 'thereness', an intensity of lived experience, especially in the morning peregrinations featuring Bloom, which is surely an indispensable part of the reading process for anyone who enjoys *Ulysses*. This phenomenon, experienced as the sensuous density of living consciousness, has the surprising effect of making the particularity of the detail irrelevant, even though the inclusion of detail is necessary. We realize that not just these details are important, but rather the presence of detail as such, as the grain of existence, existence in itself disclosed through the existence of Bloom, is what matters—and what, as readers, we are looking for even and perhaps especially when we are engaged in the differential niceties of interpretation.[13] The paradox I am driving at is even clearer in travel literature and so-called regional literature. Devotees of those genres feel an obligation that is almost moral to learn about other places, and of course they do so; yet the more vivid the sense of otherness their interpretative powers can construct, the more likely it is that what they are doing at the same time is absorbing deep infusions, as from a warm breeze, of just being in place, reinvigorating the situatedness of their own consciousness by bringing the situatedness of others into sharper focus. Just so, the minute botanizings of Dorothy Wordsworth's Journals or Coleridge's Notebooks may outwardly intend a hermeneutics of difference—chiaroscuro, taxonomy, the picturesque—subtending what Coleridge called 'multëity in unity' and his precursor James Thomson 'the varied God', but the daemon lurking in the shadow of their observations, mocking all nicety, is the sheer immanence of the earth.

What I mean by ostension plainly differs from what Wittgenstein calls ostension at the beginning of the *Investigations*—the language game in which a workman picks up a slab or beam when the foreman says those words. Speech that exists only to point exists only to mean.

---

[13] Imagist poems are so obviously concerned with this issue that they undermine it by turning it into a programmatic meaning. We can easily say that 'so much depends | upon | a red wheel | barrow | glazed with rain | water | beside the white | chickens' (W. C. Williams, 'The Red Wheelbarrow') means 'so much depends upon the vivid consciousness of lived experience'; so easily, in fact, that the underdetermination of meaning negates itself in having become an overt theme.

Perhaps most often present when language is most like noise or
tracery (humming like murmurous bees, scribbled like gathering
swallows in the sky), hence continuous with reality rather than
mimetic, what I mean by ostension points to no one thing but evokes
the thinghood of things. It discloses the non-human register of existence on which human consciousness (intention) imposes itself. (Here
I am closest to what Paul de Man frequently does with the Saussurian
sense of 'language'.[14]) Coleridge's bees in the beanfield ('This Lime-
Tree Bower my Prison') are thus ostensive, but superimposed on his
literal hum is the underdetermination of meaning: bees and beanfield
merge, efface themselves, in their common being. The supreme poet
of this phenomenon, though, is the Wordsworth of the 1799 or 'Two-
Part' *Prelude*, with its almost unmotivated emphasis on 'spots of
time' that confirm the poet's vocation without saying anything
more, really, than that such moments happened and were memorable.
Because the spots of time provoke us into dazzling feats of interpretation yet lead us finally to realize that we still cannot say what they are
about, they can be seen as prototypes of the literary experience.[15]

IV

I should like to conclude with some remarks about the professional
sources of interpretation-compulsion. In the longer view, it is less
than self-evident that interpretation is the only way we can busy
ourselves with literature. Philology and historical research may be
forms of interpretation, albeit second-order forms, but it is really a
question whether appreciation, the Paterian hallmark of the generation of scholars with which we associate the names of Sir Arthur
Quiller-Couch and William Lyon Phelps, had much that was interpretative about it. Philosophers are at all times interested in interpretation as an aspect of epistemology, but the rise (and, perhaps, the
decline) of hermeneutics as a discipline is historically conditioned.

[14] This sort of argument will be found in many of the essays in *The Rhetoric of
Romanticism* (New York: Columbia UP, 1984), for example 'Autobiography as
De-facement' and 'Shelley Disfigured'. See also 'Hypogram and Inscription' in *The
Resistance to Theory*.
[15] For elaborations of this view, see my *A Defense of Poetry*, 91–107; and 'Green to
the Very Door? The Natural Wordsworth', *Studies in Romanticism*, 35 (1996),
535–51.

Hermeneutics comes about when (*a*) it is considered crucially important that the intention of a text be understood, and (*b*) that text is in
fact difficult to understand. Sacred texts are therefore its first objects
(after the Reformation dislodges infallible authority), legal and constitutional documents next (ensuing upon the rise of constitutional
governments), historical evidence next (during the great surge of
historiography in the nineteenth century), and literature last, in the
theory-laden century now concluding. Literature had been difficult
intermittently throughout history (the early modern period begins,
like Spenser's Letter to Raleigh, with an emphasis on 'Allegory, or
darke conceit'), but it was not until the Romantic period, when a new
kind of difficulty emerged to coincide with a new kind of authorial
aura, lending polite letters a newly scriptural urgency, that interpretation began to accumulate the burden of self-consciousness we
recognize in our modern, academic enterprise.

    Throwing emphasis on the message of a text, in other words, is
historically inseparable from the belief that the message is hard to
decipher. Neither Pope nor his contemporaries troubled themselves to
say what *The Dunciad* 'means', and its 'variorum' Scriblerian notes
were an ongoing satire on drudges of textual scholarship like Theo-
bald who made hermeneutic mountains out of molehills. But in the
nineteenth century gloomy forebodings like Arnold's 'Dover Beach'
led to a positive orgy of anxiety about 'the difficulty of communication' in the twentieth. Popular psychology, 'cultural awareness'
promotion, Corporate Teamwork Retreats, and countless other
socialization industries have thrived on mending real and imaginary
breaches of communication. In my opinion, far from understanding
other people imperfectly, we understand them altogether too well,
and that predisposes me no doubt to be tired of interpretation-
compulsion; but it has to be said that the most important thinking
of this century has shared this compulsion with popular thinking.
Strange, perhaps, from a historical viewpoint, that, in describing a
'promise', an ordinary language philosopher will emphasize felicity
conditions (being serious, securing a promisee, knowing that a promise is not a wager, etc.) rather than obligations! Profound as well as
commonplace minds have witnessed the epidemic of war and atrocity
that surrounded them and reflected thenceforth on the murkiness of
human intentions. Of all these tendencies deconstruction has been
the apocalyptic finale. But the landmarks of criticism throughout the
century had long anticipated it: Types of Ambiguity, Complex Words,

Grammars and Rhetorics of Motives, Hateful Contraries, the obscurity of a Sacred Wood, or the remoteness of an Axel's Castle—all was
not well with meaning.

Naturally there is no retreat from endgames, and one's remaining
portion is to decide how to play them out. Pragmatists or 'situated
readers' typically push the social pawn, and proponents of 'rhetorical
reading' are accused at least by their opponents of pushing the
aesthetic pawn (in truth it is not clear what they are doing), while
a few others are still attempting a fork with this or that synthesis of
the mimetic and the fictive. No one is any longer able to say to anyone
else's satisfaction quite what literature is, and I would suggest in
conclusion that this is because we have now been completely blinded
by the anxiety of interpretation. In this condition, we can scarcely be
expected to see that literature is that form of discourse which is not
exhausted by interpretation.

10

Poetry, Music, and the Sacred

DAVID FULLER

> Damit es Kunst giebt, damit es irgend ein ästhetisches Thun und
> Schauen giebt, dazu ist eine physiologische Vorbedingung unum-
> gänglich: der Rausch.
>
> For art to exist, for any sort of aesthetic activity or perception to
> exist, a certain physiological precondition is indispensible:
> intoxication.
>
> (Nietzsche, *Twilight of the Idols*,
> 'Expeditions of an Untimely Man', 8)

I began university life as a music student, but I abandoned that
because I found that writing counterpoint in the style of Palestrina
and Bach, or writing harmony in the style of Haydn and Schumann,
bore little relation to what I wanted to do—to participate in more
intense and more varied ways in the beauty of works which obsessed
me, and to find the fullest possible range of other music which might
have the same exciting effects. So I gave up Music (as an academic
subject) and took up English. The people who taught me (Francis
Berry, and later William Empson) were wonderfully odd, and apparently led intellectual lives in which there was a harmonious inter-
change between the intellect and the other faculties. These people
were not, as I naively assumed, the pattern of university life; and
when I went to my second university I became conscious again of the
gap between the experience of art and the modes of engaging with
that experience. But I retained a haunting sense that this need not be
so: the gap between aesthetic experience and its institutional study
could, I continued to believe, be decreased.

Haunted dissatisfaction may be the human condition in any
sphere: it may be that imagination requires some promise of fulfil-
ment beyond present experience, whether this is an Ithaca at which
the heroic quester can actually arrive, or a Godot which can sustain

the necessary illusions and help pass the time tolerably. However, I think this dissatisfaction is also, in special and partly remediable ways, a fact about institutional study of literature. My own experience of the institutions of criticism has been complemented—even governed—by two modes of contact with art which have remained outside the toils of the institutional context—one musical, the participation in works that comes from playing them; the other through religion, where again one is a participant—in the drama, poetry, and music of liturgy. It is what I have gathered from these that I am using here—thinking, from the experience of art that they have kept alive for me, about whether an analogously full and intense experience of poetry can be better fostered within institutions.

Les Murray suggests some main aspects of my subject, and offers a way of seeing the analogy between poetry and the sacred.

Religions are poems. They concert
our daylight and dreaming mind, our
emotions, instinct, breath and native gesture

into the only whole thinking: poetry.
Nothing's said till it's dreamed out in words
and nothing's true that figures in words only.

A poem, compared with an arrayed religion,
may be like a soldier's one short marriage night
to die and live by. But that is a small religion.

Full religion is the large poem in loving repetition;
like any poem, it must be inexhaustible and complete
with turns where we ask Now why did the poet do that?

You can't pray a lie, said Huckleberry Finn;
you can't poe one either. It is the same mirror:
mobile, glancing, we call it poetry,

fixed centrally, we call it a religion,
and God is the poetry caught in any religion,
caught, not imprisoned. Caught as in a mirror

that he attracted, being in the world as poetry
is in the poem, a law against its own closure.
There'll always be religion around while there is poetry

or a lack of it. Both are given, and intermittent,
as the action of those birds—crested pigeon, rosella parrot—
who fly with wings shut, then beating, and again shut.[1]

---

[1] 'Poetry and Religion', in *Collected Poems* (Manchester: Carcanet, 1991), 272–3.

The most important thing in a religion—what it calls 'God', its sense of the divine—is a distillation of its poetry, its deeply true fictions. These give forms for intuition and ideal, forms which address and draw into a harmonious relation all the faculties of being. The common errors Les Murray contradicts are those of thinking of poetry too simply in terms of fiction, and the opposite error of thinking of religion too simply in terms of literal truth.

In talking about the sacred I am not considering religion either as a matter of belief or as a moral system. I am interested in a kind of experience, or an attitude to experience. In *The Sacred and the Profane* Mircea Eliade talks in Heideggerian terms of the sacred as 'saturated with *being*',[2] as the world of the deeply real, contrasted with other notions of reality, for example that version of 'the real world' which represents buying and selling as the highest indices of truth—a notion that anybody interested in either poetry or religion is likely to see as corrupt, however necessary some pragmatical negotiation with it may be. Eliade's 'saturated with *being*' readily suggests what such a sense of the sacred has in common with certain views of the aesthetic.

One central desideratum for an adequate understanding of poetry is intensity of attention and concentration: to paraphrase T. S. Eliot, in an ideal reading 'you are the poem while the poem lasts'.[3] My sense of this, as of much else about poetry, comes from music. One ingredient of success in musical performance is the ability to concentrate wholly. Essential to such concentration is memory: you have to know how you are shaping a piece of music, which means knowing where you aim to lead the listener's ear from the first note. The plan may change during performance, but it has to change as an organic development relating all that has happened to all that will happen. From the point of view of the listener too, memory is important to participation: it enables one to listen more fully, because it helps to fix and direct attention, and because it allows one to pace oneself emotionally in relation to the musical shape as a whole.

The musical analogy basic to this argument—and basic to my experience of poetry—does not imply a distortion of poetry. I am

---

[2] *The Sacred and the Profane: The Nature of Religion* (1957), trans. Willard R. Trask (San Diego: Harcourt Brace Jovanovich, 1959), 12.

[3] 'You are the music | While the music lasts', 'The Dry Salvages', V, *Four Quartets*. (Evidently it is germane to my argument that Eliot thinks of music as provoking such wholly absorbed concentration.)

not arguing that poetry is wholly similar to music; only that what is recognized about understanding music offers a model for what is not adequately recognized about understanding poetry: the concentrated participatory shaping that is required in musical performance and appreciation helps one to see what is required in reading and hearing a poem.

I should say that I view the possibilities of institutional improvement here gloomily, because I think the machinery of the university system as a whole too inertly strong for reasoned argument to have any great effect on what flows from its imperatives. One fruitful way to combat the consequences of setting institutions against one another to compete for funding (as they currently are impelled to in Britain) is to shift the argument from the declared aims of this competition—about promoting what is called 'excellence'—to its actual effects. One effect is to increase the power of critical fashions which suit the dominant paradigms of knowledge—quasi-scientific ones about 'research' and knowledge as 'progressive', paradigms which are at best only partially applicable to literary criticism. But it would require the brilliance of Oscar Wilde to confront these paradigms with the necessary non-utilitarian and anarchic notions of aesthetic pleasure.

One way of seeing the subject of poetry and the sacred is to historicize it as a specifically Romantic idea, as T. E. Hulme did when he called Romanticism 'spilt religion', meaning that there is a proper kind of religion which admits Original Sin and human limitation, and Romanticism was making a mess by claiming human perfectibility and trying to pretend you could have heaven on earth.[4] The Hulme view of Romanticism is currently promulgated by the sceptical materialist so-called 'New Historicist' approach to literary criticism, which attempts to present the whole Romantic movement as a historical phenomenon which we have passed beyond—or should have passed beyond, and this criticism will help us to do so. In discussing the proper reading of poetry as having analogies with religious experience first as a historical phenomenon I do not mean to accede

---

[4] 'Romanticism and Classicism', in *The Collected Writings of T. E. Hulme*, ed. Karen Csengeri (Oxford: Clarendon Press, 1994), 59–73 (quotation from p. 62). It is to say the least paradoxical that the most notable writer to enact the Hulme view in English poetry is Milton, when the archangel Michael tells Adam he can build 'a paradise within thee happier far' than Eden (*Paradise Lost*, XII. 587).

to any New Historicist polemic. On the contrary, I would argue that the connection between poetry and the sacred is as ancient as the Hebrew psalms, as ancient as Greek tragedy, as ancient as the Upanishads. But the idea takes different and more complex forms in an age which was ceasing to be religious (as was the age of Wordsworth), or has ceased to be religious (as has our own). Why this should be so is indicated by a famous comment of Matthew Arnold's, which presupposes the sort of analogy between religion and poetry suggested by Les Murray:

More and more mankind will discover that we have to turn to poetry to interpret life for us, to console us, to sustain us. Without poetry our science will appear incomplete; and most of what now passes with us for religion and philosophy will be replaced by poetry.[5]

Arnold was writing in the context of over a century of intellectual developments—the Higher Criticism of the Bible, the geology of Lyell, the biology of Darwin—which presented problems for a mistakenly literal notion of biblical truth. His argument is that much of what is valuable in religion is not its literal but its symbolic truth. In effect Arnold presents religion as poetry carried on under the guise of a simpler kind of truth which, by the late nineteenth century, it appeared that science was forcing religion to do without. This may now seem, from a religious point of view, almost quaintly Victorian: as creation theory in contemporary science becomes ever more religious, with some Big Bang theorists talking about getting near the mind of God, this sense of science as a threat to Christian truth looks remote. But whatever its value as a comment on the 'supposed facts' of Christianity it does point up the relation between poetry and religion which is my subject. And in this context it is striking to notice that I. A. Richards—not an obviously Arnoldian thinker—used the passage just quoted from 'The Study of Poetry' as an epigraph to his *Science and Poetry* (1926, 1935; rev. edn. 1970, *Poetries and Sciences*). Richards's argument endorses his Arnoldian epigraph on new grounds. Richards, of course, took a large-minded interest in science, particularly in Psychology, and this interest in

---

[5] 'The Study of Poetry' (1880), in *Essays in Criticism*, 2nd Series (London: Macmillan, 1888), 2–3. Arnold begins the essay in which these famous sentences appear by quoting another passage from his own writings which indicates the context of his line of thought: 'Our religion has materialized itself in the fact, in the supposed fact; it has attached its emotion to the fact, and now the fact is failing it' (p. 1).

Psychology provides one basis of the argument of *Science and Poetry*, which presents poetry as protecting civilization from attempts by Science to govern areas of thought which are not Science's proper concern.[6] That the same line of thought can be adopted by such different parties as Arnold and Richards is in itself evidence that it cannot be sharply historicized. Nevertheless, with the reservation that the connection between poetry and the sacred should not be seen as a specifically Romantic period idea, I shall now consider what the Romantic poets did with this, both in their statements about poetry and in poems which recast religious myths in new terms.

The *Prelude* is a narrative of a Fall (a gradual loss of the poet's childhood awareness of the divine through nature), his spiritual struggles in the fallen world (from Cambridge to Paris), and his own personal redemption ('the imagination, how impaired *and restored*'); that is to say (as many critics have observed), it is a poem analogous in the structure of its narrative to *Paradise Lost*. By expressing this pattern in his own personal life Wordsworth gives poetry a religious function: he makes it the instrument of a wider human restoration—and these social consequences are not simply left implicit. At the end of the poem Wordsworth looks forward to being, with Coleridge,

> Bless'd with true happiness if we may be
> United helpers forward of a day
> Of firmer trust, joint-labourers in a work . . .
> Of [man's] redemption. (1805, XIII. 437–41)

This means that, while the specific subject of *Paradise Lost*, and that whole mode of impersonal narrative epic, is abandoned, the personal story that replaces the Christian myth has not only the same shape, but also to a considerable degree the same meaning. The *Prelude* shows how the myth on which *Paradise Lost* is based can be experienced in the age of the French Revolution, and shows this—the poem is concerned with 'man's redemption'—in an explicitly religious context.

Though Shelley was a poet of quite different religious views, one

---

[6] See, for example, *Poetries and Sciences: A Reissue of 'Science and Poetry' (1926, 1935) with Commentary* (London: Routledge & Kegan Paul, 1970), 78: 'Our protection, as Matthew Arnold, in my epigraph, insisted, is in poetry. It is capable of saving us . . . The poetic function is the source, and the tradition of poetry is the guardian, of the supra-scientific myths.'

can present a similar argument about *Prometheus Unbound*. Shelley too is in some sense a religious poet, as is most obvious in the 'Hymn to Intellectual Beauty'. Like Wordsworth he discusses poetry in quasi-religious terms: 'Poetry redeems from decay the visitations of the divinity in man'; 'Imagination is as the immortal God which should assume flesh for the redemption of human passion'.[7] Though an antagonist of the Church, Shelley was also an admirer of Jesus, as (with Socrates) one of the truly heroic figures of history. And (despite what he saw as their vitiation by the delusions of Christianity) Milton and Dante were for Shelley the great poets of modern Western civilization. Like Wordsworth in *The Prelude*, Shelley wrote his own version of *Paradise Lost* in *Prometheus Unbound*. Here the Fall has taken place before the poem begins: Prometheus/Adam has enslaved himself to Jupiter/Satan by allowing hatred to take possession of him. (In Shelley's, as in Blake's account of Milton, it is the tyrant Father (Jupiter) who is truly Satanic.) Prometheus is redeemed by being reunited with his capacity to love. At the beginning of this process Jesus is invoked as an analogue to Prometheus in his heroic capacity for selfless love (though on Shelley's view Jesus has been betrayed throughout history by the Church's misrepresentation of him). The individual redemption of Prometheus leads to an apocalyptic transformation of the universe. Though by a different means to that proposed by Milton, it is a coda in which paradise is regained.

Moreover, various of the Romantic poets consciously saw the writing and reading of poetry as a religious activity. Wordsworth drew the analogy in his 'Essay, Supplementary to the Preface' in the *Poems* of 1815.

The concerns of religion refer to indefinite objects, and are too weighty for the mind to support them without relieving itself by resting a great part of the burden upon words and symbols. The commerce between Man and his Maker cannot be carried on but by a process where much is represented in little, and the Infinite Being accommodates himself to a finite capacity. In all this may be perceived the affinity between religion and poetry; between religion—making up the deficiencies of reason by faith; and poetry—passionate for the instruction of reason; between religion—whose element is infinitude, and whose ultimate trust is the supreme of things, submitting herself to circumscription, and reconciled to substitutions; and poetry—

---

[7] *A Defense of Poetry*, in *Shelley's Poetry and Prose*, ed. Donald H. Reiman and Sharon B. Powers (New York: Norton, 1977), 505; *The Cenci*, preface, ibid. 241.

ethereal and transcendent, yet incapable to sustain her existence without sensuous incarnation.[8]

The context of these remarks is Wordsworth's attempt to explain various forms of imperfect evaluation of poetry. His argument is that religious poetry is frequently valued mistakenly on grounds of its overt religious content. The religious reader is liable to over- or undervalue a poem depending on whether he approves or rejects its doctrines. The quality of religious poetry, Wordsworth emphasizes, has nothing to do with its overt religious content. It has to do with the analogy between poetry and religion—an analogy which holds good for the kind of poetry Wordsworth most values whether or not the subject matter of the poem is religious. The common element of poetry and religion, in this account, is symbolism, necessary because both are reaching after what cannot be directly named. Wordsworth first suggests that the two connect through a different relation to the common element, reason, which is of itself inadequate (poetry and religion relate to this inadequacy in different ways). Then (suggesting a more complete parallel), both use the sensuous world to point to something beyond itself (not necessarily in the obvious religious sense of in some wholly other mode of reality).

Coleridge proposed a yet more comprehensive analogy, seeing religion as 'the Poetry of all mankind', and giving as his final and 'grandest point of resemblance' that

Both have for their object (he knew not whether the English language supplied an appropriate word) the perfecting, the pointing out to us the indefinite improvement of our nature and fixing our attention upon that. It bids us while we are sitting in the dark round our little fire still look at the mountain tops struggling with the darkness, and announces that light which shall be common to us all, and in which all individual interests shall dissolve into our common interest, and every man find in another more than a brother. Such being the case we need not wonder . . . that at all times the Poets . . . should have joined to support all those delicate sentiments of the heart, (often, when they were most opposite to the reigning philosophy of the day) which might be called the feeding streams of Religion . . .
In the poet was comprehended the man who carries the feelings of childhood into the powers of manhood: who with a soul unsubdued, unshackled by custom can contemplate all things with the freshness, with the wonder of a child, and, connecting with it the inquisitive powers of his manhood, adds, as

---

[8] *The Prose Works of William Wordsworth*, ed. W. J. B. Owen and J. W. Smyser, 3 vols. (Oxford: Clarendon Press, 1974), iii. 65.

far as he can find knowledge, admiration, and where knowledge no longer permits, admiration gladly sinks back again into the childlike feeling of devout wonder . . . What is old and worn out, not in itself, but from the dimness of the intellectual eye brought on by worldly passions, he makes new: he pours upon it the dew that glistens, and blows round us the breeze which cooled us in childhood.[9]

For Coleridge the moral value of poetry lies in the imaginative extension it provokes: we are led, as by religion, to see ourselves in a large context which acts as a deflating perspective on the narrow concerns of immediate circumstance. It is finally a matter of a certain kind of feeling that is provoked: 'all those delicate sentiments of the heart . . . which might be called the feeding streams of Religion'; 'devout wonder' (an idea to which I shall return in discussing W. H. Auden). Coleridge's unexpected example in this lecture is the so apparently secular *Romeo and Juliet*. For Coleridge *Romeo and Juliet* is a religious work because it makes the reader feel the beauty of the idealizing tendency brought intensely into play by love. This suggests a more general nobility of human aspiration and potential, the ultimate form of which Coleridge regards as necessarily religious.

For Wordsworth and Coleridge poetry has, in different ways, a quasi-religious function, but there is a clear hierarchy: Christianity is truth; poetry is an approach to, or analogous with that truth. Blake is more radical.

The ancient poets animated all sensible objects with Gods or Geniuses, calling them by the names and adorning them with the properties of woods, rivers, mountains, lakes, cities, nations, and whatever their enlarged & numerous senses could perceive. . . . Till a system was formed, which some took advantage of & enslav'd the vulgar by attempting to realize or abstract the mental deities from their objects; thus began Priesthood.
    Choosing forms of worship from poetic tales.[10]

This is a more combative version of Les Murray's claim: for Blake all religions originate as, and properly understood really are, poems—

    [9] J. P. Collier's transcription from his own shorthand notes of a lecture given by Coleridge in Dec. 1811; in *Lectures 1808–19: On Literature*, ed. R. A. Foakes, *The Collected Works of Samuel Taylor Coleridge*, vol v (Princeton: Princeton UP, 1987), I. 325–6.
    [10] *The Marriage of Heaven and Hell*, pl. 11, in *The Complete Poetry and Prose of William Blake*, ed. D. V. Erdman, commentary by Harold Bloom (New York: Doubleday, 1965; rev. edn. 1988), 38.

metaphoric forms of perception—the personifications of which are projections from the mind onto the world. The Church, and much in the Bible itself, is in this account a cheat designed to impose on people by reading metaphors as literal truth. For Blake the bard of English tradition combines the roles of poet and religious figure, as the prophet (whose method of communication is often metaphoric or symbolic) did in Hebrew tradition. In his later work Blake continues to associate poetry and religion,[11] as is indicated in his myth by the identification of Los, the spirit of poetry, with Jesus (*Jerusalem*, pl. 96). It is in this context that we are to understand Blake's most uncompromising indentification of poetry and religion in the aphorisms of his late *Laocoön* engraving.

Prayer is the Study of Art
Praise is the Practice of Art
Fasting &c. all relate to Art
The outward Ceremony is Antichrist
A Poet, a Painter, a Musician, an Architect: the Man
Or Woman who is not one of these is not a Christian
You must leave Fathers & Mothers & Houses & Lands
    if they stand in the way of ART (Erdman edn., 274)

If the gospel enjoins exercise of the imagination then a Christian must be some sort of an artist. Jesus affirms the reward of those who leave father and mother and house and lands 'for my sake and for the gospel' (Mark 6: 29). Blake's reformulation—'You must leave Fathers & Mothers & Houses & Lands if they stand in the way of ART'—emphasizes his interpretation of the whole gospel as concerned with 'the liberty . . . to exercise . . . Imagination' (*Jerusalem*, pl. 77). By identifying religious activities as artistic—not vice versa: not 'the study of art is a form of prayer'—Blake emphasizes the primacy of what Wordsworth and Coleridge see as subsidiary. Religion is not now, as it was in *The Marriage of Heaven and Hell*, condemned as an imposition on poetry; but Blake's ordering insists on the primacy of the symbolic meaning of any religious action—as he makes clear in concluding that 'The outward Ceremony is Antichrist'.

So far I have discussed writers in the Romantic tradition: apart

---

[11] See the preface to the final chapter of *Jerusalem*: 'I know of no other Christianity and of no other Gospel than the liberty both of body & mind to exercise the Divine Arts of Imagination' (pl. 77; Erdman edn., 231).

from those from the Romantic period—Arnold, influenced by Wordsworth; and I. A. Richards (however unlike Arnold he may be), influenced by Coleridge. I shall also invoke two writers who comment in similar terms and are decidedly not in this tradition—Joyce and W. H. Auden.

In *A Portrait of the Artist as a Young Man* Joyce describes the hero, Stephen Dedalus, as 'a priest of eternal imagination, transmuting the daily bread of experience into the radiant body of everliving life'.[12] Allowing for the mild rhetorical inflation by which he sympathetic-ally satirizes Stephen's pretensions, Joyce seriously means here that the function of the artist is a quasi-religious one: the artist trans-mutes the temporal into the eternal. The artist offers a form of religious experience, but one not circumscribed by sect and dogma. Shem, the writer figure of *Finnegans Wake*, more than a priest, per-forms, as artist, Christlike miracles: 'he lifts the lifewand and the dumb speak' (p. 193). It is in keeping with this view of the artist that Joyce uses the term 'epiphany' (derived from the manifestation of Christ to the Magi)—by which he means 'a sudden spiritual mani-festation, whether in the vulgarity of speech or of gesture or in a memorable phase of the mind itself'—for what he discovers and records.[13] The artist, in this account, is engaged in a struggle which can be understood in terms of a religious symbolism, radically reor-iented, cast free of what are to Joyce unnecessary frameworks of doctrine and belief. Joyce reworked the epiphanies he collected as a young man into *A Portrait*, *Ulysses*, and *Finnegans Wake*, and he used the concept with his usual comic seriousness in the *Wake*'s climactic confrontation (p. 611), which Joyce described as 'defence and indict-ment of the book itself'.[14]

Auden, similarly, is not a writer in the Romantic tradition. He described Romanticism as 'unawareness of the dialectic'—this in a poem which, while his English publisher (T. S. Eliot, at Faber) gave it

---

[12] *A Portrait of the Artist*, ed. Richard Ellmann (London: Jonathan Cape, 1956), 225. Cf. Stephen's religious view of 'the instant of inspiration': 'In the virgin womb of the imagination the word was made flesh. Gabriel the seraph had come to the virgin's chamber' (p. 221).

[13] *Stephen Hero*, ed. Theodore Spencer (1944), rev. John J. Slocum and Herbert Cahoon (London: Jonathan Cape, 1956), 188. Cf. Stephen's alternative reference to the eucharist, *Stephen Hero*, 33.

[14] *Letters of James Joyce*, 3 vols.; vol. i, ed. Stuart Gilbert (London; Faber, 1957; reissued with corrections, 1966); vols. ii and iii, ed. Richard Ellmann (London: Faber, 1966); i. 406.

the title *New Year Letter*, Auden himself called *A Double Man*, indicating by an epigraph from Montaigne about the inevitability of self-division that dialectic was his subject. Auden, the anti-Romantic, is, however, quite as clear as Joyce about the necessary connection between poetry and the sacred:

It is from the sacred encounters of his imagination that a poet's impulse to write a poem arises. Thanks to the language he need not name them directly unless he wishes . . . Some poems are directly *about* the sacred beings they were written *for*: others are not, and in that case no reader can tell what was the original encounter which provided the impulse for the poem . . . Whatever its actual content and overt interest, every poem is rooted in imaginative awe. Poetry can do a hundred and one things . . . but there is only one thing that all poetry must do; it must praise all it can for being and for happening.[15]

Auden's formulation makes it clear that the connection between poetry and the sacred need not be explicit: the poem itself may contain no hint of the religious impulse in its inception. Nevertheless, Auden also often treats apparently secular subjects in a religious spirit, for example in the sequence about his house, 'Thanksgiving for a Habitat', where the thanksgiving is eucharistic, an acknowledgement of divine goodness and mercy which is expressed in a religious vocabulary. For Auden, as for Joyce, it is not the subject matter in itself which makes a poem religious.[16] It is the poet's attitude to his or her material which gives the artist in some sense a priestly function, mediating between the reader and the divine. An aphoristic epitome of the whole line of argument (again from the Romantic tradition) is offered by Wallace Stevens: 'After one has abandoned a belief in god, poetry is that essence which takes its place as life's redemption.'[17]

---

[15] 'Making, Knowing and Judging', in *The Dyer's Hand* (London: Faber, 1963), 59–60.

[16] 'There can no more be a "Christian" art than there can be a Christian science or a Christian diet. There can only be a Christian spirit in which an artist, a scientist, works or does not work. A painting of a Crucifixion is not necessarily more Christian in spirit than a still life, and may very well be less.' 'Christianity and Art', ibid. 458.

[17] 'Adagia', in *Opus Posthumus: Poems, Plays, Prose*, ed. Samuel French Morse (New York: Alfred Knopf, 1957), 158. Cf. 'Poetry is a means of redemption' (p. 160); 'God is a symbol for something that can as well take other forms, as, for example, the form of high poetry' (p. 167).

I have now to consider the consequences of this view of poetry for criticism, and the relevance of the analogy between poetry and music with which I began. In an essay of 1964 Susan Sontag argued 'against interpretation',[18] by which she meant the translation of works of art into more abstract terms—primarily thematic ones, though it is the abstract mode not the nature of its content to which she objected. She criticized interpretation by means of what was, even then, a caricature of what has now become much more sophisticated, but this does not affect her argument about the need to dislodge the dominance of critical activities which either (as with the target of Susan Sontag's polemic) re-present works in terms which purport to extract a supposed hidden essence, or in other ways treat the beauty of the particular articulation as subsidiary to some other focus of interest. The implication of the most sophisticated hermeneutics is that a poem can really be better presented to the mind in terms other than those of its characteristic mode of existence—that surfaces are only valuable in so far as they imply inexplicit depths. Susan Sontag gives some excellent examples of foolish reading-in of 'profundities', and makes well the point that the interpreter who habitually seeks to read a surface in terms of some inexplicit depth will really be expressing a lack of response to the words, the images, the sounds of the work in themselves. It is clear what Susan Sontag opposes: 'interpretation is the revenge of the intellect on art.' It is less clear what she proposes. Her essay ends with a pointed enigma: 'in place of a hermeneutics we need an erotics of art.' This is a provocative final sentence, and though Susan Sontag does not expand on what she means, it is clear that her presuppositions are Lawrentian: sensory and emotional knowledge in intellectuals is underdeveloped; the art criticism of intellectuals is a symptom of this, though art properly understood could be a cure for it. I am in sympathy with that, as with the cognate drive for aesthetic pleasure in the stress on 'jouissance' or 'le plaisir du texte' of Roland Barthes. But I want to add something more mentalistic and quasi-religious than I suspect a Lawrentian such as Susan Sontag or a cultivated hedonist such as Barthes would like— that a real erotics is about finding the inward beauty of the spirit reflected in the outward grace and loveliness of the lineaments. A true delight in aesthetic surface means that the poem (or picture, or song)

<hr/>

[18] 'Against Interpretation' and Other Essays (New York: Farrar, Straus & Giroux, 1966), quotations from pp. 7 and 14.

is treated as analogous to a lover's body, beautiful both in itself and because it is an emanation of spirit. One can mention the spirit—the depth which the surface reveals—because on this view only a lover bamboozled by Neoplatonism will want delight in surfaces refined out of existence. What is needed are ways of participating in those surfaces, and all they imply, more completely. Interpretation can be one of these only so long as it is carried on in a way that recognizes its status as preparatory—that recognizes that its aim is to return the reader to the work able not to abstract some essence from it after reading, but to be more fully present in it during the reading.

One should be in awe of the mysteriousness of great art. One should approach it with a decent tentativeness about how little the intellect is able to re-present that mysteriousness adequately, and understand that attempts which have too great a pride of intellect are worse than the innocence of uncomprehending awe, because they encourage too exclusive a reliance on modes of knowledge which give an illusion of understanding by providing something to say, and so evade the proper and necessary sense of how mysterious and resistant to the intellect art can be. Recognizing that, one begins in the right place; whereas making the tongue wag may keep the spirit dumb.

If one does not become an adequate lover by talking too readily, how is this to be done? I argued earlier that memory is important to full concentration. Another important and neglected issue is orality. In introducing his anthology *The Poet's Tongue*, W. H. Auden puts the claims of orality in extreme form: 'No poetry . . . which when mastered is not better heard than read is good poetry.'[19] Auden's exaggeration is a corrective to the tendency inherent in the usual modern practice of silent reading to ignore the aural experience of poetry, though oral performance, in association with memory, can be decisive in its effect on participation. The reader who has a poem in his memory, and who has spoken it through and through until its words have become naturalized into his own voice, who can bring to bear on it all the faculties of being that vocal presence can convey— not, as the New Critical slogan has it, as 'words on the page', but as words in the memory and in the whole vocal mechanism—is in the position of the musician for whom music is not in the score but in the ears and in the fingers, or in the position of the dancer for

[19] *The English Auden: Poems, Essays and Dramatic Writings, 1927–1939*, ed. Edward Mendelson (London: Faber, 1977), 327.

whom the choreography is in that memory which any dancer will recognize as seeming to inhere in the body. Socrates was sceptical about claims to wisdom in poetry because the poets could not tell him, he claimed, what their poems meant[20]—by which he meant they refused to translate their work into his mode of knowledge. Poets do refuse. When T. S. Eliot was asked what he meant (in *Ash Wednesday*) by 'Lady, three white leopards sat under a juniper-tree' he famously replied, 'Lady, three white leopards sat under a juniper-tree'—by which he meant, the questioner was looking for knowledge in the wrong terms. Blake provides the poet's answer: 'Plato has made Socrates say that Poets & Prophets do not Know or Understand what they write or Utter[;] this is a most Pernicious Falshood. If they do not, pray is an inferior Kind to be calld Knowing[?]'[21] I am not looking, in some quasi-Platonic gesture, to banish literary critics from the commonwealth. The critical, sceptical consciousness which Socrates demands is a necessary complement to the activities of the Homeric rhapsode. Participatory enthusiasm without the complement of a sceptical critique is the recipe of the Nuremberg rallies. However, the danger in the university is not of the sceptical intellect being undervalued: the danger is of its being the only thing that is valued. I am looking, therefore, *contra* Plato, to reinstate the thoroughly interiorized mode of knowledge of the rhapsode, and something of the kind of participation in poetry that the rhapsode inspired in his auditors.[22] To do that one has to scale down the pretensions which scholarship and criticism claim for their necessary but (as Blake puts it) inferior kind of knowing.

This is one way in which the analogy between poetry and music can help. One thing performing musicians learn is to shape aural structures. The process of studying a musical work to perform it does not usually involve replacing the characteristic modality of the art by another mode. The musician considers meaning as sound—how to shape, articulate, project particular congeries of notes. Experiments in thinking stay within the medium: you play the notes one way, you play them another. All the decisions you make cumulatively amount to a decision about what the piece means. Of course, you may be able to explain your decisions in words, but you think about them as

[20]   *The Apology* 21c; *Meno* 99c–e; *Laws* 719c.

[21]   'A Vision of the Last Judgement', Erdman edn., 554.

[22]   This is described in the dialogue on poetic inspiration and the nature of the rhapsode's knowledge between Socrates and Ion (*Ion* 535–6).

sound. It is possible to experiment with thinking in a similar way with a poem—to try the words one way, to try them another. It is quite possible to make experiments with critical thinking which stay with the words of the poem. Finding solutions to problems of reading aloud makes clear how much reading aloud is a mode of criticism. Some of the problems will be simple local ones of tone, emphasis, and shaping, but beyond these there are more general problems, for example, how to handle the sometimes opposite demands of syntax and form—an especially important problem because expressive energy often arises from a conflict between their demands. Obviously I am hampered in discussing this in writing: in reading poetry aloud so much happens that is untranscribable that adequate demonstration has to be oral. However, I can describe my own general preference, which is for a negotiation that gives approximately equal weight to the demands of the regular metrical structure, the feeling of which must never be wholly absent, and rhetorical stress, that is the demands of sense where these conflict with those of the regular metre. These two will often be distinct, but in a successful poem they will always be in some expressive relation, never entirely at odds.[23]

Reading aloud has also to tackle at a practical level the problem of the relationship in critical understanding between acknowledging the otherness of a poem—the fact that it comes from an imagination, a sensibility, and was written for a voice not one's own[24]—and recognizing that a poem (like any work of art) only achieves its full existence when it becomes alive in the whole being of a person who did not invent it. This means that to read a poem you have to be able to use all the resources of your own real voice as you use it in the rest

[23] In an otherwise fine essay on the issues involved in reading poetry aloud Yvor Winters, despite the usual rationalistic emphasis of his criticism, favours a quasi-incantatory delivery which, where necessary, sacrifices rhetorical to metrical stress ('The Audible Reading of Poetry', in *The Function of Criticism: Problems and Exercises* (Denver: Alan Swallow, 1957)). Winters derives the fundamental orientation of his argument from Valéry (*A Discourse on the Declamation of Verse*, extracts from which are given in *Paul Valéry: Selected Writings*, trans. Louise Varèse (New York: New Directions, 1950)).
[24] In *Poetry and the Physical Voice* (London: Routledge & Kegan Paul, 1962) Francis Berry discusses the supposed actual voices of various poets, largely as these can be reconstructed from the printed page. He does not consider the reader's voice except in so far as it can approximate to that of the poet. In *The Printed Voice of Victorian Poetry* (Oxford: Clarendon Press, 1989) Eric Griffiths argues the importance of imagining poetry in performance, how the spoken word may be inferred from the written, and the subtleties of meaning that can be derived from so doing.

of your life, responding to the poem's inflections of tone and implication, but also to its level of stylization. Again the musical analogy helps here. 'Richter's Schumann' does not mean some peculiarly eccentric distortion of Schumann: it means in the first place a revelation of the music itself, but filtered through a particular sensibility which, in so far as one admires it, one judges peculiarly able to co-operate with the music to reveal its character. What this means with a poem is that the reader has to strike some relationship between trusting the words in themselves, being a quasi-anonymous vehicle, while also using all the resources of feeling and understanding that exist in his or her own vocal being.[25] Learning to do this means acquiring a significant critical skill, one that helps make reading poetry the kind of wholly absorbed, completely concentrated experience it should be—'intoxication' 'saturated with *being*' that 'concerts | our daylight and dreaming mind'.

[25] In an essay stressing the critical importance of reading aloud F. R. Leavis draws a musical analogy to make a similar point: 'Faithfully reading out a poem . . . one should think of oneself as both the violinist and the violin, and not as an impressively personal elocutionary voice blessed with an opportunity' ('Reading out Poetry' (1972), in *Valuation in Criticism and Other Essays*, ed. G. Singh (Cambridge: Cambridge UP, 1986)).

Part III

Criticism and the Ethical

11

The Aesthetic, the Cognitive, and the Ethical

Criticism and Discursive Responsibility

SEÁN BURKE

Literary criticism inevitably entertains a curious relationship to the object of its investigation. The practice of literary interpretation or formal reading exists in some indefinite region between the creative acts it studies and a philosophical discipline which has often been in quarrel with the idea of a truth discoverable in literature. Indeed, one might argue that the *ethos* of criticism is closer to philosophical analysis than to the creative and poetic acts which constitute its objects. Certainly, its attempts at disinterested analysis make its mode of being both adjacent to and yet incommensurable with the literary works which it studies. In this sense, criticism flourishes at an intersection between aesthetic, cognitive, and ethical ways of knowing.[1] While its objects are aesthetic, literary criticism translates those objects according to a language of cognition rather than feeling; when justifying itself as a cultural practice, criticism's strongest appeals are to the ethical significance of studying literature. Even advocates of pure aesthetic experience, when asked to justify their endeavours, will admit to an ethical mission in terms of the benefits to society of broadening access to such experience. Literary criticism proceeds from a variety of impulses which, while often hostile to one another, none the less betray ethical convictions. Humanist critics seek to

---

[1] The categories of aesthetic, cognitive, and ethical are not treated as mutually exclusive: rather, the argument proposes that the ethical realm can be malignly invaded by mixed discourses which draw from aesthetic resources in the presentation of (supposedly) pure cognitive claims. It is the fluidity rather than fixity of these boundaries that gives rise to ethical concern.

defend the aesthetic as an ethical act; critics opposed to humanist values will find an ethical imperative in reducing the aesthetic to the ideological. Such critical positions are readily identifiable, perhaps because they are *positioned* in relation to a clearly defined set of beliefs about the social function of texts. Less visible but no less pervasive, however, is a general ethic which sees criticism as an activity designed to guard against the ethical dangers of textual claims overspilling into social practices. This latter function of criticism also incorporates philosophical scepticism and discourses on the ethics of science as well as literary criticism. It is this broader sense of criticism as a regulative and defensive interrogation which will form the main focus of my discussion.[2]

Criticism begins with the Socratic method of question-and-answer and its development in Plato's dialogues. Taking Plato's work as the most compelling instance of the convergence of the cognitive, the aesthetic, and the ethical, I will argue that—long before Kant— rationalist philosophy was attempting to separate cognitive knowledge from aesthetic experience in such a manner that philosophy would succeed poetry as the dominant influence on the realms of ethics, social ordering, and education.[3] This determination explains why Plato puts such emphasis on discursive containment, on the necessity of preventing poetic and sophistic texts from exerting malign or irresponsible influences in the world of politics and social order. However, as I will argue in the second phase of this essay, the Platonic philosophy has only an insecure place within the cognitive realm which it represents: dialectical philosophy's uneasy status as a discourse suspended between poetry and science—its insecurity as a science—led to the Platonic philosophy exerting the very dangerous influence on the ethical sphere which it thought to have detected in poetry. The final section contends that speculative philosophy rather than poetry has exhibited all the dangerous tendencies which Plato discerned in the poetic tradition. The essay concludes by outlining the

---

[2] On my argument, Plato provides the only sustained account of the ethics of discursive transmission. In our era, a most insightful contribution is made in Jacques Derrida, *The Ear of the Other: Autobiography, Transference, Translation: Texts and Discussions with Jacques Derrida*, trans. Peggy Kamuf and Avital Ronell (New York: Schocken Books, 1986).

[3] All references to Plato will be made to *The Collected Dialogues of Plato, Including the Letters*, ed. Edith Hamilton and Huntington Cairns, Bollingen Series LXXI (Princeton: Princeton UP, 1961). Page numbers and letters are given parenthetically within the text.

(hopefully) robust future of criticism as an activity which unmasks the surreptitious use of mythic, aesthetic, or sophistic strategies by which speculative discourses present themselves as discourses of truth. Throughout, I will be concerned with the capacities of different genres and disciplines to monitor or delineate the legitimate field of their own reception. An ethically responsible discourse, I will contend, is one which frames itself securely in the realms of the cognitive or the aesthetic. This concern with reception, I will insist, is an ethical issue which centres on the dangers of a discursive *telos* being (mis)translated onto the plane of history, 'ethics' here being addressed only under the aspect of textual ethics.[4] In the first instance this demonstration involves registering the quarrel between philosophy and poetry in terms of an ethics of discursive reception.

1. Aesthetic

In so far as literary criticism begins with Plato, it begins in a spirit of antagonism toward literature.[5] The predominantly oral culture of poetry had relied on memorization and performance to keep the Homeric tradition alive in the collective consciousness.[6] Both the performing rhapsode and his audience would strive to become one with the world evoked by the poem—a species of identification exactly the reverse of that activity which we call literary criticism, an activity which typically involves standing back from the poem, judging it as an event external to its performance. The first concerted attempt at this objective questioning of the literary work occurs in Plato's dialogues. When Plato recalls his master in the *Apology* it is as that radical who asked the so-called men of wisdom what they understood by wisdom. It is also as that primordial literary theorist who asked the poets what they meant by their poems, who called for a rational agent to step out from the world

---

[4] The scope of this essay does not allow for a discussion of ethics *qua* ethics. On contemporary philosophical ethics, see Bernard Williams, *Ethics and the Limit of Philosophy* (London: Fontana, 1985). On 'textual ethics', a lively account is given in Jay Bernstein, *The New Constellation: The Ethical-Political Horizons of Modernity/ Postmodernity* (Cambridge: Polity Press, 1991).

[5] Cf. *Republic*, bks. 2, 3, 10.

[6] For a brilliant but highly speculative account of the oral culture of Greek poetry, see Eric A. Havelock, *Preface to Plato* (Cambridge, Mass.: Belknap Press of Harvard UP, 1963).

of poetic identification. Socrates was disappointed in his assumption that the authors of these works might provide a rational account of their work:

> It is hardly an exaggeration to say that any of the bystanders could have explained those poems better than their actual authors . . . I decided that it was not wisdom that enabled them to write their poetry, but a kind of instinct or inspiration, such as you find in seers and prophets who deliver all their sublime messages without knowing in the least what they mean. (*Apology* 22b–c)

Plato's Socrates confronts discourses with departed, unknown, or intellectually deficient agents. Whether memorized or inscribed, poetic works proliferate in society without a responsible subject who will answer for their shortcomings, explain ambiguities, and guard against abuse of their cultural authority.

This anxiety is also apparent in the *Ion* where Socrates looks to the rhapsodes for an explanation of poetic meaning. Most famous for its celebration of the poet as possessed by a divine madness, the *Ion* is seen to contradict Plato's banishment of the poets in the *Republic*. The romantic reading sees this contradiction as issuing from an unconscious competition between the poet and philosopher in the Platonic psyche: another reading will neutralize the contradiction by seeing Socrates' praise of the poet as ironic. Both readings, however, deny that the poet has any conscious control or interpretative provenance over the work. Whichever way the dialogue is taken, philosophy's claim to be the best judge of poetic meaning is reinforced: the way is thereby paved for the *Republic*'s gesture of banishment. In the *Ion*, Socrates does not confront the poet but the bearer of his posthumous word, the rhapsode. Ion lectures on Homer in addition to performing from the *Iliad* and the *Odyssey*, but he shows himself powerless to answer questions, to reconstitute intention, even to offer plausible interpretations of passages from Homer. The discourse entrusted to the rhapsodes is thus unprotected, open to all order of rhetorical abuse, prey to fall into any hands, to reappear on any tongue: the rhapsodes themselves are pseudo-authorities, men without the wisdom to counter (mis)appropriation of poetic content. The argument is clearly not intended as any criticism of Homer: here, as elsewhere, an anxious debt of influence and admiration is acknowledged (cf. *Republic* 10. 595c). Nor is Socrates' target Ion himself, but the absence of a tradition, of an heir who could safeguard the Homeric inheritance against misreading. In choosing as Socrates'

interlocutor one of the finest rhapsodes—Ion has just won first prize
at Epidaurus—Plato seeks to show that the authorized legatees of the
Homeric *paideia* provide little or no defence against misappropriation. They are not villainous in themselves, but rather poor sentries at
the gates of tradition:

SOCRATES: From both the *Odyssey* and the *Iliad* I picked out for you the
passages belonging to the doctor, the diviner, and the fisherman; now you
likewise, since you are better versed than I in Homer, pick out for me the sort
of passages, Ion, that concern the rhapsode and the rhapsode's art, the
passages it befits the rhapsode, above all other men, to examine and to judge.
ION: *All* passages, Socrates, is what I say! (539d–e)

Naturally, the Socratic premiss is absurd when considered from an
aesthetic point of view: a poetry expert will judge precisely that
which is poetic in poetry rather than treat each line as a constative
statement. One would not, for example, seek out a veterinarian to
consult on a reading of Baudelaire's 'Les Chats', still less a geologist
to explain Malcolm Lowry's *Under the Volcano*. In the same spirit,
though in heavier tones, the *Republic* reduces the poem to prosaic
statement so as to separate out the aesthetic from the cognitive
(*Republic* 3. 393c–394b). Stripped of its tropes, the poetic 'argument' will no longer beguile, capture unwary travellers, or offer itself
to those who call its authority to their questionable ends. The reduction of the poetic to prose statement serves to separate aesthetic from
cognitive and reveals the insufficiency of poetry as an ethical guide.

These strategies will seem absurd and insensitive to us today, yet
our response is precisely a measure of their success. The more ridiculous the idea of reducing a poem to a prose statement sounds to us,
the more sure we can be that the poetic has been distanced from the
constative. In a society which had not arrived at even the provisional
Kantian separation of the cognitive, ethical, and aesthetic realms, the
Iliad and the *Odyssey* were taken not only as (Arnoldian) touchstones
but as discourses of unquestionable truth and guides to everyday
action. Faced with a culture in which Sophocles was elected a general
because people were so impressed by his *Antigone*, Plato's mission to
separate the cognitive from the poetic acquires a validity and urgency
quite alien to our own sense of the relations between literature and
cognitive knowledge. One need only imagine a contemporary situation in which Pound's *Cantos* had become the dominant educational
resource of the twentieth century to find some sympathy with this

Socratic/Platonic anxiety. Plato was not the first to criticize the hold
of the poets over Greek consciousness: both Heraclitus and Xeno-
phanes (though a poet himself) had challenged the concept of poetic
authority. But Plato's extensive concern with the effect of poetry on its
audience, its potential contribution to the spread of false wisdom,
reveals an ultra-civilized determination to treat discourse as an ethical act of the sternest significance. The Socratic practice of asking the
poets what they meant—of demanding an alternative syntax—
amounts to enjoining the poet not only to be a reader, a literary
critic of his or her own work, but also to take ethical responsibility
for that work. In this regard, the Socratic interrogation constitutes a
clear demand that poets sign their texts in the full sense of signing for
the future, for misreading, for unintended meaning. Only by separating out the personality of the poet from the content of the poem, by
enforcing a critically reflective distance between person and poem,
can Plato ensure that the artificer takes as much responsibility for the
artifice as a parent for its child. Furthermore, we can see how the
practice of dialogue serves this ethical aim. The method of question
and answer *in the presence of the speaker or author of the text* is
necessary to ensure that context is perpetually reanimated and expli-
cated anew. Eluding the fixities of poetic or scribal words, dialectical
logoi seek to ensure that discourse cannot proceed from ear or eye to
the psyche without understanding having been achieved. In this way
alone can we have the assurance that discourse is an ethically responsible act rather than a dangerous abandonment.

   This ethical concern connects with the critique of writing in the
Phaedrus. Here Plato addresses the afterlife of a written work, the
problems that writing poses to the future by travelling without a fixed
destination, by exceeding the field in which an author can oversee its
reception. Although poetry is not specified in the main argument,
there are clear connections between Plato's distrust of the poets and
his distrust of written discourses in general. Written words are mute
like paintings; when you ask a question of them, they do no more
than repeat themselves (*Phaedrus* 275d). Of poetry, the *Protagoras*
complains: '[n]o one can interrogate poets about what they say'
(347e). Writing is ethically troublesome in the same manner as
poetry. In the *Apology*, Socrates says of the poets he has questioned:
'the very fact that they were poets made them think that they had a
perfect understanding of all other subjects, of which they were totally
ignorant' (22b–c). In its myth of writing as a divine gift refused, the
Phaedrus puts writing in the same case:

it is no true wisdom that you offer your disciples, but only its semblance (*doxan*), for by telling them of many things without teaching them you will make them seem to know much, while for the most part they know nothing, and as men filled, not with wisdom (*anti sophōn*), but with the conceit of wisdom (*doxosophoi*), they will be a burden to their fellows. (275a–b)

In a culture of writing, texts will fall into the hands of the ill-befitted without benefit of a teacher's wisdom or the tutelary presence of their authors. The concern is clearly ethical in that the spread of false wisdom will have a malign effect on social order. Where the speech situation allows the dialectician to monitor the reception of his discourse, writing

drifts all over the place, getting into the hands not only of those who understand it, but equally of those who have no business with it; it doesn't know how to address the right people, and not address the wrong. And when it is ill-treated and unfairly abused it always needs its parent (*patros*) to come to its help, being unable to defend or help itself. (*Phaedrus* 275e)

The scruple itself is simple and severe. Whereas an oral teacher can distinguish those who can benefit from a discourse without abusing its terms, a written text has no power of selection over who receives its words. The written word can mutiny against its subject's intentions. Like poetry, writing is defenceless before misreading: it is incapable of discriminating between those who understand (*tois epaïousin*) and those who do not. The *Phaedrus* thus militates against writing in what would seem to be a universal manner.

However, Plato's discourse is in some contradiction with itself. First, the *Phaedrus* is a written document and the arguments are therefore implicated in a self-referential paradox.[7] Secondly, no sooner than insisting on the self-presence of speaker to discourse, Socrates describes 'legitimate' speech as that which 'goes together with knowledge, and is written on the soul of the learner (*hos met' epistēmēs graphetai en tēi tou manthanontos psuchēi*), that can defend itself, and knows to whom it should speak and to whom it should say nothing' (*Phaedrus* 276a). How can the presence of the parent or author be absolutely essential (at 275e), while certain discourses can flourish without their subject, defend or help themselves just as well as their author (at 276a)? Within the *Phaedrus*,

---

[7] On the self-referential paradox of writing against writing, see Mary Margaret Mackenzie, 'Paradox in Plato's *Phaedrus*', *Proceedings of the Cambridge Philological Society*. NS 28 (1982), 64–76.

insulation is provided by the speech situation, by ensuring that speaker and audience occupy the same place in space and time. However, for the *Phaedrus* itself, which is a written text, the situation is different. How does the text or its author propose to appeal to its suitable readers and to repel its unsuitable readers? Having castigated poetry and written discourses for a failure to legislate for their reception, how is dialectic to answer these charges when they are turned on itself? Socrates says on the next page:

> The dialectician selects a soul of the right type, and in it he plants and sows his words founded on knowledge, words which can defend (*boēthein*) both themselves and him who planted them, words which instead of remaining barren contain a seed whence new words grow up in new characters (*en allois ēthesi*), whereby the seed is vouchsafed immortality. (*Phaedrus* 276e–277a)

This statement is close to claiming a priori status for dialectical judgements. Unlike poetic or sophistic productions, the truth of a properly philosophical discourse can be entrusted to the future. Its *logoi* can be maintained and added to (in new characters), just as a truly gifted pupil in logic or mathematics will extend logical inferences from the axioms of his teacher or precursor. In placing dialectical philosophy on the side of scientific discourse, the *Phaedrus* might be seen to continue Plato's agon with the poets in the *Republic* as also with the sophists. Once again poetry and sophistry would be characterized as lower-order discourses, this time in terms of their inability to help themselves, their dependence on a source or agent.

However, Socrates' claim that dialectical judgements possess apodeictic certainty raises more problems than it solves for the status of the Platonic philosophy. Whereas one can envisage a set of mathematical axioms travelling through history with a degree of security, to make such a claim for a body of philosophical work would seem overly optimistic. The work of a pure science such as that achieved by Euclid might surrender its axioms to the future without risk of significant distortion. How, on the other hand, might a text or tradition such as dialectic avoid the fate of misreading? To address this question we must consider the model of scientific agency and ask how—as a discourse stranded between *muthos* and *logos*, sophistics and science—dialectical philosophy measures up against its own model of impersonal knowledge.

2. Cognitive

No method which embraces the ideal of scientificity will affirm the concept of an author. Whereas an authority has achieved mastery over a certain field, an author is thought to have generated a field. The goals of science cannot be created but wait innocently to be discovered much as America awaited Columbus. Plato's dialogues repeatedly assert the requisite impersonality of knowledge. The *Symposium* affirms that whilst one may counter Socrates, the truth is beyond contest: 'It's the truth you find unanswerable, not Socrates,' the master declares to Agathon (201c). Similarly the *Charmides* insists: 'the point is not who said the words, but whether they are true or not' (161c).[8]

Plato aimed *toward* this scientific model of truth, and yet was always aware of the ethical dangers of abandoning that work to sophistic plundering. Unlike pure mathematics, the discipline of dialectical reasoning cannot walk abroad freely in the knowledge that its axioms will assimilate to the very discipline it strives to institute. Lacking the precision of a pure science, it finds itself bound not only to a speaker, a spokesman, an accredited adept in its methods, but also to a small school of auditors judiciously selected and educated. Without such attendance, the discipline lacks inherent means of distinguishing between its proper and improper uses. Dialectic cannot attain scientificity because the uses made of its own elements are not governed by the systematic interplay of those very elements. Although the philosopher may be raised to the apprehension of intuitively given truths such as those of the *eidos*, or the a priori knowledge attainable through geometry, the statements of dialectic itself are not shielded by the principles of coherence and compulsory agreement sought in Euclidean geometry, Aristotle's syllogisms, or the axiomatic structure of the Cartesian 'regulae'. Following Parmenides, Plato himself accepts that mathematical entities alone possess the immutable intelligibility required by the objects of a true science. Whilst dialectic and geometry are both concerned with the 'eternally existent' (*Republic* 7. 527b), the dialectical work that outlives its author will always be ethically portentous but epistemologically ambiguous: that is, dangerous, open to ethical misinterpretation, misappropriation.

[8] See also *Republic* 1. 336a.

208 SEÁN BURKE

In many ways the anxieties expressed in the *Phaedrus* concerning dialectical legacy centre on that curious discursive property that we now refer to as iterability. If we take iterability to denote 'that ability of locutions to be separated from the intentional context that gave them birth [whereby] each repetition is inevitably a rebirth, a rejuvenation, sucking in the life juices of other contexts and other intentions',[9] then it is clear that philosophical statements (those of formal logic aside), those of the human sciences or dialectic, are always and everywhere prone to drift out of context. Mathematical formulae, on the other hand, do not lend themselves to restatement outside the system, nor do they need to be restored to a framework of original intention. Intention is far from being a compelling category in mathematical science: the very attempt at a proof establishes an operative intention and the success or failure of the proof determines whether that intention has been achieved. Intelligibility rather than intention provides the context of a mathematical statement and insulates it from iterability. Divorced from context, a mathematical lemma resists appropriation in a heterogeneous series of statements or axioms.[10] Responsible reception occurs within the very disciplinary parameters themselves and independently of *œuvre* effects, detailed statements of intention, history, or surrounding discourses.

In his *Sophistical Refutations*, Aristotle was to register the insufficiency of dialectical method as science. He does so in a critique which adduces iterability in everything but name. Comparing mispractice in dialectical argument and geometrical demonstration, Aristotle observes:

The contentious argument stands in somewhat the same relation to the dialectical as the drawer of false diagrams to the geometrician; for it beguiles by misreasoning from the same principles as dialectic uses, just as the drawer of a false diagram beguiles the geometrician. But whereas the latter is not a contentious reasoner, because he bases his false diagram on the principles and conclusions that fall under the art of geometry, the argument which is

---

[9] Zygmunt Bauman, *Postmodern Ethics* (Oxford: Blackwell, 1993), 102.
[10] While pure mathematics does indeed offer itself to ethical misapplication if its formulae are used for reprehensible ends, it is never open to ethical misreading or expropriation *per se*. This is a matter of both disciplinary boundaries and orders of discourse: the languages of pure mathematics and the languages of the ethico-political are absolutely incommensurable.

subordinate to the principles of dialectic will yet clearly be contentious as regards other subjects.[11]

This overspill, the excess of the iterable, constitutes an ethical threat which the making of a false diagram could never pose to society. Being immune from translation into other contexts, geometrical science is incapable of infecting adjacent orders of discourse, of finding its statements reconstituted in any other syntax or system. Dialectical discourse, on the contrary, carries with it the potential for generating ethically pernicious statements, extrapolations that are foreign to its *ethos* but not to its syntax.

Secondly, there is the related danger that the absence of intrinsic disciplinary parameters will allow irresponsible, amateurish, or sophistic imitators to practise the interrogatory method. Plato is himself repeatedly alert to the danger of ill-willed attempts to utilize the resources of dialectical philosophy. But once again, competence and incompetence in the discipline is not made apparent by the discipline itself. Incompetent mathematical reasoning will reveal itself as the failure to produce intelligible proofs, even as the failure to make mathematical propositions: ethical or dogmatic distortions of philosophical statements, on the other hand, will retain the appearance of statements.

The absence of such disciplinary parameters impels Plato to the establishment of extramural parameters: legacy, constraints on circulation, and the formation of an Academy take the place of disciplinary autonomy. The risk of misprision is at the very heart of Platonic rationalism, in its statements, its 'system', its methods, and ethos: 'all great things are precarious' (*Republic* 6. 497d), Socrates declares of dialectic. In *Republic* 7, having approved mathematics and geometry as requisite objects of learning, Socrates will be altogether more circumspect when admitting pupils to the study of dialectic for fear that unsuitable souls will discredit 'the whole business of philosophy' (*Republic* 539c).

Because dialectic does not possess the intrinsic resources to distinguish between the proper and improper uses to which it is put, legacy must be ensured by the presence of the dialectical master, by an institution which ensures responsible succession. At a crossroads which we will see re-encountered by Marxism and Freudianism in the preoccupation of their founders with forming and presiding over

---

[11] Aristotle, *De Sophisticis Elenchis*, trans. W. A. Pickard-Cambridge in *The Works of Aristotle*, ed. W. D. Ross, vol. i (Oxford: Clarendon Press, 1928), 171^{b}35–172^{a}2.

legacies, it is the very insecurity of dialectic as science which dictates that the parent of a discourse be always at hand, keep watch over its effects in a protective, rescuing proximity. Whilst work in a science, in particular mathematics, passes not so much into its author's corpus as into the space, the axiomatic reserve of the discipline itself, discourses such as Marxism and Freudianism must draw a line and a structure of inheritance on the basis of the *œuvre*. A science will not need an institution in the sense that the First International, or Plato's Academy, were institutions, since the discipline self-regulates to a far greater extent: for this reason we might wish to distinguish the idea of a scientific community (which refers back to the principles of the discipline) from that of an interpretative institution (which takes its bearings from the overall distribution of forces within the *œuvre*). Having insisted on agency to draw a culture of poetic identification into a *polis* dominated by rational subjectivity, Plato's discourse yet failed to establish itself on the disciplinary model by which a science might prescribe what is true and untrue of itself. Which is another way of saying that dialectic itself is also in the place of that defenceless writing, that discourse in need of its parent to come to the rescue.

Plato evolved the most sophisticated account of discursive ethics that we have as reference, even today. On the other hand, he transgresses the terms of his ethic by the very fact that the *Phaedrus* is a written work, a work which *eo ipso* takes its chances with uncertain destination, with unsuitable readings. The Platonic philosophy is thereby summoned to its own tribunal, as a dangerous instance of the general dangers of writing. Homer has not had a more dangerous effect upon society than Plato, no more than the *Iliad* or the *Odyssey* have affected the political organization of society in anything like the manner of Plato's *Republic*. Certainly, no one would claim that Plato's text managed to distinguish between its suitable and unsuitable readers. We might here hold Plato both 'irresponsible' and 'responsible', terms which are interchangeable in any mature ethics. That his *Republic* should have provided the blueprint for every subsequent projection of an idealized order onto the plane of history was doubtless an accident that he could never have foreseen. In his view of writing as blind consignment, however, he self-condemns by taking the wager, but letting loose his *logoi* in the knowledge of their uncertain destination, in the knowledge that no text could defend itself against unsuitable readers.

What then protected Homer, Aeschylus, Sophocles, and Euripides

THE AESTHETIC, COGNITIVE, AND ETHICAL   211

from the dangers of socially constructive misreading? What jeopardized Plato? What has made a certain mode of philosophy so open to misreading, to misapplication? Why should it be that the discourse and discipline that banished the poets on the grounds of their dangerous effects on society should have shown itself altogether more dangerous than poetry?

3. Ethical[12]

This question can be answered in terms of textual frames, of a work's capacity to prescribe the boundaries of its own legitimate influence. It is also a question of the frames provided by the distinction between *muthos* and *logos* and of the dangers of mixed discourses which combine aesthetic strategies with seemingly scientific assertions. Plato succeeded in showing how poetry should not be taken as a discourse of truth, but he could not foresee the extent to which philosophy would covertly appropriate literary devices in the propagation of deterministic theories of history. Although Socrates referred to the Ideal State as a 'city in words', the *Republic* does not insist on its fictional frames in anything like the manner of More's *Utopia*, or Morris's *News from Nowhere*, nor does the dialogue discourage the idea that its vision might be realized on the plane of human history. Plato thus prefigured the realm in which speculative philosophy would unfold, and yet provided the most systematic exposition of the dangers of utilizing aesthetic strategies toward cognitive ends. In this sense Karl Popper is *partly* correct in linking Platonic dialectic and the dialectical philosophies of Hegel and Marx, but egregiously one-sided in neglecting Plato's insistence on responsible legacy and the principle of dialogue.[13] What 'dialogue' there is in the Hegelian or Marxist systems occurs only within the system itself. The movement from thesis to antithesis may mimic a dialogue within history, but the very idea of historical inevitability is monologic in denying people the right to be in dialogue with the history in which they live.

Furthermore, speculative philosophy developed in the wake of

---

[12] Parts of the following section are indebted to the work of Hans Vaihinger and Frank Kermode (as cited below).

[13] See Karl Popper, *The Open Society and its Enemies*, i: *The Spell of Plato*, ii: *The High Tide of Prophecy: Hegel, Marx, and the Aftermath* (London: Routledge & Kegan Paul, 1945).

religious belief as a culturally unifying force. Mobilized by a newly secularized *telos*, philosophy is now borne on the back of a history whose course the speculative text partly directs. Quasi-religious providentialism is disguised as scientific process: thus the socialism of Marx and Engels will cover over its own fictionality by claiming scientific status for the narrative of conflict and resolution by which its utopian ends were to be achieved. This simultaneous deployment and occultation of aesthetic devices allows speculative philosophy to exceed the frames imposed by philosophical discipline: latent appeals to mythic and redemptive patterns of history extend the influence of nineteenth-century dialectic beyond its texts. Attempting to master the very fabric of a history which it can at best study, speculative philosophy further advances its influence through insupportable and self-aggrandizing dicta which tell us that the point of philosophy is not to interpret but to change the world, or that the rational is the real. Reflection on history is construed as historical substance; mentalistic events are confused with physical events; concepts mistake themselves for the concrete. An instrument for *approaching* history presumes to determine historical reality. It is as if the map of a river's course were to alter the course of that river itself. The boundaries that separate the fictional and the cognitive are breached as the text of speculative philosophy writes itself as the future.

We have seen how the work of pure mathematics exists within clear disciplinary parameters. Critical philosophy of the kind practised in the Anglo-American tradition also insulates itself against spectacular misreading: in these instances we encounter cognitive discourses without negative ethical overspill. Might we make any such case for the literature of modernity, in particular for the status of poetry in our world? The movement toward self-consciousness in poetry, pronounced since at least the Romantic era, can be read as retreat of the work from its world. However, such an inward turn also defends poetry against misreading as dogma or constructive myth. As Vaihinger has argued, a poem will insist on a hypothetical frame, on the fact that it is articulated 'as if . . .'.[14] Yet the poem inhabits conditionality perpetually rather than provisionally: unlike the scientific hypothesis, it never aspires to shuffle off the hypothetical frame.

[14] Hans Vaihinger, *The Philosophy of As If: A System of the Theoretical, Practical and Religious Fictions of Mankind*, trans. C. K. Ogden (London: Routledge & Kegan Paul, 1924).

A hypothesis wishes to become a demonstrable truth; a poem dreams only of being a poem. As Wallace Stevens writes in 'An Ordinary Evening in New Haven': 'The poem is the cry of its occasion, | Part of the res itself and not about it'.[15] Self-conscious uses of aesthetic strategies, the reminder to the reader that what is being read exists within the realm of the imagined, the capacity of literature to be in dialogue with itself—all these metafictional cues do the serious work of reminding us that literary events are not to be construed as imperatives in the broader ethical realm. This is not naively to build up a forcefield between the poetic and the real, the fictive and the lived, but to commend the sense of ethical responsibility assumed in a poem drawing attention to its existence *qua* poem, a novel reminding us of its status as novel. The framing 'what would it be like if . . .' is sanctified by the modern poet, just as it is suppressed by the speculative philosopher. In 'Of Modern Poetry', Wallace Stevens tells us that the modern poem:

> has
> To construct a new stage. It has to be on that stage
> And, like an insatiable actor, slowly and
> With meditation, speak words that in the ear,
> In the delicatest ear of the mind, repeat,
> Exactly, that which it wants to hear.[16]

This insistence on poetry finding its own realm is not an evasion of responsibility: it resists the solidification of the work into dogma or myth, prevents it from invading the political order. On this stage, the aesthetic contains all mutinies within itself. The poetry of Keats, for example, is altogether enriched by the treacheries of his language: these treacheries feed back into the enclosed labyrinth of the work. Nor again is this to deny the power of literature to allow us to reflect critically on ethical issues: indeed, as Martha Nussbaum might argue, the novel provides a splendid forum for the consideration of social, moral, and ethical dilemmas,[17] but does so within the splendidly elaborate yet consequence-free setting of a hypothetical situation. Similarly, a Balzac or a Dickens invites us to pass judgement on a significant moment in history but in novels which seek to understand

---

[15] Wallace Stevens, *Collected Poems* (London: Faber & Faber, 1955), 473.
[16] Ibid. 240.
[17] See Martha C. Nussbaum, *Love's Knowledge: Essays on Philosophy and Literature* (New York: Oxford UP, 1990).

rather than to drive history. These containments seem essential if we are not to allow fictions to masquerade as truth, to become myths which people refuse to recognize as myths. As Frank Kermode reminds us: 'If we forget that fictions are fictive we regress to myth . . . "making human sense" is something that literature achieves only so long as we remember the status of fictions.'[18] Kermode also goes on to say: 'World history, the imposition of a plot on time, is a substitute for myth.'[19] Anticipating by a long time Lyotard's call for a war on totality, Karl Popper too teaches us that History is an unjustifiable abstraction from the many and real histories that people live through. The genius of literature is to remind us of these resonant singularities even as speculative philosophy worked to deprive thought of this meagre but invaluable knowledge.

The same critical eye which resists totalizations is today most acutely trained on the claims of contemporary science. No doubt scientific investigation can and should continue to develop on objective lines; but it can and must submit to both epistemological scepticism and ethical scrutiny. This is not to say that scientific work should be limited, only that discoveries should be passed through a tribunal similar to the one which the Socratic-Platonic philosophy hoped to make of itself some 2,500 years ago. As that philosophy said, in words that would have enormous relevance to contemporary debates in the ethics of science:

when they have captured what they hunted . . . huntsmen and fishermen hand over to the cooks. Geometers and astronomers and calculators—for these are a sort of hunters too, since they are not mere makers of diagrams, but they try to find out the real meanings—so because they do not know how to use them, but only how to hunt, they hand over their discoveries, I take it, to the dialecticians to use up, at least all of them hand over who are not quite without sense. (*Euthydemus*, 290c)

The twentieth century affords us grotesque examples of the inadequacy of politicians or law-makers to intervene or arbitrate in the uses to which scientific discoveries are put. In Plato's scheme, the scientist would not be charged with responsibility as an ethical being, but neither would scientific discovery be independent of ethical judgement. That judgement would be provided not by those with an interest in political expediency, but by the dialectician or philosopher:

[18] Frank Kermode, *The Sense of an Ending: Studies in the Theory of Fiction* (London: Oxford UP, 1966), 41.   [19] Ibid. 43.

all products of science, like those of discourse, would then be subject to philosophical and ethical interrogation before being allowed to circulate as discoveries in society at large. Here again we arrive at a model of criticism in the most strenuous sense—criticism as a regulative rather than constitutive practice, as an interrogatory activity governed by ethical considerations.

As we see in this collection of essays, as we see all around us, there is once again a crisis in our distinctions between the realms of the aesthetic, cognitive, and the ethical. We have witnessed the aestheticization of science in this century; we have also encountered the doomed project to make a science of the aesthetic; we have seen the lethal consequences of aestheticizing the political. If we are witnessing an upheaval in epistemological categories, and should knowledge become answerable to any of these three categories, then it must be the ethical that is established as the highest tribunal. And for us, as for Socrates, there is no other forum for an ethics of discourse than that of dialogue or multilogue. We can never fully recapture the culture of spoken discourse, but criticism provides its closest approximation. Criticism dialogizes, it forces the work to keep answering for itself, enacts across temporal chasms what spoken dialogue achieved in the animate present. It supplements the mortality of the author and finds its own unique way of eliciting responses from the changeless form of the written. While criticism produces misreadings of its own, it also produces challenges to those misreadings in a continuous exchange which defends the text from ossification within one particular structure of misreading. It enacts its own *ekphrasis* by generating movement in the static object that is a sequence of written words.

Perhaps this is why criticism in its gentlest, its most gentlepersonly form, manifests itself as literary criticism because great works of art are always already in critical discussion with themselves: the experience, for example, of reading one of Keats's great odes is that the poetic movement undoes itself as dogma, subsumes every seemingly constative statement in an endless spiral of reflection. Following that experience, opening it up to new readers, allowing the poem to 'speak to the delicatest ear of the mind', is the very fine business of the literary critic. Something else again is asked of the philosophical critic: the philosopher-critic is called to challenge every truth-claim she encounters. It is her no less august calling to ask: 'what does that mean?'; 'how can you claim X when Y has been asssumed?'; it is her duty to carry forward the relentless task of refutation begun by Plato's Socrates, to work toward a society in which nothing can be claimed until everything has been asked. Hopefully criticism can continue to develop upon the dialogic principle which Plato visibly enshrined *within* his work.

Criticism derives etymologically from 'crisis'. This alerts us to its enduring function, for the deep structures of our ethical contracts only manifest themselves with clarity during times of crisis. Our era faces crises in knowledge which only ethical discourse seems capable of addressing. In a theocratic or properly monarchic society, the realms of the aesthetic and cognitive and ethical were subject to the constraints of power. With the demise of such cultural authority, the ethical asserts its independent claim upon thought. Perhaps this is what Kant envisaged some two centuries ago when he declared that of pure reason, aesthetic judgement, and practical reason, the latter deserves first rank in our thought. Criticism interposes practical reason between the claims of the aesthetic and the cognitive. As activity, it does not derive from an impulse to create but from an impulse to intervene between a text and its reception. If we were to seek the source of this interventionist imperative we would not find it in the aesthetic or cognitive realms. For these reasons, criticism is neither an art nor a science but an ethical realm and a realm of the ethical.

12

Literature and the Crisis in the Concept of the University

TIMOTHY CLARK

1. Introduction

In the summer of 1995 an article in the *TLS* by Daniel Dennett opened with an observation he had made during a recent visit to Oxford: that when he was there in the 1960s he felt that it was a university whose ethos and sense of purpose came from academics and they employed others to administer them. Now, his impression was that, in conformity to a model already long apparent in the USA, they were working for the administration. Yet, he adds, where can any idea of the university reside if not in its academics?[1] This is part of the situation the late Bill Readings has in mind in his polemical book *The University in Ruins*.[2] This claim is not novel. A. H. Halsey's *The Decline of Donnish Dominion* argues that academics are in the process of becoming a new form of proletariat: that is, workers whose labour is owned by others.[3]

This is a common complaint. However, Readings's book is not the lament of a member of an élite looking back to some dubious cultural ideal and blaming the government or so-called postmodernists for spoiling it all. His book considers the profound changes that are befalling the university at a time that is seeing economic integration on a global scale, the universal triumph of free-market capitalism, and the decline of the nation-state. The end of the old university

---

[1] 'Our Vegetative Soul: The Search for a Reliable Model of the Human Self', *TLS* (25 Aug. 1995), 3–4 (p. 3).
[2] *The University in Ruins* (Cambridge, Mass: Harvard UP, 1996).
[3] *The Decline of Donnish Dominion: The British Academic Profession in the Twentieth Century* (Oxford: Clarendon Press, 1992), 124–5.

should be seen as an opportunity. His optimism is forced but contagious. Readings finally attempts to transvalue the crisis in the university, 'rethinking the categories that have governed intellectual life for over two hundred years' (p. 169).

My essay applies some of Readings's arguments to the issue of the uniquely problematic relation between the university and the discipline calling itself 'English'. English has always had a peculiar and troubled place in the university. 'Literary Criticism' was institutionalized in the nineteenth century as the object of an attempt to fit a practice of writing previously confined mainly to journalism and belles-lettres to a model of research with a defensible place in the modern research university.

My thesis is that many of the debates going on within the walls of English departments, about the canon, the authority of tradition, the nature of interpretation, and so on, are unsolvable because they are not questions that can be formulated and addressed within defined disciplinary boundaries (the way, for instance, that a proof of Fermat's last theorem is a task that belongs safely to the mathematicians). Many major questions in literary studies cannot be solved *in* literary studies, but immediately involve other fields, such as history or sociology, the cultural mission of the humanities, and an 'idea of the university'.

It might be objected that this situation is not peculiar to literary studies. Take the example of the kind of problems that arise in genetics: how much choice should parents have as to the characteristics of their child, should this be limited to screening for serious disease or disability, or can they choose its sex or disposition? Yet these ethical questions, it could be answered, are not inherent in the status of genetics as a science: they do not inhabit its axioms or procedures of experiment. In literary studies it is clearly different: ethical judgements are inherent in the very designation of something *as literature*, as a work of cultural value. The diabolical question 'what is literature?', if it is to have an answer with proper academic credentials, sends us to fields as diverse as history, psychology, aesthetics, ethics, sociology, semiotics, psychoanalysis, anthropology, and so on. Literary studies is, in its very constitution, a field whose object embraces issues that transcend the competence of any one discipline: like an unfigurable topology of a greater space contained in a smaller. 'English', I think, has been less an academic discipline in itself than an unstable and valuable place of intersection and con-

testation between various other disciplines, as well as debates outside
the university. This volatile status is apparent in the way questions in English, by
transgressing the possibility of academic compartmentalization, cannot but raise questions about the university as a whole. The debate
about the canon is the most obvious instance of this. It is an issue that
is often posed in terms that look, superficially, as if they can be
contained within the limits of recognized areas of expertise, as being,
for example, about the nature of the novel, the merits of Dickens as
compared to Mary E. Braddon, the autonomy or otherwise of
aesthetic value, and so forth. Let us focus on the contention that
the canon serves to reproduce unjust or unrepresentative forms of
cultural authority. It is a debate that will never be solved in English
departments because it is ultimately, surely, a debate about the nature,
function, and authority of the university, and about university access.
The problem is that it is no longer certain *who* the university is
responsible for and to whom it is responsible. 'The question is, of
course, what and whose history, community, knowledge, and voice
prevails?'[4]

The vitality of literary criticism in raising questions of this kind
has recently been intense. This is manifest in the virulence of the
so-called 'PC' wars in the USA. What is called the crisis in English
might be taken as a direct ratio of its health, its transcendence of
being a merely academic subject, as, say, analytic philosophy might
now be described. Criticism has never performed so vigorously
Matthew Arnold's prescription, 'to turn a stream of fresh and
free thought upon our stock notions and habits'.[5] The study of
literature has been a space in which major debates about cultural
values, about multiculturalism, the status of women, have first been
heard in our culture. Literary study is not only the site for the
detailed study and analysis of literary works: it is simultaneously a
place in which the kinds of language a culture uses about itself are
continually up for reconfirmation or revision. It is a space in which
our culture—or cultures—attempt to define what they are or might

---

[4] Henry A. Giroux, 'Liberal Arts Education and the Struggle for Public Life:
Dreaming about Democracy', *South Atlantic Quarterly*, 89/1 (1990) ('The Politics
of Liberal Education'), 112–38 (p. 115).
[5] As quoted and reaffirmed by Richard Hoggart, *The Way We Live Now* (London:
Pimlico, 1995), 90.

be through a reconsideration of what they have been in texts that still seem to challenge our closest reading, and resist interpretation. It is this function of criticism—criticism as continual critique— that is now at risk as a result of the changes besetting the modern university, both within and without.

2. *Professional Oblivion*

Until recently, general discussion of the concept of the university was rare among academics. It has been as if the institution itself somehow produced a forgetting of the issues closest to those people within it. This structural oblivion could be related to the professionalization of intellectual life. The term 'professional' seems to go without saying as its own commendation. And of course all of us in universities take pride in being 'professional' in our work, either as academics, students, or administrators. However, the concept of the professional may be double-edged. Samuel Weber has studied the emergence of the notion of the professional in the nineteenth century, how it provided the middle classes with a category for organizing and regulating their affairs and their power.[6] The rise of the university is also bound up with the emergence of the professions in their modern form. It still serves to regulate the passage of young people from the family to a profession. The problem that bothers Weber concerns the transformation of intellectual life that befalls the university when it is itself professionalized into a series of discrete departments and areas of expertise. The regulative idea of the '*professionalist paradigm of knowledge*' (p. 147) is the absolute autonomy of the individual discipline. Each discipline is construed as a self-contained 'field' of investigative procedures and knowledge held to be universally valid within the confines of its unproblematized space. Professionalism is vital to academic rigour, and the procedures which govern the rationality that maintains a discipline. It is also important to the maintenance of academic freedom: it ensures that, for example, only historians will judge the work of other historians. However, these virtues stand in a contradictory relation to some insidious effects. By conforming to the ideology of professionalism, expertise in a

---

[6] *Institution and Interpretation* (Minneapolis: University of Minnesota Press, 1987), 18–32.

particular field becomes cut off from broader intellectual life. 'Indeed, the very notion of academic "seriousness" came increasingly to exclude reflection upon the relation of one "field" to another' (p. 32). The disclaimer that such questions are 'not part of my field' is only the flip side of the vacuously pious claim to be pursuing an area of research for 'its own sake'. Both prop up the fiction of disciplinary autonomy and subserve the ideology of professionalism. The overall effect is that the question of the idea of the university as a whole is forgotten, except as a place to compete with other disciplines for students, space, or money. Professionalism seems to legitimize the individual field but at the cost of surrendering the university to an idea of administration. This leads to the absurd situation we have today in which nine out of ten academics, if asked to refer to any of the documents on which the idea of the modern research university is founded, cannot even name them, let alone discuss the issues.[7]

Yet the idea of the university is assumed in some form in every seminar, research paper, and administrative memorandum. A good example of our blindness to this might be read even in the term 'criticism' itself. As we all know, there are heated debates going on about the function of criticism, the problematic relations between knowledge and power. Claims are made that criticism is too 'politicized' or is not political enough, and so on. What does not seem to get said is that, in the practice of English departments, criticism is actually administered under another category, that of *research*. With this term all the fashionable questions about knowledge, power, and institutions are immediately at work, though not this time in ways we seem to be so eager to discuss. Another example is the discrepancy between the scrupulous attention to the minutiae of words and concepts within the institutions of criticism, and the crass jargon used in representing these activities to the public by the university administration. We have all seen such phrases as 'Investing in Excellence', 'A Quality Place', 'Making the Grade', and so on (this last one is especially ridiculous, suggesting a new paradigm of the academic as marine—the soldier, the slave as hero). What disturbs me about such corporate, hard-sell language is not just that it is banal, but that presuppositions about the nature of the university are being made, and generally imposed, without being discussed.

[7] See Aharon Aviram, 'The Nature of University Education Reconsidered', *Journal of the Philosophy of Education*, 26 (1992), 183–99 (p. 183).

3. A Romantic and Idealist Institution

Shelley wrote of modern European civilization: 'we are all Greek.' An academic, even a literary critic, must say 'we are all German', or even 'ich bin ein Berliner'.

It is surprising to find that the research university is not primarily a child of the Enlightenment but of German Romanticism and Idealism. A decisive event was, famously, the foundation of the University of Berlin in October 1810, according to the plans proposed by Wilhelm von Humboldt. Although he is the principal figure in the establishment of the university, his thinking simply gave official form to an idea of the university that had emerged in the 1790s, especially at the University of Jena, which Humboldt had attended from 1794 to 1797. The key texts for the idea of the modern research university are: Schiller's lecture at Jena in 1789,[8] Kant's *The Conflict of the Faculties* (1798),[9] Fichte's lectures on the duty of the scholar,[10] Schelling's lectures of 1803, again at the University of Jena,[11] and Friedrich Schleiermacher's proposals in 1808 for the University of Berlin.[12] Many arguments of these German founding texts are largely repeated in Cardinal Newman's *The Idea of a University* (and Karl

---

[8] 'Was heisst und zu welchem Ende studiert Man Universalgesichte', in *Sämtliche Werke*, 5 vols. (Munich: Carl Hanser, 1980), iv. 749–67. Useful general accounts can be found in Elinor S. Shaffer, 'Romantic Philosophy and the organisation of the Disciplines: The Founding of the Humboldt University of Berlin', in Andrew Cunningham and Nicholas Jardine (eds.), *Romanticism and the Sciences* (Cambridge: Cambridge UP, 1990), 38–54; Theodore Ziolokowksi, *German Romanticism and its Institutions* (Princeton: Princeton UP, 1990), 218–308. The founding documents for the University of Berlin are gathered in *Idee und Wirklichkeit einer Universität: Dokumente zur Geschichte der Friedrich-Wilhelms-Universität zu Berlin*, ed. Wilhelm Weischedel (Berlin: Walter De Gruyter, 1960). For an abridged English translation of von Humboldt's proposal see 'On the Spirit and the Organisational Framework of Intellectual Institutions in Berlin', *Minerva*, 8 (1970), 242–50.
[9] *The Conflict of the Faculties*, trans. Mary J. Gregor (Lincoln, Nebr.: University of Nebraska Press, 1979).
[10] 'Einige Vorlesungen über die Bestimmung des Gelehrten', in Johann Gottlieb Fichte, *Gesamtausgabe*, 4 parts (Stuttgart: Friedrich Fromann, 1964–78), I. iii. 3–68; 'Über das Wesen des Gelehrten', *Gesamtausgabe*, I. viii. 39–139; *Deduzierte Plan einer zu Berlin zu errichtenden höhern Lehranstalt* (1808), in *Die Idee der Deutschen Universität*, ed. Ernst Anrich (Darmstadt: Wissenschaftliche Buchgesellschaft, 1956), 127–217.
[11] *On University Studies*, trans. E. S. Morgan (Athens, Oh.: Ohio UP, 1961).
[12] *Gelegentliche Gedanken über Universitäten in deutschen Sinne* with an 'Anhang über eine neue zu errichtende Universität' (1808) in *Die Idee der Deutschen Universität*, 221–308.

Jaspers's work of almost the same title),[13] as well as in large sections of numerous official documents since. Although its German provenance is long forgotten, this idealistic model of the university as a centre of disinterested research and cultural legislation still lies behind many complaints that the university is betraying its mission. All of these German documents were responding in part to the questions raised by the French Revolution, and most of them were written during a time of warfare with Napoleon, or during the French occupation. The French Revolution had been an attempt to replace traditional, feudal structures of power with a republican state founded entirely on rational principles—instituted in accordance with a notion of politics as a science. The following question governs the foundation of the modern university: can a life of reason be institutionalized without becoming other to itself, as it manifestly had in France? Kant's *The Conflict of the Faculties* presents a model of the university as the institution in which reason gives itself its own law (which is still the crucial component of the idea of academic freedom). Although the university must be allowed to legislate in all matters of knowledge, it is subordinate in power to the state. The state, however, has a duty to protect the university from any abuse of power that would interfere with the autonomy of reason. Reason is instituted primarily in the so-called lower faculty of 'philosophy' (a term that would cover the humanities and natural sciences in today's language). The three so-called higher faculties—law, medicine, and theology—are primarily devoted to the training of a professional class in service to the state—lawyers, doctors, and clergy. Yet they are also expected to submit to the legislation of philosophy, of reason, in their own affairs. In this way, the university becomes the site for the peaceful diffusion of enlightenment throughout the state.

The Germans kept the old name of university for what was essentially a new Romantic/idealist institution. Three defining characteristics stand out. (*a*) First is the ideal of *Wissenschaft*. This cannot be translated by the modern English word 'science'. It means a fully grounded knowledge, unifying the disciplines, and articulated in a systematic form. It is not merely the compiled knowledge of the Enlightenment encyclopedia. Schiller's lecture had affirmed the place of the university as providing a midpoint (*Mittelpunkt*) from which

[13] John Henry Newman, *The Idea of a University* (Oxford: Clarendon Press, 1976); Karl Jaspers, *The Idea of the University*, ed. Karl Deutsch (London: Peter Owen, 1960).

the unity of all the disciplines can be grasped.[14] (*b*) Knowledge is not a static body of information but an organic process, one that involves the scholar and student in an ethical manner: the pursuit of *Wissenschaft* has redemptive qualities. A student earns a place in the system by personally working through the stages of the knowledge in a discipline. The organic, process-like nature of learning demands that the teacher be engaged in research. Later documents remain close to Schiller in stressing more than Kant the ideal of culture—of *Bildung*—as the defining purpose of the university. *Bildung* names the intellectual process whereby tradition and the life of the people are infused with the spirit of rational enquiry and grounded in an understanding of the unity of all knowledge. As a synthesis of custom and reason, the ideal of *Bildung* is partly a reaction against a radical, abstract, and Jacobin rationalism associated with the French wars and conquest. 'Culture', then, and often since, named a reformist notion of the gradual development of customs and forms of consciousness, the reconciliation of reason and history. (*c*) An opposition is made between the genuine scholar—defined by commitment to the previous two ideas—and the mere specialist or philistine, with their merely departmental or instrumentalist attitudes to knowledge. Schiller's lecture of 1789 makes a famous distinction between the genuine scholar and what he terms the *Brotgelehrte* ('Bread Scholar'), so called because his main concern is earning a crust and getting a qualification. This straw man reappears in various guises in all the other foundational documents. Of the philosophical spirit, however, we read: 'From early on he has convinced himself that in the realm of reason, as in the world of the senses, everything is related, and his vigorous drive for integration cannot content itself with fragments. All his strivings are directed towards the completion of his knowledge.'[15] The genuine scholar unites and redeems the fragments of mere *Brotwissenschaft*. Another distinguishing feature of the genuine scholar is openness to new discoveries. The poor *Brotgelehrte*, on the other hand, wants nothing less than to hear about some radical and exciting new development in his field just a week before exams.

The genuine scholar, in pursuing the aim of a total and unified knowledge, is simultaneously engaged in a process of self-cultivation that will render him a rare embodiment of unalienated humanity. The goal of the new University of Berlin, Fichte argued, should be to

---

[14] *Sämtliche Werke*, iv. 752–3.   [15] Ibid. 752.

produce 'scientific art' (*wissenschaftliche Kunst*), and 'the art of scientific understanding'—phrases that sound oxymoronic within the terms of the contemporary conflict of faculties in Anglophone universities.[16] Lecturing to the University of Erlangen in 1805 he affirmed that 'The concern for this uniform development of all human abilities presupposes the knowledge of [the scholar's] total abilities, the science of all his impulses and needs, the completed measure of his entire being.'[17] Conceptions of disinterested non-instrumentalist research are in effect not finally disinterested but essential to humanity's realization of its essence.

The university, then, legitimizes itself as the central institution in which the culture of the nation-state knows itself, grounds its historical customs and traditions in reason, and, thus grounded, develops them further. In doing so it also serves freedom, ennobling the human race by making it free from the compulsions of nature.

4. Three Relations between the Claims to Legitimacy of English and the University

Nowadays, there seems to be a pervasive lack of knowledge about issues which relate to the university as a whole and a striking lack of an adequate vocabulary whereby to discuss these things. The German idea of the university—as a place simultaneously for disinterested research, cultural legislation, and the realization of the human essence—rested on forms of idealist philosophy which are no longer an option for us, but its idealistic programme still pervades contemporary clichés. Nostalgia for the German idea of the university certainly seems to highlight much that is deficient in the contemporary 'University of Excellence' (to use Readings's nickname). Nevertheless, such nostalgia needs to be resisted; it blinds us to the series of exclusions on which the notion of *Bildung* was actually predicated—the obvious class and gender bias at work, and the implicit or explicit forms of nationalism inherent in the idea of the university as the self-realization of a national culture. Nostalgia for Germany can be no more than a covert expression of disquiet about the multicultural and multiracial climate in which the modern university lies. Barry Hindess cautions that the 'idea of the university' may perform an 'insidious

---

[16] *Deduzierte Plan*, 133, 136.   [17] *Gesamtausgabe*, I. iii. 52.

service, which is to promote—especially among academics and their
better students—a view of the distinctive character (and, often,
indeed, of the superiority) of Western civilisation as embracing a
unique relationship both to truth and to freedom'.[18]

The German idea of the university should be re-examined as a
source of guidance in our present predicaments, but not uncritically.
The German idea of the university haunts many an academic cliché.
For instance, the statement that we should do science—or whatever—
'for its own sake' is surely a distant echo of German ideals of
achieving unconditional knowledge, but shrunk into a platitude.
We also fall back on vague liberal remarks about the university
getting people to 'think for themselves', or the extraordinary and
oddly English debate about whether knowledge should have a use or
not, and the various uses of 'useless' knowledge.[19]

What follows is an attempt to schematize three major ways in
which English has legitimized itself in relation to both the university
and to society as a whole.

1. This first I touched on earlier: the attempt to make English a
model of disciplinary knowledge, not in the German sense of
Wissenschaft but according to the ethos of professionalism, in the
form of a self-contained autonomous university discipline. The conflicting notions, or cultures, of 'science' and 'art' must also be seen as
partly the effects of lines of professional demarcation whose terms
would be foreign to the modern research university in its original
idea. In the UK the pressure to conform to the professionalist paradigm meant usually that criticism tried to model itself on procedures
made prestigious elsewhere in the university, such as in the natural
sciences, that is notions of empirical investigation or formal system
modelling, or positivistic historical scholarship. Such ambitions char-
acterize various movements in criticism throughout the century, such
as Russian formalism, versions of structuralism, and aspects of the
New Criticism.

What may be of concern about such critical schools, considering
them from the angle of the university as a whole, is the extent to which

[18] 'Great Expectations: Freedom and Authority in the Idea of a Modern University',
Oxford Literary Review, 17 (1995), 29–49 (p. 48).
[19] See Robert J. C. Young, 'The Idea of a Chrestomathic University', in *Torn Halves:
Political Conflict in Literary and Cultural Theory* (Manchester: Manchester UP, 1996),
184–221.

their aims and methodologies seem driven by institutional ends. Louis Menand asserts: 'There is a sense in which the establishment of literature as a field was not a precondition for the establishment of literary criticism as a discriminable field of endeavour but the other way round.'[20] The institutional demand to compartmentalize knowledge in disciplines and departments seems to have had effects that pervade the minutiae of critical debate. Russian formalism, for example, has been described as representing 'one of the earliest systematic attempts to put literary studies on an independent footing, and to make the study of literature an autonomous and specific discipline'.[21] In this case it took the form of attempting to isolate some pure concept of *literariness*, focusing on the techniques of defamiliarization that can be said to render language 'literary'. We see a similar formalist drive in the aim of the American New Critics. The drive to isolate a clean, demarcated area of study, with its own methodology, making criticism a self-sufficient discipline, was a major factor in the lasting appeal of the New Criticism, as well as notions of practical criticism and decontextualized close reading adapted from the experiments of I. A. Richards. These ideas still dominate the way literature is read at A level: they would have the critic study only the 'words on the page', and then, with the words thus conveniently decontextualized, to construct all their interrelations in the forms of notions of 'paradox', 'complexity', and 'irony'.[22] These last, finally, are then passed off as the essence of literary language. Clearly, the desire for professional autonomy has taken the form of a drive to resist, deny, or repress the inherent fuzziness of the concept of literature—that, for instance, one can read Gibbon's history of Rome as literature, or, conversely, *Uncle Tom's Cabin* as history. Throughout the twentieth century, repeated calls were made to read 'literature as literature'— whatever that may mean. One suspects all such attempts to be little more, finally, than institutional policing operations. They cannot but foreclose the explosive but uncomfortable interdisciplinarity of literary practice. One might offer, in response, the genuinely paradoxical

---

[20] Quoted from John Harwood, *Eliot to Derrida: The Poetry of Interpretation* (Basingstoke: Macmillan, 1995), 101.

[21] Ann Jefferson in Ann Jefferson and David Robey (eds.), *Modern Literary Theory: A Comparative Introduction* (2nd edn. London: B. T. Batsford, 1986), 25.

[22] The widespread irritating use of the term 'paradox' in anglophone literary culture finds its source here: any seeming conflict of implication in a text, almost anything requiring thought, now finds itself blessed as a 'paradox'.

claim: that the peculiar force of those texts we still call literary lies in direct proportion to the difficulty with which one can treat them merely 'as literature'.

2. A second view of the relation of English to the university was the dominant one until about the mid-1980s, and is still strong in many older institutions.

English is both a subject and a meta-subject. It is claimed that English can have the legitimacy of a professionalized, scholarly discipline but that its status also transcends that. Literature is placed at the centre of a general idea of liberal education.

A famous example is the proposal for an English School made by F. R. Leavis during the Second World War. English is Leavis's panacea, 'because it is a humane school, and the non-specialist intelligence in which the various studies are to find their centre'. The university will find its centre in a 'special—but not specialist—discipline', the literary-critical, 'a discipline of sensibility, judgement and thought which, of its essential nature, is concerned with training a non-specialist intelligence'.[23]

In this sense the legitimacy of English was not that it formed a subset of the research project of the university *in toto*, but that it either constituted its animating centre (as in F. R. Leavis's proposal for an English School) or offered a supplement to it in the form of a non-specialized liberal education addressed to the person 'as a whole', rather than as a technician or mere specialist. The discipline saw itself as cohesive and redemptively unifying, a synthetic rather than a merely factional form of knowledge, opposed to the dominant values of what Leavis neatly termed 'technologico-Benthamite civilisation'.

One of the things that meets most resistance in courses on the nature of literature is the discovery that, strictly speaking, there was no such thing as 'literature' in the sense we now employ it prior to the eighteenth century. 'Literature' in the modern sense of imaginative writing is a concept mainly of the Romantic period. Previously the term 'literature' simply meant the totality of written texts in a culture. There were diverse arts of language, including poetry, the novel, oratory, drama, sermons, and essays, each defined by a set of artisanal techniques geared to the production of rhetorical effects as time and place required. That there was something called 'literature', a set

[23] *Education and the University: A Sketch for an 'English School'* (London: Chatto & Windus, 1943), 43.

embracing many previous arts of language and transcending rhetoric, and whose value is to express or embody some essential human attribute, such as 'creativeness', the 'imagination', some capacity for moral growth, and so forth—this idea emerges in the late eighteenth century, finding its deepest philosophical defence in early nineteenth-century Germany. It is later transplanted into English by writers such as Coleridge, Shelley, Carlyle, G. H. Lewes, George Eliot, and Matthew Arnold.

The broad vague concept of literature as imaginative writing alters decisively the perception of those texts to which it is applied, granting them a certain cultural and even pedagogic value. Literature means, in effect, something that teaches—if not in a narrowly didactic sense—or which is to be taught. Literature becomes conceived as part of the national culture's legitimization of its origins, a source of pride, a touchstone of authenticity and identity, a sort of linguistic National Trust, but plural and seemingly open to everyone.

The concept of literature as imaginative writing, the site of humane values, was forged in a nineteenth-century struggle for dominance between two factions of the bourgeoisie in the early industrial era—the managerial/technical/utilitarian, and the liberal-humanist. In effect, literary studies, in the very nature of its institution and its constitutive ideas, continued this battle throughout the twentieth century. The idea that literature can be the centre of a scheme of liberal education is a watered-down English translation of the German ideals of *Wissenschaft* and *Bildung*, filleted of anything so difficult as transcendental philosophy, except in the heavily disguised form of the notion of the 'the imagination'. Literature is offered as a unique form of knowledge not an object of it, as a defence of the imagination in a world dominated by utilitarianism and political economy, its antagonist being not religion (the implicit antagonist of *Wissenschaft* in the German scheme), but a caricatured view of science as a monstrous calculating machine, murdering to dissect.

The idea of the university, in its German form, and literature are mutually implicated. Both are defined by an understanding of the redemptive notion of culture. One cannot then simply oppose the university on one side and literature on the other: they are born together, at roughly the same time, in a complex symbiosis we are only now beginning to unravel. For instance, it is one of the distinguishing features of German Romanticism that it took place within a university context, and involves all the academic figures already

230   TIMOTHY CLARK

discussed. Often divided into three periods, early, middle, and late, the first two of these schools of German writers are now known by the names of the universities with which they were associated, Jena, and Heidelberg.[24] The contrast with British Romanticism here is striking—Oxford and Cambridge figure in the careers of Wordsworth, Coleridge, Byron, and Shelley largely as sub-ecclesiastical grotesques to be overcome and then ignored. The progressive cultural agenda that led to the foundation of the modern research university in Germany found an outlet in England, prior to the inauguration of the University of London in 1828, mainly in grandiose publishing ventures, such as Wordsworth's *The Recluse* or Coleridge's attempt to become a one-man walking talking university. Elsewhere in Europe since the foundation of Humboldt's institution, even the most anti-academic modernist avant-garde has also been an alternative idea of the university.

The fact that the literary critic was probably the last academic species to embrace professionalization is evidence for, not against, this intimate link. For a long time literary criticism still remained separate from and not necessarily dependent on the university. Its function of cultural legislation was not just a departmental affair but remained parallel to that of the university as a whole.

The legitimization of English through the notion of liberal education was so successful that it defined for most people simply what it meant to be an English department. This is the contradictory demand constitutive of English in the university, to be a kind of intellectual anti-intellectualism, to be *wissenschaftlich* but also non-academic, or more than academic. The danger with such a position is obvious: literary culture becomes too easily merely a form of anti-intellectualism. To outsiders, an old-fashioned English department did often present a peculiar subculture, both intellectually undefined and socially patronizing, in conceiving itself as the one department of the university that somehow stayed in touch with authentic 'experience'; which echoed Harold Bloom's sneer that 'Cultural criticism is another dismal social science, but literary criticism, as an art, always was and always will be an élitist phenomenon;'[25] which was suspicious

---

[24] Crabb Robinson in a letter of Jan. 1802 observed that 'The Litery Characters of Germany are almost all Univery Men' [*sic*], *Crabb Robinson in Germany 1800–1805: Extracts from his Correspondence*, ed. Edith J. Morley (London: Oxford UP, 1929), 104.
[25] *The Western Canon: The Books and School of the Ages* (1994; London: Macmillan, 1995), 17.

of the natural sciences and rude about sociology, or about any form of knowledge that seems merely 'abstract', not addressed to the so-called 'whole person'. It promulgated, under the name of ideals of self-discovery and expression, a conservative ideology of national character first forged in the English response to the French Revolution, one based on so-called 'common-sense, on a resistance to generalised thought'.[26] Terry Eagleton makes a similar observation: 'The opposite of poetry in England is not prose but Jacobinism; and if the phrase literary theory seems to some an oxymoron, it is because literature for the English is an alternative to systematic enquiry, not an object of it.'[27]

The odd and unique status of English as a would-be meta-subject became apparent in the irrational reception given to anyone who desired to pursue what would elsewhere be humdrum university business: that is, posing the question 'What is literature?' and then researching its answer systematically. Literary theorists found themselves, to their bemusement, being addressed on the seeming assumption that they must belong to some secret society of conspirators, named perhaps the SDLD—or 'The Society for the Demolition of the Lake District'. Perhaps that should not be meant entirely as a joke, after the incalculable damage which an image of the Lake District has done to English culture for 200 years. The main place of literature in modern society is now the heritage and tourist industry, part of the commodification of the past and of national difference.

3. We have so far surveyed two ways in which academic criticism has offered credentials of legitimization: (1) as a field of professionalized scholarship, with the same autonomy as any other department of the university as to the integrity of the object that defines it and in its disciplinary procedures: (2) as a meta-subject, the unique vehicle of liberal education, and the defender of a vague Romantic psychology of the 'whole self' against the intellectual reifications of other parts of the university.

The consensus about literature as the central institution of liberal education has long since collapsed. Since 1979 the liberal humanists have been increasingly marginalized. Technologico-Benthamite civilization has staged a massive counter-attack upon the universities.

---

[26] David Simpson, *Romanticism, Nationalism, and the Revolt against Theory* (Chicago: University of Chicago Press, 1993), 4
[27] *The Crisis of Contemporary Culture: An Inaugural Lecture Delivered before the University of Oxford on 27 November 1992* (Oxford: Clarendon Press, 1993), 16.

English can no longer rely on a correspondence between a generally accepted idea of the university and a notion of literary education to protect its autonomy as an intellectual field. Moreover, in the form of 'literary theory', other disciplines have, so to speak, turned upon English once more with a plethora of theories and methodologies associated with linguistics, historiography, psychoanalysis, continental philosophy, anthropology, and so on.

Nowadays, a bizarre situation has come about in which the legitimizing stance taken by critics in the university tends increasingly to be opposed to the institution in some way or another. The controversy over so-called 'political correctness' is one example. It has taken the form of attacks from academics writing in the press, defending the old ideals of cultural consensus against the supposed domination of the humanities by factional interest groups. Oddly, the charge made, from the popular forum of the media, is that literary studies have become *too* academic and full of jargon, a betrayal of the ideal of common values. In fact, these sorts of claims have been made about new trends in criticism for as long as English departments have existed. Literary theory, which has often been difficult, has fed into those attacks on the professionalization of criticism that have been going on since 'English' was initiated.

Conversely many of the so-called radicals under attack also see themselves as a vanguard for excluded or marginalized groups or forces outside the university. To that extent, they also take an anti-institutional stance. I cannot be the only one to have noticed that, in the early 1980s, as many traditional critics tried to refashion themselves as literary or cultural theorists, the tweed jacket was widely replaced by the leather jacket. A situation has arisen almost the reverse of that within the university culture in early nineteenth-century Germany, where students formed a distinct caste and dismissed anyone outside the university as a 'Philister' or philistine. The controversy in English can lead to a lot of fantasy politics on both sides. One worker in cultural studies, for example, describes himself as an 'intellectual freedom-fighter'.[28] Academia becomes conceived less as an ivory tower than as a kind of prison: postmodern thinkers in leather jackets agonize about how we might ever

---

[28] Cornell West, in 'The Postmodern Crisis of the Black Intellectual', in Lawrence Grossberg et al. (eds.), *Cultural Studies* (New York: Routledge, 1992), 689–705 (p. 689).

escape being trapped in our representational schemas, to get out of 'the prisonhouse of language' to the 'real world' outside. Others fall back on a naive identity politics, and talk about 'speaking as a Jew' or 'speaking as a woman' or 'speaking as someone who grew up in *blah blah blah*'—as if referring to some extra-academic identity could be a better guarantee of intellectual authenticity. The clamour that criticism should be 'political' often represents similar anxieties about legitimization.[29] Literary theory has also been the occasion for what is, in effect, a revolt against the ideology and effects of over-professionalization.

What is striking about the controversy is the implicit and almost total agreement about the kind of claim to legitimacy that criticism is making or should make: both appeal, in different ways, to a non-academic public. The appeal to public understanding is part of an intensifying struggle as to the conditions which we set for the legitimization of discourse. The problem is how one legitimizes criticism in the university, from within or from without? Peggy Kamuf writes: 'it is not, in other words, a difficulty at the level of concepts, but at the level at which one accepts or resists the conditions of one's *own* address, one's *own* meanings, one's *own* intention and, consequently one's *own* "self".'[30] Debates in criticism cannot be confined within the walls of some safe disciplinary or even interdisciplinary problematic—such as whether criticism can be a science or not. They also concern the nature of the university as a whole and the status of its claims to legitimacy.

5. Conclusion

Back, finally, to *The University in Ruins*. The power of Bill Readings's argument is that it gives us a broad understanding of the controversy in criticism, and where it really belongs—not as matter of dispute within English studies, as academic issues that might be solved there, but in relation to the university institution as a whole.

The crux of Readings's argument is that we mislead ourselves if we continue to try to understand universities primarily as sites of

---

[29] For these points see Robert J. C. Young's superb 'The Dialectics of Cultural Criticism', in *Torn Halves*, 10–30.
[30] Peggy Kamuf, *The Division of Literature: Or the University in Deconstruction* (Chicago: University of Chicago Press, 1997), 160.

cultural legislation (or 'ideological state apparatuses'), but that they now function merely as one relatively autonomous bureaucratic organization among others. Debates about criticism have raged around the issue of inclusion or exclusion from what are taken to be centres of cultural power. But arguments, whether on the 'left' or the 'right', that the other side has an unjust hold over the institutions of culture, each presenting itself shrilly as marginalized by the other, mask the deeper issue that the centres of power in contention no longer really function as privileged sites of national cultural self-definition. No sooner do, say, radical feminists or cultural materialists see their work included in university curricula—as they have loudly campaigned for years that it should be—than the agonizing begins about the dangers of being incorporated into 'the institution', institutionalized, rendered just another academic subject, and so on. It is not just that the university is no longer a centre for cultural legislation, a prize to be fought for and cherished, but that culture no longer has a centre. One television serialization will change the public perception of Jane Austen more than decades of expert scholarship. The problem here is that debates in criticism have proceeded with a displaced virulence that might suggest that the battle was for the prince's palace, not for a neglected old *Schloss* in the suburbs.

Readings traces this situation to nothing less than the globalization of the world economy. As the nation-state dwindles to a marginal and increasingly powerless player amidst the international flow of capital, the notion of a national culture undergoes a terminal change. The idea of culture is no longer able to legitimize the work of the humanities in the eyes of increasing numbers of people. As a consequence, critics' appeals to culture and to 'human richness' look increasingly irrelevant and élitist. Culture has become a market place in a society that has shed ideological pretence and reduced even the British royal family to a soap opera. We see the almost total saturation of what used to be termed culture by market forces, as in the practices of the various television companies, each ultimately engaged in the business of selling audiences to advertisers. We are living through the demise of 'the linking of nation-state and symbolic life that has constituted the idea of "national culture" since the eighteenth century',[31] of which, one might add, the notion of a national literature was a major part. Instead we see the emergence of a global petty bourgeoisie,

[31] Readings, *The University in Ruins*, 51.

wearing similar clothes and even watching similar television programmes. The decline of the nation-state, of course, has consequences for institutions even more crucial than the university: the
notion that you are living in a democracy becomes less credible than
ever when your society is no more than a localized point in global
transfers of capital.

Let me recapitulate my thesis: that many of the debates going on
within the walls of English departments, about the canon, the authority of tradition, even the status of close reading, are unsolvable
because they are not ultimately academic problems but immediately
involve the cultural mission of the humanities in general and the idea
of the university. The broader issue is that the cultural mission of the
humanities has become an anachronism and that the humanities have
lost their institutional mission to the ethos of professionalism and the
meaningless pursuit of 'excellence'. This cant term is now used so
frequently in vice-chancellors' speeches and university publicity that
it has become, in effect, the contemporary idea of the university. The
problem is, of course, that 'excellence' is tautologous: it means
almost nothing, it refers to nothing more than the doing well of—
whatever it is universities do! The main point of Readings's book is
this: 'the appeal to excellence marks the fact that there is no longer
any idea of the University, or rather that the idea has now lost all
content. [Excellence] is a non-referential unit of value entirely internal to the system . . . All that the system requires is for activity to
take place, and the empty notion of excellence refers to nothing other
than the optimal input/output ratio in matters of information'
(pp. 38–9). In other words, the university has lost its old mission of
cultural legislation and, like many other bureaucratic organizations,
it really has no higher idea than its own maximized self-perpetuation.
The notion of liberal education has lost its *raison d'être*, the idea of
culture as both the origin and the *telos* of the human sciences. 'The
human sciences can do what they like with culture, can do Cultural
Studies, because culture no longer matters as an *idea* for the institution' (p. 91).

What can we do? I do not think things are yet quite as terminal as
Readings presents. It is clear we cannot go back to old and discredited
dreams of general cultural legislation, but I feel that Readings's
account of the traditional university's definitive relation to national
culture is a little simplistic. It does not make allowance for the many
sorts of specific or local cultural engagements that can and do go on,

without universities thereby passing them off as the realization of some grand cultural essence for the nation.

However, I do not share Readings's optimism that the decline of the university also opens new opportunities for reform. It is one of the ironies of the erosion of the status of the university as a cultural centre that it has also enabled fairly 'radical' forms of critique to flourish. Some of these may seem to resist old demarcations and departmental boundaries in productive ways, usually those calling themselves something 'studies'—women's studies, queer studies, subaltern studies have all become powerful forces in the less conservative universities. Yet, as Readings acknowledges, the vitality of criticism may be in direct proportion to a decline in the kind of impact it can make.

Readings also proposes that the general trend towards dissolving English and humanities departments into departments of cultural studies be transformed into a revision of the departmental as the basis for intellectual life:

> The argument has to be made to administrators that resources liberated by the opening up of disciplinary space, be it under the rubric of the humanities or of Cultural Studies, should be channelled into supporting short-term collaborative projects of both teaching and research (to speak in familiar terms) which would be disbanded after a certain period, whatever their success. I say 'whatever their success' because of my belief that such collaborations have a certain half-life, after which they sink back into becoming quasi-departments with budgets to protect and little empires to build. Or to put it another way, they become [as departments are now] modes of unthinking participation in institutional-bureaucratic life. (p. 176)

Utopia! Nevertheless, the departmental structure is so deeply built into the university's administration—administrative and intellectual categories are more mutually implicated than ever—that I cannot see this proposal having much chance of success, especially given the fact that university administrators increasingly run the institution by setting up artificial internal markets, whose effect is to polarize colleagues and departments in competition against each other.

Two things seem clear from the discussion so far. (1) The uniquely volatile place of criticism, both within the university and in relation to it outside, has already suggested the need for a much closer consideration of ways of engaging the media, and forms of genuine public relations, that is, something more than the production of glossy illustrated brochures with corporate slogans and churchy towers poking through every skyline as a mark of social exclusiveness. In criticism, it may mean a much closer involvement in contemporary literature, its production and broadcasting. There should also be continued de-nationalizing of literature, by which I do not mean privatizing it but critical work which resists the general public appropriation of literature as a kind of verbal 'stately home' or national nature trail to be visited for edifying weekends or used as a backdrop for costume dramas.

(2) It seems clear that not only is there very little awareness of issues relating to the university as a whole, but that the modern professionalized university systematically produces this lack of awareness. In effect, an element in the modern, professionalized university is inherently self-destructive. Reason has institutionalized itself in a way that has often rendered it an empty formalism. We need to create a new institutional space that will generate rather than repress general discussion on the idea—or ideas—of the university as a whole, both among staff and also students (many of whom are unaware that their teachers do research). At the very minimum, this might take the form of setting up various interdisciplinary modules, one in each faculty, which would be compulsory for all first year students, called (say) 'university studies'. It would include discussion of the history of the concept of the university, its purposes, its duties in relation to society as a whole, the difference between pure and applied research, between the idea of scholarship and vocationalism. It would need to include an element that might be called 'science as a humanities subject' covering the basics of scientific method, the ethics of science, and the status of science in society. Such a course in 'university studies' might also help produce a genuine sense of corporate spirit, loyalty, and mission among students and staff. It might also be compulsory, as a condition of employment, for all people appointed as administrative officers.

If every university student since 1945 had taken a course like the one proposed, would universities be quite so alienated from public life as they now seem to be?

13

The Metaphysics of Modernism
Aesthetic Myth and
the Myth of the Aesthetic

MICHAEL BELL

1. Why Myth?

The use of myth in modern writers such as Eliot, Joyce, Lawrence, and Yeats has passed into the academic reception of the period in the now derided form of the 1950s 'myth kitty'; and Marc Manganaro has acutely shown the line of transmission from Frazer, through Eliot, to Northrop Frye as the continuation of a mistaken ethnographic method.[1] In the world of Anglo-Saxon academic criticism myth has deserved its bad name, while on the larger stage of European thought it has come to be associated with sinister political movements as the Marxist critique in Adorno and Horkheimer's *Dialectic of Enlightenment* has won out over the efforts of Thomas Mann and Karl Kerenyi to maintain its progressive and humanistic potential.[2] But this familiar story obscures the true significance of modernist myth-making, and to that extent of the literature itself, for modernist myth has a liberal and progressive aspect as well as a nostalgic and conservative one. What has been obscured is its philosophical, and through that its critical, import even for the present. I will show this by noting first how some earlier Romantic aspirations towards a philosophical mythopoeia were unwittingly realized in British and American modernism. I then take Nietzsche as a discursive model to

---

[1] See Marc Manganaro, *Myth, Rhetoric and the Voice of Authority: A Critique of Frazer, Eliot, Frye and Campbell* (New Haven: Yale UP, 1992).

[2] See Theodor Adorno and Max Horkheimer, *Dialectic of Enlightenment*, trans. John Cumming (London: Verso, 1986), and Thomas Mann and Karl Kerenyi, *Mythology and Humanism: The Correspondence of Thomas Mann and Karl Kerenyi*, trans. Alexander Gelley (Ithaca, NY: Cornell UP, 1975).

reconsider the function of the aesthetic in the metaphysics of modernism and, after a brief survey of some key writers, I conclude by suggesting the relevance of this history to the present-day practice of criticism.

It is generally recognized that literary modernism is a further expression of the Romantic impulse complicated, among other things, by the assimilation of much anti-Romantic reaction and a very different intellectual, cultural, and political context. Burton Feldman and Robert Richardson, in their survey of uses of the term 'myth' from early Enlightenment to modern times, note that the Romantic and modern periods are the twin peaks of its positive ambition.[3] Hence, the German Romantic thinkers influenced by J. G. Fichte at the University of Jena in the 1790s still give important clues on the question of myth although they were not directly influential on anglophone modern writers.

Friedrich W. J. Schelling, at the high point of German idealist philosophy, believed poetry might express what philosophy could not articulate. His turn to poetry, the aesthetic, and to myth, arose from problems in the philosophical legacy of Immanuel Kant. Where Kant had dissolved the Cartesian split between self and world, and along with it the associated scepticisms of the eighteenth century, J. G. Fichte's subjectivist interpretation of Kant posed a different dilemma. Instead of world being split from mind, the two were now so thoroughly collapsed into each other that either the world is an aspect of the mind or the mind an aspect of the world. There must therefore be an 'Absolute' beyond this dichotomy, and Schelling turned to myth as a mode in which the subjective and objective are dissolved; although, as he suggested in his *System of Transcendental Idealism* (1800), the creation of such a 'new mythology' would be a poetic task achieved only by a future generation.[4] Likewise, Friedrich Schlegel, in his *Dialogue on Poetry* (1800), sought a 'new mythology' as the basis of a true modern poetry.[5] The quest for a new mythology has continued in German thought right down to the present, and has been discussed extensively by Manfred Frank, but the very

[3] Burton Feldmann and Robert D. Richardson, *The Rise of Modern Mythology: 1680–1860* (Bloomington, Ind.: Indiana UP, 1972), 301.
[4] 'But how a new mythology (which cannot be the invention of an individual poet but only of a new generation that represents things as if it were a single poet) can itself arise, is a problem for whose solution we must look to the future destiny of the world and the further course of history alone.' See ibid. 322.   [5] See ibid. 309–13.

self-consciousness of that project has obscured its unexpected fulfil-
ment in the modernist decades.[6]

The modernist moment, by contrast, followed the general collapse
of idealist philosophies and, while several writers of the period
embodied in literary form a new conception of myth, its internal
logic was resistant to philosophical articulation, which is why I
describe such mythopoeia as being 'embodied', rather than, say,
'used' or 'invented'. The modernist moment included a strongly
anti-metaphysical, anti-philosophical, strain. Indeed, there was a
suspicion of abstract thought as such; an attitude most strikingly
epitomized in T. S. Eliot's obituary compliment to Henry James on
having 'a mind so fine that no idea could violate it'.[7] Hence,
although the Jena Romantics were equally critical of abstraction,
the 'new mythology' of Schelling and Schlegel was itself an *idea*
called up by a discursive process of reflection, whereas the modernists were myth-*makers* who recognized that a too explicit reflection
would rob myth of its mythopoeic power, would translate it back
into merely reflective terms. Yeats, for example, was steeped in
myth, but virtually never used the word in his poetry. The modernists' *obiter dicta* make clear that they all understood what they were
variously doing, but they avoided placing myth conceptually within
a reasoned philosophy. The more self-conscious it became, the less
truly mythopoeic it would be.

For modernist myth is not a project so much as a way of being. It is
not most essentially a content, whether traditional or invented, nor
even a literary structure, but a mode of apprehending the world.
Hence modernist mythopoeia, rather than the creation of 'new'
myth, is the recognition that we cannot *but* live mythopoeically,
whether consciously or not. Myth is modernity's form of philosophical self-knowledge. At its most abstract level, the point can be seen in
Martin Heidegger's definition of modernity as the 'age of the world
picture':

The expressions 'world picture of the modern age' and 'modern world
picture' both . . . assume something that never could have been before,
namely, a medieval world picture and an ancient world picture. The world
picture does not change from an earlier medieval one into a modern one, but

---

[6] See, for example, *Der Kommende Gott* (Frankfurt: Suhrkamp, 1982) and *Gott im
Exil* (Frankfurt: Suhrkamp, 1988).
[7] 'In Memory of Henry James', *Egoist*, 5 (1918), 1–2.

rather the fact that the world becomes picture at all is what distinguishes the essence of the modern age.[8]

Heidegger's claim is not just that there is a distinctively modern world picture but that a defining feature of modernity is to be aware of this relativity. That recognition came crucially into consciousness in the teens and twenties of the present century, and not least in the literature we think of as modernist. But why put this recognition under the tendentious and problematic sign of myth? Among many factors, the rise of anthropology, even though this was itself still in a scientifically primitive condition, was clearly important. Whereas anthropology started as the supposedly neutral scientific study of other peoples and their myths, these myths increasingly became an emblem of any set of living convictions making up a world-view, including therefore science itself. The microscope of anthropological science turned out to be a mirror. And it is the shock effect of this, the denaturalizing of your own world-view even as you perform its most sophisticated and committed functions, that the notion of myth keeps alive. Whereas the term 'myth' is usually a relational see-saw whereby one person's belief, religion, or science is looked down on as another's myth, the mythopoeic consciousness of modernity combines these two viewpoints in a difficult balance. However positivistic your beliefs, as a citizen of modernity you inhabit a world of conscious myth, for the mythic lies not in the belief itself but in the internal relation to it. Hence the use of archaic myth in *Ulysses* or *The Rainbow* is emblematic of the ontological status of the modern world that is being represented. Of course, the particular content and provenance of these myths is important too, and has received plenty of recognition, but their underlying function of emblematic philosophical self-reflection is constantly missed. By the same token, to say that science is mythic, of course, is not to deny its truth value; it is only to note its function as an authoritative organization of values within the culture. Myth is an evaluative, as well as a cognitive, form.

Heidegger's essay, while referring to a long sweep of post-Renaissance modernity, still finds it necessary to make this point, to bring it fully into consciousness, even as late as 1938. The awareness came slowly and it was furthered in the early twentieth century

[8] *'The Question Concerning Technology' and Other Essays*, ed. and trans. William Lovitt (New York: Harper & Row, 1977), 130.

by the increasing pressure of a global political, as well as an internal historical, sense of cultural relativism. The colonial era was beginning to break up, if not yet institutionally, then in thought, and since the retrospective wisdom of post-colonial critique mainly sees modernism as still within an unreconstructed colonial mentality, and there is of course much truth in this, it is important to emphasize that the conscious relativity of the period was laying the foundations for a critical viewpoint which by the end of the century has become conventional wisdom.[9] It is only paradoxical until you think about it, that Europeans would begin to understand the real Africa by first understanding the Africa within; that the heart of darkness is in Europe not Africa. This slow process of recognition was part of a more general awareness of living, not just in a world, but in a worldview. The accent is on living, as conviction and value, what you know in some sense to be relative. The double consciousness of actually *living* a world-view *as* a world-view is the true significance of literary myth in the period.

In that respect, the problematics of modernist mythopoeia are still those of Friedrich Schiller's essay 'On Naive and Sentimental Poetry' (1795–6), which might be translated as spontaneous and self-conscious poetry. At the purely logical level, it is manifestly impossible to combine the self-conscious and the unselfconscious, but literary texts can overcome such apparent contradictions and, in quite different ways, and with different degrees of success, this is what several writers of the period achieved. Writers such as Joyce, Lawrence, and Yeats, although highly self-conscious as artists, are remarkably implicit in this particular respect. They do not wear their 'metaphysic', to use Lawrence's term, on their sleeves, or make it their main point. In them, we experience a way of being rather than a reflective definition of it. The mythopoeic status of their represented world is a half-subliminal premiss; the small print, as it were, of the artistic contract. One may think here of Nietzsche's remark that 'truth is a mobile army of metaphors'.[10] His recognition that all language is metaphor, which is in effect the microcosmic, or linguis-

[9] I develop this point more fully in relation to post-colonial reading of *Heart of Darkness* in *Literature, Modernism and Myth: Belief and Responsibility in the Twentieth Century* (Cambidge: Cambridge UP, 1997), 148–58.
[10] 'On Truth and Falsehood in a Non-moral Sense' in *Philosophy and Truth: Selections from Nietzsche's Notebooks of the Early 1870s*, trans. and ed. Daniel Breazale (London: Humanities Press, 1990), 840.

tic, dimension of modernist mythopoeia, is so radical and encompassing that it makes at once all the difference and no difference. It does not invalidate the everyday distinctions we make between the literal and the metaphorical, and it leaves the world, to outward appearances, as it was. Modernist mythopoeia has the same kind of encompassing, or *überhaupt*, status which enables it to be put, in some sense, at the back of the mind even as it governs the ultimate significance of the world represented in the text.

Several features emerge, then, from this brief account of modernist mythopoeia: it is not a specific content so much as a mode of being; and it is not a project we can choose to create, as the Jena Romantics supposed, so much as the condition of consciousness in the world. It is especially problematic in being not primarily a cognitive question so much as one of living conviction or value, and also because, although it is an awareness, or it is nothing, it has to be largely subliminal or naturalized. But to understand it more fully we must take up another hint from the Jena Romantics, and from Schiller, in seeing that modernist mythopoeia characteristically functions under an aesthetic sign. At first glance, the term 'aesthetic' is even more slippery than 'myth', and to invoke it here may seem like oiling one's hands to climb a greasy pole. But the word mythopoeia links myth to poetry and it is only when the relationship of both terms, the 'mythic' and the 'aesthetic', is understood that the true impact of the aesthetic, increasingly lost since Schiller, becomes clear. This is best approached through Nietzsche's proto-modernist transformation of a nineteenth-century conception of the aesthetic.

2. Nietzsche and the Aesthetic Turn

An important legacy of Enlightenment thought was its identification of the aesthetic as an autonomous order of consideration, distinct from the cognitive and the ethical; a separation classically reflected in Kant's three critiques. Like many legacies, however, this one has proved ambiguous, has led to quarrels, and had unintended effects. The Kantian distinction of orders is now often taken to be a separation of realms whereby the aesthetic is *divorced* from the ethical. I believe this is a mistake reinforced by cultural developments over the course of the nineteenth century. Romantic thinkers, as the first generation to absorb the autonomous significance of the aesthetic, saw it not as separate but as aspectival and gave it a crucial role in the ethical life. Schlegel and Schelling understood the function of the aesthetic in the context of German idealism, but as the idealist tradition generally came under critical pressure in the course of the nineteenth century, the autonomy of the aesthetic was increasingly understood as a counter-term to other values; a development most notably enshrined in the literary aestheticism from which modernism partly grew. The trouble is that the ghost of aestheticism still exerts on discussion of the aesthetic a mischievous, subliminal influence which it is a principal purpose of this essay to combat by seeing the connection with myth. For this purpose, Schiller, who kept a distance from the Jena Romantics, is a crucial figure; both in his own right and as setting some of the terms for Nietzsche.

The important watershed in interpretation of the aesthetic occurs between Schopenhauer and Nietzsche and, since it is often misappreciated, it needs to be rehearsed here despite its familiarity. In Schopenhauer's philosophy of the will, human consciousness was the product of a blind, inhuman process of nature. But the irony of consciousness is that it fulfils its function by imagining itself to be independent and purposive; as if nature would endow a billiard ball with consciousness so that it should move by its own desire when required. For Schopenhauer, therefore, all human purposes and meanings are illusions and the supreme importance of the aesthetic domain is to be a conscious illusion. Art is the realm in which human beings can escape, albeit only mentally and momentarily, from the blind process which consciousness otherwise serves. The aesthetic sets the conscious illusion of art against the compelling and unconscious illusions of life, and Schopenhauer was read sympathetically by aesthetes and Symbolists. This was the model that Nietzsche would both use and invert.

In his still early *The Birth of Tragedy out of the Spirit of Music* (1872) Nietzsche's thinking on the aesthetic derives from a sympathetic reading of Schopenhauer. He twice uses the aphoristic formula that 'Only as an *aesthetic phenomenon* are human existence and the world eternally *justified*.'[11] This is an anticipatory sketch of his own life's work, for the claim that the aesthetic could 'justify' human existence was eventually to require a full-scale reversal of

---

[11]   *The Birth of Tragedy out of the Spirit of Music*, trans. Walter Kaufmann (New York: Random House, 1957), 52, 141.

Schopenhauer's pessimism. Yet one reason the reversal could not be immediate was that its significance depended in the first instance on a thorough assimilation of Schopenhauer's metaphysics of illusion. While seeing tragedy as ultimately affirmative, which is his point of resistance to Schopenhauer, Nietzsche still placed this affirmation within the context of a nihilistic conception and, furthermore, one for which the modality of dream is essential: 'Let us imagine the dreamer: in the midst of the illusion of the dream world and without disturbing it, he calls out to himself: "It is a dream. I will dream on"' (*Birth of Tragedy*, 44). But what for Schopenhauer was a scandalized and tragic vision of human being in a world of Darwinian process *avant la lettre* became increasingly for Nietzsche simply a working conception of the human psyche. Nietzsche's proto-modernist metaphysic was a fully digested and transformed Schopenhauer and, by assimilating the elements of life and art so completely that they ceased to be separably apparent, he offers an important clue to the metaphysics of literary modernism. I have suggested that in several defining works of modernism the mythopoeic metaphysic disappears into the texture of the living experience, or of the text, achieving a naturalness which has effectively disguised the metaphysical implication of the aesthetic form. The same process is foreshadowed in Nietzsche's thought by the gradual, apparent disappearance of the separable category of the aesthetic as he inherited it from Schopenhauer; a transformation to be seen in his very different treatment of Schopenhauer in one of his very last works, *Twilight of the Idols* (1888)

Having inherited Schopenhauer's use of the aesthetic as a counter-term to life, Nietzsche gradually assimilated the one realm to the other while keeping a sense of their contrastive meanings. This is not aestheticism. Aestheticism is the adoption of art as an order opposed to life. Nietzsche did something quite different. He affirmed life on the model of art. The separate realm of the aesthetic retains its meaning as a position in thought in order to define a living posture. Kant's formula of 'purposiveness without purpose' now applies not just to the aesthetic, but to the human, realm.[12] This is the essential shift by which modernist writers, such as Joyce, were to assimilate naturalism to aestheticism, and it is why Nietzsche stands to

---

[12] Immanuel Kant, *Critique of Judgement* (1790), trans. J. H. Bernard (New York: Hafner, 1972), 55.

modernism as Schopenhauer stood to the aestheticist and Symbolist movements.

Nietzsche's conception of the aesthetic was so far from being neutral *vis-à-vis* the values of life as to be actually merged with his vitalism. There is nothing unusual about this position in itself, only perhaps in the perspicacity and force with which Nietzsche understood both the complexity and the simplicity of the aesthetic relation to life. The simple, or ultimate, relation he expressed as follows: 'Nothing is beautiful, only man. On this piece of naivety rests all aesthetics, it is the *first* truth of aesthetics. Let us immediately add its second: nothing is ugly but *degenerate* man—the domain of aesthetic judgement is therewith defined.'[13] But although the aesthetic may be evaluatively bounded by life it also has its internal aspect. Art, precisely because it is a human product, is inescapably an object of judgement in a way that objects in reality are not. Trees, or even people, are not good or bad in the sense that poems or cooking are. For this reason, too, seeing life under an aesthetic sign, as Nietzsche suggested, is far from putting it outside the realm of ethical judgement, or relegating it to some specially aesthetic domain. On the contrary, the implicit process of judgement which is the inescapable condition of conscious being comes more sharply and urgently into focus in the response to a work of art. Indeed, as Schiller argued in his *Letters on the Aesthetic Education of Man* (1795), because there is no instrumental purpose being served, the critical function is unusually conscious and focused; it *is* the internal *telos* of the work. Values are considered *per se*. Of all the arts, imaginative literature is most inescapably a specific organization of values to which one responds, to be sure, in an intrinsic or contemplative rather than an immediately practical mode, but to which one cannot respond neutrally. That is the sense in which it provides a model for the Nietzschean conception of life understood aesthetically. Life is lived *as* an intrinsic, rather than *for* an instrumental or teleological, value and, this being the case, it involves a rigorously intrinsic self-critique.

This point is often misunderstood partly because of the residual pull of aestheti*cism* in the word 'aesthetic', and partly because the discourse of philosophy is unsuited to critical response. Philosophical discussions of the 'aesthetic' tend to focus on its metaphysical aspect

---

[13] *Twilight of the Idols*, trans. R. J. Hollingdale (Harmondsworth: Penguin, 1968), 90.

THE METAPHYSICS OF MODERNISM 247

and to miss, what is just as important, namely the evaluative and the critical. Jay Bernstein, Peter Alan Dale, Alan Megill, and Robert Pippin have all written over the last decade excellent books on this topic, yet they all understand the aesthetic only in its aspect of separation as enshrined in the word 'aesthetic*ism*'.[14] Alan Megill explicitly reads Nietzsche's aphorism about the aesthetic justification of human existence and the world as if existence itself were at stake; as if Nietzsche had claimed that the *world* is an aesthetic phenomenon. As Megill puts it: 'If it could be shown that the world really is an aesthetic phenomenon, then we would have to concede that in his essentials Nietzsche was right.'[15] But existence is merely Nietzsche's premiss; his claim relates to the evaluative question of *justification*. It is because Nietzsche never slighted the evaluative dimension that, whatever other problems his writings raise, he remains indispensable to the present question; and the indissoluble link of the aesthetic and the living was focused for him, as for later modern writers, in the holism of myth.

Two further passages bring this home. In his early essay on 'The Uses and Disadvantages of History for Life' Nietzsche defines it as a 'universal law' for 'every living thing' that, if it is to be 'healthy, strong and fruitful', it must be able to draw 'an horizon around itself'.[16] The horizon image, with its emphasis on living commitment, is the concise image of mythopoeia as a lived world-view, whether this be self-conscious or not. Meanwhile, in *The Birth of Tragedy* myth is linked to aesthetic response in the following way:

Whoever wishes to test rigorously to what extent he . . . is . . . the true aesthetic listener . . . needs only examine sincerely the feeling with which he accepts miracles represented on the stage: whether he feels his historical sense . . . insulted by them, whether he makes a benevolent concession and admits the miracle as a phenomenon intelligible to childhood but alien to him, or whether he experiences anything else. For in this way he will be able to determine to what extent he is capable of understanding *myth* as a

---

[14] Jay Bernstein, *The Fate of Art: Aesthetic Alienation from Kant to Derrida and Adorno* (Cambridge: Polity Press, 1992); Peter Alan Dale, *In Pursuit of a Scientific Culture* (Madison: University of Wisconsin Press, 1989); Alan Megill, *Prophets of Extremity: Nietzsche, Heidegger, Foucault and Derrida* (Berkeley and Los Angeles: University of California Press, 1985); Robert Pippin, *Modernism as a Philosophical Problem* (Oxford: Blackwell, 1991). [15] Megill, *Prophets*, 102.
[16] *On the Advantage and Disadvantage of History for Life*, trans. Peter Preuss (Indianapolis: Hackett, 1980), 10.

concentrated image of the world that, as a condensation of phenomena, cannot dispense with miracles.

(*Birth of Tragedy*, 134)

This differs from Coleridge's classic formulation of a poetic 'suspension of disbelief' which implicitly reinforced the boundaries between the poetic and the extra-poetic. For Nietzsche, by contrast, myth is the condition, not just of entering a poetic world, but of living in any world. You can suspend disbelief with respect to miracles, but myth is not a category you can *escape*, only fail to *recognize*, and the identification of the mythic and the aesthetic works both ways. Just as the aesthetic is not autonomous in the separatist sense, so the mythic is never a merely arbitrary relativism. The Nietzschean horizon is centred around a particular concentration of values, and, just as we cannot read a poem neutrally, so the living world-view of the Nietzschean subject is itself a matter for inevitable justification. Aesthetic justification, that is to say, is a reflexive relation. In so far as the aesthetic opens itself to judgement, the Nietzschean subject lives a life open to justification. Shorn of theological or metaphysically grounded justifications, this aesthetically conceived mythopoeia is an intense form of responsibility.

3. Myth in Literature

If Nietzsche is the closest discursive equivalent for the metaphysic characteristically embodied in a number of modernist writers in more implicit or emblematic ways, the question of a directly Nietzschean influence in any given case has to be treated with care since his thought was often received in reductive ways even by authors for whom he had radical affinity. Lawrence's *Women in Love*, for example, presents Gerald Crich as the Nietzschean figure, yet it is clear that Gerald's 'will to power' is of the compensatory kind that Nietzsche disapproved of as much as Lawrence, while the truly Nietzschean figure in the book is Rupert Birkin. It may be that Lawrence was not merely affected by a reductive reception of Nietzsche, but had elided precisely those aspects of Nietzsche's thought which he had already worked out in his own way. Likewise, Yeats and Joyce found in Nietzsche echoes of their own prior thinking, so that his position in relation to modernism is one of brilliant prescience as much as influence. He remains the best discursive model for appreciating the common significance of mythopoeic writers who are otherwise widely divergent and for whom space allows only a brief, suggestive listing.[17]

Yeats's poems are most essentially mythopoeic not in their use of legendary material such as Leda and the swan, nor even in their use of a personal mythological system. Their mythopoeia lies in their careful internal definition of their own viewpoint, or their ontological status, even when making the apparently all-encompassing statements that end 'Easter 1916', 'Among School Children', or 'Lapis Lazuli'. Lawrence's *The Rainbow*, which has so often been misread as merely an Edenic projection of his own nostalgia on to the English rural past, is actually a dynamic conflict between biblical and Darwinian conceptions of the world, both being understood as myths of origin. And myth here does not refer primarily to the past, imaginary or otherwise, it refers to a permanent dynamic within the psyche as each generation of the Brangwen family is caught between the Edenic need to stay rooted in their familiar environment, and the equal, evolutionary, need for an internal development realized in the exploration of the outer world, by leaving the Marsh. Once it is realized that the book is creating competing world-views, rather than a world, it becomes apparent that even its narrative form of a nineteenth-century historical family saga is internally appropriate to the process depicted rather than being an old-fashioned mode imposed by the author. By the same token, *Women in Love* required a spatialized, modernist structure as it became a study of different world-views jostling in the same historical moment and reflecting the different psychic conditions of its characters. Nordic and African are the poles of a psychic geography. Joyce's *Ulysses* is, of course, the classic instance of the modernist play of world constructions under the sign of myth, although the very overtness of this as a principal thrust of the work goes with a less direct concern for the moral and political choices constantly to the fore in Yeats and Lawrence. Whereas they think mythopoeically, but implicitly so, Joyce makes mythopoeia itself his theme.

It may be that differences between authors are not merely personal for, once it has become self-conscious at all, the balancing act required to present a mythopoeic conception without lurching into

---

[17] I discuss these authors more amply in *Literature, Modernism and Myth*.

excessive self-consciousness is only possible within a relatively brief historical moment. By the time of E. M. Forster's *A Passage to India* (1924), for example, the sense of competing world-views, however worthy in its liberalism, is already too self-conscious and schematic. Although this is a feature of Forster's novels generally, and he is a lesser writer than those mentioned so far, the schematism of his last novel has a partly epochal sharpness. Such an epochal shift is borne out by Thomas Mann's *The Magic Mountain*, of the same year, which thematizes the question of competing world-views in the most overt and discursive way. Mann makes this the very subject of the work and, within a few years, he had moved into his consciously mythic phase with the Joseph novels. Mann is the most encompassing and self-conscious, if not the most profound, exponent of modern mythopoeia. In an *œuvre* spanning the first fifty years of the century, he fought a long struggle against his own Romantic and nationalistic commitments derived partly from Nietzsche. Yet his mythic phase, for which the Joseph tetralogy was the first major expression, drew upon Nietzsche to present a liberal mythopoeia. And in *Doctor Faustus*, as he faced his personal and national past in a spirit of tragic critique, and modelled his modern Faust partly on Nietzsche, it was still a Nietzschean, mythopoeic, conception through which he conducted the critique. Myth, he seems to suggest, can only be fought with myth.[18] Even evil myth is not evil *as* myth, myth is merely the condition of human life and community, and seeking to destroy the mythopoeic as such is not only a lost cause but can exacerbate the condition. Properly understood, mythopoeic consciousness is a prophylactic against fanaticism and dogma.

But this, of course, is to put it at its best, and there are modern writers for whom a form of mythopoeia acted as a collusion with rather than a protective from sinister authoritarianism, just as there are others for whom such a conception does not significantly apply at all. Virginia Woolf, for example, affirms the special horizon of female experience, but she does not draw upon a mythopoeic conception in the sense defined here, perhaps because the female horizon seemed so

---

[18] Mann's humanist narrator, Zeitblom, speaks of 'the horizon that every life needs in order to develop values, through which, however relative they are, the character and capacities are sustained. They can, however, do that, humanly speaking, only if the relativeness remains unrecognised. Belief in absolute values, illusory as it always is, seems to me a condition of life.' *Doctor Faustus*, trans. H. T. Lowe-Porter (Harmondsworth: Penguin, 1947), 63.

much more imposed than chosen, and this raises a larger question about gender in modernism. The mythopoeic conception I have been describing does seem to have a strongly, but not I think intrinsically, masculine orientation. The poetry of H.D., for example, would be a counter-case. But perhaps the most important problematic instance in understanding the present definition of modernist mythopoeia is T. S. Eliot, since his use of the Grail legend in *The Waste Land*, along with his praise of Joyce's 'mythic method' in *Ulysses*, has strongly governed subsequent perception of myth in relation to literary modernism.

Eliot's use of myth in *The Waste Land* was precisely that, a *use* of myth, rather than an embodying, or inhabiting, of it as a mode of being. His own comment in the *Ulysses* review, that myth 'is simply a way of controlling, of ordering, of giving a shape and significance to the immense panorama of futility and anarchy that is contemporary history', is revealingly ambiguous.[19] He stresses the imposing of an artistic order to highlight, rather than mythopoeically to transform, the futility and anarchy. Meanwhile, in *The Waste Land* itself, the borrowed fertility myth stands in contrast to the desert of modernity, and is itself belied by the sexual distaste in the poem. In effect, the Grail myth in this poem proved to be a placeholder for the religious belief which was to be Eliot's true subject, and, as a great modern religious poet, particularly in the *Four Quartets*, Eliot came closest to the mythopoeic conception in so far as, poetically speaking, he did not rely on his own, or a reader's, faith. These poems actively create their religious sense of the world. Yet even so, in his discursive essays, Eliot could not accept that his own religious belief could have a mythopoeic status. There is, in other words, a large subject here in discriminating precisely how the mythopoeic conception applies, or does not apply, to individual authors, but Eliot's well-known prose comments, and his apparently most obvious use of myth, are highly misleading with regard to modernist mythopoeia. He rather shows us what it is not.

The most problematic case, perhaps, is Ezra Pound. Ten years younger than Thomas Mann, he also had a long career encompassing much of the most disturbed history of the century. But whereas Mann found a mythically based recovery from reactionary politics, Pound started, along with his coeval Lawrence, as one of the most naturally

---

[19] 'Ulysses, Order and Myth', *Dial*, 75 (1923), 483.

mythopoeic imaginations of his generation, yet descended into fascistic dogma. For Pound lacked the mythopoeic relativity which I have been describing, except perhaps in the Pisan Cantos. The *Cantos* as a whole are an essentially mythic reading of history which does not recognize its own status in this regard. Their method of 'ideogram-mic' compression rests on a suppressed, and tendentious, historical argument, which seems to have no means of questioning itself. They become not myth, but ideological dogma, and on the basis of this example, we may infer that myth which is not aware of itself as myth, as in Thomas Mann, is in danger of ossifying into ideology, and that leads to my final emphasis. So far, I have defined an epochal recognition which has been largely obscured in the subsequent reception of modernism. I wish now to indicate its present import for the function of criticism.

4. Myth, Narrative, and Ideology

I have emphasized the positive function of modernist mythopoeia because the fortunes of the term 'myth' are now at their lowest. For many academic practitioners of literary study, myth is merely mystification. But the meaning of this decline lies partly in what has taken over the function of the word 'myth', and I will conclude by looking at two important terms which attempt to do so. One is a positive attempt to continue the mythopoeic recognition by other means while the other seeks to destroy it. These are, respectively, 'narrative' and 'ideology'.

Over the last two decades especially, several writers have appealed to 'narrative' as the form in which ethical and communal being are created. Alasdair MacIntyre and Martha Nussbaum are among the best known, and rightly respected.[20] But the true value of these contributions lies in their closely engaged reading of literary texts to highlight the relative impoverishment of other forms of ethical understanding such as analytic philosophy and law. As I have argued elsewhere, narrative, while providing, as we have always known, the most complex form in which to rehearse and examine the complex-

---

[20] See Alasdair MacIntyre, *After Virtue* (London, Duckworth, 1981); Martha Nussbaum, *The Fragility of Goodness: Luck and Ethics in Greek Tragedy and Philosophy* (Cambridge: Cambridge UP, 1986) and *Love's Knowledge: Essays on Philosophy and Literature* (Oxford: Oxford UP, 1990).

ities of the ethical life, cannot actually create or ground such a life.[21] Or rather, any narrative which does do so is already more than a narrative, it is functioning mythopoeically. Hence, although the word 'narrative' seems more technical, unsentimental, and politically neutral than myth, its stronger claims depend upon an optimistic sleight of hand in assuming as a premiss the very matter that is to be proved. The word 'myth' by contrast is frankly problematic. It is a disturbing term, and rightly so. It insists that at any moment we carry with us the responsibility of living an ungroundable view of the world which can have no purely rational precedence over others, including those we consider evil. Any precedence has to be earned, and is a matter of intrinsic judgement like the different weights which, consciously or not, willingly or not, we accord to poems. Indeed, the value of literary art from this point of view is that it objectifies a world-view and allows it to be seen as an external object, in the round so to speak, in a way that is not possible in the living of it. But the impossibility of seeing one's own life in the round, of raising the implicit to full consciousness, leads to the second, and more widespread, challenge to the mythopoeic, namely the ideological.

'Ideology' is now a favoured term to designate a lived world-view while 'myth', for the ideologically minded critic, means false consciousness, a merely naive or unconscious ideology. Now much good contemporary criticism is ideologically inspired, it seeks to expose the unconscious ideological premisses of texts and cultures, and I applaud this gain in cultural self-critique. But it carries its own dangers, and particularly in so far as it is a cultural assumption disseminated well beyond its more distinguished practitioners. There is an increasing assumption among students of the humanities that ideological exposure is the essential function of criticism. At a superficial level this may be what is now known as political correctness and, without pretending that political correctness is merely a right-wing projection, I can accept it as the inevitable accompaniment of a serious process. It stands to ideological critique as Sunday School piety stands to Christianity. But there is the more disturbing possibility that ideological critique is only a more sophisticated version of political correctness, and particularly when an oppositional tone and posture are actually reinforced by group solidarity. The problem here

---

[21] See 'How Primordial is Narrative?' in Cris Nash (ed.), *Narrative in Culture* (London: Routledge, 1992), 172–98.

is that ideological critique, by concentrating on the unmasking of others, tends to occlude the problem of its own standpoint. Modernist mythopoeia, by contrast, was a responsible awareness of the implicit values within which we all live, whether as individuals or as cultures.

Of course, this does not mean that by virtue of the mythopoeic conception individuals or communities would always get things right. Therein lies a world of discrimination, once known as criticism, as I have hinted in relation to several modern authors. What is at stake is rather a different kind of awareness although not, of course, a total raising to consciousness of the implicit world as such. That would be impossible. Borges's fable of 'Funes the Memorius', which is itself borrowed, I would surmise, from a few sentences of Nietzsche, expresses this point.[22] When Funes acquires total perception and recall, he is also paralysed, and he dies of congestion. Indeed, far from being a complete raising into self-consciousness of the implicit, mythopoeia is the awareness of the impossibility of doing so. And the importance for criticism is that this truth applies internally to any work of the imagination. For the world represented in the work is not just to be judged *by* an ideology, it is itself a means of *judging* the ideology. The value of a world outlook lies in how it is lived, or the life it enables. There are many different potential worlds, some admirable, some less so, within the abstract ideologies of Christianity or of Marxism. It is not just that both world-views accommodate brutes and saints, but that the brutality and the sainthood are lived as expressions of these world-views, which is why the ideology by itself does not tell you what you most need to know about them. Imaginative literature is a unique means of understanding and assessing this complex interplay, and detecting the ideology in the text is, therefore, not the end, but merely the first step in criticism. Taken as the end, it becomes a reductive, and self-fulfilling, short cut. In affecting to understand its opponents, it is in danger of reifying them; and precisely in the medium, imaginative literature, which should most educate against this. Henry James's Lambert Strether has a confident ideological judgement of Madame de Vionnet until he gets to know her.

---

[22] *Advantage and Disadvantage of History,* 9–10. 'Funes the Memorius', in Jorge Luis Borges, *Labyrinths*, ed. Donald A. Yates and James E. Irby (Harmondsworth: Penguin, 1970), 87–95.

These remarks will be obvious to some, and unacceptable to others. The vantage-point of ideology is jealously guarded, and the supposed mystification of its opponents is one of its standard preemptive tactics in which the autonomy of the aesthetic has a crucial function. The charge of mystification outlaws that appreciative submission to the work which is the first phase of criticism, and implies that only ideological critique performs the critical function at all. Jochen Schulte-Sasse provides a conveniently bald statement of this tactic:

The ideological function of 'organic' works of art depends on a balance between an internal semantic plenitude that escapes simple fixations and ideological demarcations that enclose the work of art from external considerations. Countless books on aesthetics developed in line with the institution of art simultaneously permit ideological exclusions and the subjective experience of fullness.[23]

He has a real point, of course, but it is obliterated by the tendentiousness, and the black or white dualism, with which it is conceived. The phrase 'internal semantic plenitude' reduces to linguistic mystification the specific weight of experience which constitutes a writer's authority. The quality, that is, which makes us attend to Primo Levi; or if that example is too close to sheer memorial, then to the fiction of J. M. Coetzee. But from Schulte-Sasse's ideological altitude 'experience' itself is merely 'subjective fullness'. Meanwhile, the 'ideological exclusions' are conceived as purely negative and dishonest. But no text, or individual, can sustain, or needs to sustain, all its living premises simultaneously in consciousness, and in literature many exclusions are, in fact, appropriate to given occasions. What matters is the nature of the artistic contract, which is itself a matter for specific critical judgement. It is the interaction of these two dimensions, the experiential and the ideological, which provides the arena for criticism, but in recognizing this you forgo the privileged viewpoint of the ideological critic. Schulte-Sasse's dualism reveals his vested interest in maintaining the notion, or might one say the myth, of the aesthetic as not merely autonomous, in Schiller's sense, but as separatist.

The power of this modern myth is exemplified in Terry Eagleton's *The Ideology of the Aesthetic*, for which his discussion of Schiller's

[23] See foreword to Peter Bürger, *Theory of the Avant-Garde*, trans. Michael Shaw (Manchester: Manchester UP, 1984), p. xxxix.

Letters on the Aesthetic Education of Man is a crucial moment. Schiller combined Kant's sense of the autonomy of the aesthetic with the Rousseauvian tradition of moral sentiment to form one of the most cogent arguments we have for the moral value of aesthetic experience. He presents aesthetic disinterestedness as an intense awareness of human values, as the recognition of responsibility as such, so that it sends us back into the world morally charged and tuned up, as it were, for action although the aesthetic experience as such, of course, gives no immediately practical or didactic guidance. On this last point, Eagleton quotes Schiller's caveat that 'if we find ourselves disposed to prefer some one mode of feeling or action, but unfitted or disinclined for another, this may serve as infallible proof that we have not had an aesthetic experience'. Eagleton then comments: 'As the very taproot of our moral virtue, the aesthetic is apparently invalid unless it predisposes us indifferently to murder or martyrdom.'[24] But Schiller does not present the aesthetic as the 'taproot' of moral virtue, only as a crucial modulation of the moral feelings, and the firm boundary he sets to the aesthetic is precisely to avoid the confusion Eagleton exemplifies. Yet Eagleton's reading is representative and symptomatic. An argument of such scope and ambition as he attempts may well be vulnerable in detail, but the misreading of Schiller is a central point of reference for his whole subsequent case. It seems that Eagleton's commitment to seeing the aesthetic as separate blinds him to what Schiller actually says and it is suggestive that it should be Schiller's moment which is misread. For that is the moment when the aesthetic was understood as aspectival rather than separate and it is a moment from which we could yet gain insight, as Nietzsche suggests by the use he makes of Schiller in *The Birth of Tragedy*.[25] In short, Schulte-Sasse and Eagleton maintain the myth of aesthetic separatism as their necessary opponent whereas the aesthetic mythopoiea seen in Nietzsche and several modern writers would enforce a more self-inclusive form of critical responsibility.

[24] *The Ideology of the Aesthetic* (Oxford: Blackwell, 1990), 110.
[25] The positive connection between Schiller and Nietzsche is recognized in Nicholas Martin, *Nietzsche and Schiller: Untimely Aesthetics* (Oxford: Oxford UP, 1996).

Notes on Contributors

MICHAEL BELL is Professor of English at Warwick. His publications include *Primitivism* (1972), *The Context of English Literature, 1900–1930* (1980), *The Sentiment of Reality: Truth of Feeling in the European Novel* (1983), *F. R. Leavis* (1988), *D. H. Lawrence: Language and Being* (1992), *Gabriel Garcia Marquez: Solitude and Solidarity* (1993), and *Literature, Modernism and Myth: Belief and Responsibility in Twentieth Century Literature* (1997).

JACQUES BERTHOUD is Professor in the Department of English and Related Literature in the University of York. His publications include (with Christina van Heyningen) a book on the South African novelist and playwright Uys Krige (1966), *Joseph Conrad: The Major Phase* (1978), and editions of novels by Trollope (*Phineas Finn*, 1982) and Conrad (*The Nigger of the 'Narcissus'*, 1984; *The Shadow Line*, 1986; and *Almayer's Folly*, 1992). His recently completed edition of *Titus Andronicus* is forthcoming from Penguin (1999).

SEÁN BURKE lectures in English at Durham. He has written *The Death and Return of the Author: Criticism and Subjectivity in Barthes, Foucault and Derrida* (1992; 2nd rev. edn. 1998) and *Authorship: From Plato to the Postmodern: A Reader* (1995). He is currently writing on value and canonicity.

TIMOTHY J. A. CLARK is Reader in English at Durham. He is the author of *Embodying Revolution: The Figure of the Poet in Shelley* (1989), *Derrida, Heidegger, Blanchot* (1992; repr. 1995), and *The Theory of Inspiration: Composition as a Crisis of Subjectivity in Romantic and Post-Romantic Writing* (1997). He is also co-editor of the *Oxford Literary Review* and editor (with Jerrold E. Hogle) of *Evaluating Shelley* (1996). He has recently completed a book on Charles Tomlinson for the series *Writers and their Work*.

DAVID E. COOPER is Professor of Philosophy at Durham. He is the author of nine books, most recently *Metaphor* (1986), *Existentialism: A Reconstruction* (1990), *World Philosophies: An Historical Introduction* (1995), and *Heidegger* (forthcoming). He has edited several books, including *A Companion to Aesthetics* (1993), and has co-edited two books on environmental thought, *The Environment in Question* (1993) and *Just Environments* (1995). He is currently writing a concise introduction to philosophy for Blackwell, and preparing a book on the limits of language and mysticism.

PAUL H. FRY is William Lampson Professor of English at Yale and Master of Ezra Stiles College. He is the author of *The Poet's Calling in the English Ode* (1980), *The Reach of Criticism* (1983), *William Empson: Prophet against Sacrifice* (1991), and *A Defence of Poetry: Reflections on the Occasion of Writing* (1995).

DAVID FULLER is Reader in English at Durham. He is the author of *Blake's Heroic Argument* (1988), *James Joyce's 'Ulysses'* (1992), and (with David Brown) *Signs of Grace* (1995) (on literary treatments of the sacraments). He has also edited *Tamburlaine the Great* for the Oxford English Texts edition of the complete works of Marlowe (1998). He is currently writing a book on Romanticism and contemporary critical theory.

DORIS LESSING was born in Persia (modern Iran), spent most of her early life in Southern Rhodesia (modern Zimbabwe), and came to England in 1949 just before the publication of her first novel, *The Grass is Singing* (1950). Her many publications include the five novels of the series *Children of Violence—Martha Quest* (1952), *A Proper Marriage* (1954), *A Ripple from the Storm* (1958), *Landlocked* (1965), and *The Four-Gated City* (1969)—and the five novels of the space fiction series *Canopus in Argos: Archives—Re: Colonised Planet 5, Shikasta* (1979), *The Marriages between Zones Three, Four and Five* (1980), *The Sirian Experiments* (1981), *The Making of the Representative for Planet 8* (1982), and *Documents Relating to the Sentimental Agents in the Volyen Empire* (1983). Other novels include *The Golden Notebook* (1962), *Briefing for a Descent into Hell* (1971), *The Summer before the Dark* (1973), *Memoirs of a Survivor* (1975), *The Diaries of Jane Somers* (1984), *The Good Terrorist* (1985), *The Fifth Child* (1988), and most recently *Love, Again* (1995). She has also published several collections of novellas and short stories, many on African subjects, and a number of works of non-fiction. The first volume of her autobiography, *Under my Skin*, appeared in 1994, and the second, *Walking in the Shade*, in 1997.

DAVID LODGE was formerly Professor of English at the University of Birmingham. His critical works include *The Language of Fiction* (1966), *The Novelist at the Crossroads* (1971), *The Modes of Modern Writing* (1977), *Working with Structuralism* (1981), *Write On* (1986), *After Bakhtin* (1990), and *The Practice of Writing* (1996); and his novels *The Picturegoers* (1960), *Ginger, You're Barmy* (1962), *The British Museum is Falling Down* (1965), *Out of the Shelter* (1970), *Changing Places* (1975), *How Far Can You Go?* (1980), *Small World* (1984), *Nice Work* (1988), *Paradise News* (1991), and *Therapy* (1995). He has also written for stage and television.

MICHAEL O'NEILL is Professor of English at Durham. He is author of *The Human Mind's Imaginings: Conflict and Achievement in Shelley's Poetry* (1989), *Percy Bysshe Shelley: A Literary Life* (1989), *Romanticism and the*

Self-Conscious Poem (1997), and a collection of poems, *The Stripped Bed* (1990). He is co-author (with Gareth Reeves) of *Auden, MacNeice, Spender: The Thirties Poetry* (1992), and the editor of *Shelley: Longman Critical Readers* (1993). He was also an editor of the magazine *Poetry Durham*. He has edited a volume in the Garland series *Bodleian Shelley Manuscripts* (1994), and has co-edited (with Donald Reiman) a volume of Garland's *The Manuscripts of the Younger Romantics* (1997). He has also edited *Keats: Bicentenary Readings* (1997), and *Literature of the Romantic Period: A Bibliographical Guide* (1998).

RAYMOND TALLIS is Professor of Geriatric Medicine at the University of Manchester and Consultant in Health Care for the Elderly at Hope Hospital, Salford. Apart from his many publications in medicine he is also the author of *In Defence of Realism* (1988), *Not Saussure: A Critique of Post-Saussurean Literary Theory* (1988; 2nd edn. 1995), *Newton's Sleep: The Two Cultures and the Two Kingdoms* (1995), *Enemies of Hope: A Critique of Contemporary Pessimism* (1998), *Theorrhoea and After* (1998), and three volumes of poetry, most recently *Fathers and Sons* (1993).

PATRICIA WAUGH is Professor of English at Durham. She is author of *Metafiction* (1984), *Feminine Fictions: Revisiting the Postmodern* (1989), *Practising Postmodernism/Reading Modernism* (1992), and *Harvest of the Sixties: English Literature and its Background, 1960 to 1990* (1995). She has edited *Postmodernism: A Reader* (1992), and *Revolutions of the Word: Intellectual Contexts for the Study of Modern Literature* (1997); and has co-edited (with Philip Rice) *Modern Literary Theory: A Reader* (1989; 3rd edn. 1996). She is currently writing *Views from Nowhere: Literature, Science and the Good Society*, a book on utopian fictions.

Index